# The French Broad

# The French

by

## Wilma Dykeman

*illustrated by* DOUGLAS GORSLINE

THE UNIVERSITY OF TENNESSEE PRESS • KNOXVILLE   TENNESSEE

# Broad

Library of Congress Catalog Card Number:   54-9349

*Fourth Printing, 1965*
*Fifth Printing, 1966*
*Sixth Printing, 1973*
*Seventh Printing, 1985*
*(ISBN 0-87049-056-7) cloth*

University of Tennessee Press paperback, 1985; 2nd printing, 1987
(ISBN 0-87049-440-6) paper

## Introduction to *THE FRENCH BROAD*

The French Broad has been called the classic example of an Appalachian mountain river. Ten years ago, when this book was written, such a statement might have held little intellectual meaning or emotional nuance for a majority of readers. Today national attention is focused on Appalachia, however, and even the stranger to this region has his own vivid mental picture of its problems and potential.

More often than not this image is an assorted confusion of contrasts: rugged scenery inhabited by ragged people, riches of folklore made picturesque by a poverty of cash, isolated mountain coves existing next door to crowded tourist meccas, sturdy independence of spirit flourishing in a generation of welfarism. All of these do exist, often side by side and interdependently. For instance, there are still wild tangled areas of the Great Smokies where "laurel slicks" make it easy for a lonely wanderer to lose his way and his life; at the same time, the Great Smoky Mountains National Park is now visited by more than five million people each year.

The instant images, the quick categories, the long-distance analyses of the French Broad country—and the rest of Appalachia —are apt to be deceptive. Problems which are most immediately obvious and simply stated may in the long run be most subtle and complex of solution. Promises which seem abundant and readily fulfilled are often illusory, built on high hopes rather than broad understanding. This book was, and is, an effort to increase understanding and appreciation for a rare region, a tough and fragile people and their hard and lovely country.

As I have said elsewhere, this is the chronicle of a river and a watershed and a way of life where yesterday and tomorrow meet in odd and fascinating harmony. During the decade since its publication, yesterday has faded a little farther into the past, tomorrow has accelerated its pace in becoming the present. Interstate highways are unrolling their wide concrete ribbons through hillside fastnesses and gorges once considered impassable by armies of weary soldiers and mud-stained stock drovers. Industries new and shiny are manufacturing gadgets and necessities for the age of space and automation. Consolidated schools increase in size and number. Where the rambling verandas of an old tavern were still sitting between the river and the railroad as recently as a decade ago, a pink motel now stands beside the highway. Where cities and industries wantonly dumped tons of raw sewage and manufacturing offal into the French Broad and its tributaries, today every municipality on the French Broad has built—or is building—sewage treatment plants, and the majority of industries are making purposeful efforts to solve, rather than evade, their water pollution responsibilities. Dwellers of the French Broad country are learning an ancient lesson in all their natural resources: it is easy to destroy overnight treasures that cannot be replaced in a generation, easy to destroy in a generation that which cannot be restored in centuries.

The landscape changes. The mountains remain. Many of the people do not. Certain counties of the French Broad region decreased in population during the past ten years. Natives went elsewhere in search of a livelihood while outlanders came here in search of refuge from the urban blight. It is one of the ironies, and perhaps one of the hopes, of much of Appalachia that many of its people have found the secret of making a way of life where they often could not find means of making a living.

For the French Broad country, like most of the mountain region which surrounds it, nourishes paradox. That is the source of much of its allure—and despair. The roots of the paradoxes, the problems, the promises, run deep into the past. This is one glimpse into that past, and one glance at the present. Perhaps it provides some perspective for the future.

Wilma Dykeman
Newport, Tennessee
March 21, 1965

This book is for
Bonnie and James
without whom it would not have been written

# Contents

## Chapter

13  THE ONLY THING FREE WAS THEIR ENTER-            195
    PRISE

14  THE CHATEAU AND THE BOARDINGHOUSE               210

15  THE BIG LAW AND THE LITTLE LAW                  228

16  BREAD AND BUTTER                                248

17  TV's AND V8's                                   267

18  WHO KILLED THE FRENCH BROAD?                    280

19  THE HIGH SHERIFF                                294

20  NO COKES IN HELL                                311

21  THE CHATTERING CHILDREN                         330

    ACKNOWLEDGMENTS                                 347

    BIBLIOGRAPHY                                    349

    INDEX                                           357

# The French Broad

# 1

# Long Man, The River

On a winding dirt road near the top of the watershed, you stand above a tree-thick basin, and the slight man in clean mended overalls turns his blue eyes toward you as he cocks his head.

"Hear that racket down there? That's your French Broad. Raises right under the Devil's Courthouse. Listen!" He listens. You listen together and hear the distant voice of "your" river. The man is slight, but he's tough as a laurel burl. You go over miles of the basin with him and he remembers.

"I first come in here on a lumber crew. Mighty rough times, but the country would have pleasured you to see. The Flowery Flats we called one spot where pines grew so thick they looked from above like big green bunches of flowers.

"The Negro camp was near those Flowery Flats. I remember sharp because I was paymaster there—and because they died off so fast. They didn't work in the lumber, just on road building. One I reckon I'll never forget. He was a giant of a man, dark as three o'clock, come in with the regular crew, but I found out pretty soon that none of the rest of them knew him. Not even his name. I never did have a full name down in my daybook for him, just Sam or Joe or somesuch, I can't recollect that now. But I can recollect how he looked and worked, how he eat to hisself and stood apart. When he took fever, there still wasn't anybody he'd talked to. And he just layed there on his bunk and stared at the slab-sided wall for two days. That was all it took. Great husky carcass of a man, the fever snuffed him out like a firefly.

"There wasn't a paper on him, never a word of where he come from or why—or *who* he was that had come amongst us and died. So all we could do was fix him up a box. We used one of those big wholesale crates that shoes come in for the store down the road, and wrapped him in an army blanket. I couldn't tell you today just where his grave was—and is, I reckon. Things change so. But he was a strange one and no denying."

This is the beginning of "your" river. And its ending too. In the memories of people, in the simple stories of strangers in a strange land. In the beauty of its water and the splendor of its mountains. Like flashes of lightning across the sky, their stories break briefly across the river's landscape in a sudden illumination.

Which is the time to know the river? April along the French Broad is a swirl of sudden water beneath the bending buds of spice-wood bushes, a burst of spring and a breath of sweetness between the snows of winter and the summer's sun. August is a film of dust on purple asters along the country roads of the lower river, and a green stillness of heavy shade splattered with sunlight beside the upper river. October is a flame, a Renaissance richness of red and amber, the ripeness of harvest in husk and bin. It is the golden span between the dry rattle of September's end and November's beginning.

In this mountain country, November is the month for classic beauty. Lines are clear and simple. Colors are subdued earth shades. Only those who know well and deeply these hills and rivers and their valleys can find them beautiful in this starkness, as a doctor may find a skeleton beautiful in its precision of bone and joint without the camouflage of flesh. November strips the trees and leaves their branches in etched design against the sky, strips the hills and reveals their contours—every winding path and rocky ridge and scooped-out gully—and finally reveals the river. No

longer laced overhead with green
limbs or half hidden under banks
of bush and fern, the streams and
springs and rivulets, as well as the
river they feed, emerge in each
sharp twist, each lazy pool, and become dark liquid lines threading
the mountains and valleys. It is a
fit time to trace the river's course.
It is a fit time to meet the country
and its people.

Now there is nothing hidden
by summer's rich growth, which is
past, or winter's soft snow, which
will come. Now the pasture gates
swing on stout hinges or sag in careless sloth, town streets stir brisk with
purpose or swarm with aimless in-
dolence, and now the river rushes
cold clear green with the first winter rains or mines a thick red-yellow
mud from barren hills and fields.
Now it is November.

The Devil's Courthouse looms
nearly six thousand feet in one of

the most remote corners of Western North Carolina's Transylvania
County. Down the ridge to its south rise the rivulets that become
the North Fork of the French Broad River. Over the ridge to the
north of the Devil's Courthouse begin the waters of the Big Pigeon
River. Though they rise less than a mile apart, the French Broad
does not receive this second largest tributary for almost a hundred
and fifty miles and in another state.

South out of the green heights of Pisgah National Forest the
North Fork of the French Broad tumbles past Piney Mountain and
Spice Cove and Panther Mountain to join the West Fork of the
river. For a unique feature of the French Broad is that it begins
with four large tributaries flowing from the four cardinal points of
the compass and all called by the river's final name. From the little
township of Rosman where the four join to create the main stem
of the French Broad, it follows a sinuous northerly course through
narrow but fertile bottom lands and receives two more rivers, the
Davidson and the Little, before it enters Henderson County, twice
the population of its neighbor Transylvania, where the bottom
lands become wider and Mills River quietly joins its course and
Mud and Cane Creeks enter from the east. Just south of Asheville
the plain Hominy and the poetic Swannanoa become part of the
French Broad.

At Asheville the whole character of the river changes. Its direction turns northwest. Instead of fertile fields and gentle fall,
suddenly it plunges between steep mountains in a bed so narrow
there is scarcely room for the railroad that follows where an old
turnpike used to cling to this passage cut by the river, now providing Asheville's only rail outlet to the west. From Asheville to
Paint Rock, only forty-three miles, the river drops seven hundred
and fourteen feet. Strewn with jagged boulders, shut in by perpendicular mountains, the French Broad falls swiftly here, receiving
many little mountain tributaries: Beaverdam, Reems and Flat
Creeks in Buncombe County, Sandymush Creek on the Buncombe-
Madison line, and Ivy Creek, Hayes Run, Walnut, Big Laurel,

Spring Creek and Upper Shut-in in rugged Madison County. A mile below the Paint Rock of prehistoric ages, and over a hundred miles from its beginnings, the French Broad leaves North Carolina and crosses through the Bald Mountains into Cocke County, Tennessee. Flowing almost due west now, the river begins to lose the wildness of its leap through the gorge. Wolf and Rock Creek, Mooneyham Branch and a dozen smaller feeders come before the literal Long and Clear Creeks, and finally, at the town of Newport, the Big Pigeon River enters again the orbit of the French Broad. Having risen in Haywood County, North Carolina, the Pigeon has drained, by a northwesterly course, the whole southern portion of the French Broad basin, including three of the largest streams heading in the Great Smoky Mountains National Park, North Carolina's Cataloochee and Big Creeks and Tennessee's Cosby Creek. Now, in the wide Irish Bottoms of Tennessee, the Pigeon and French Broad come together.

Four miles farther along this same bottom land, its other major tributary meets the French Broad. The Nolichucky, by a southwesterly course, has drained the whole northern portion of the basin. Rising in the high fastnesses of a corner of Avery County (Roaring Fork and North Toe) and the bulk of Mitchell and Yancey (Crabtree Creek and South Toe), the Toe and Cane Rivers join near the postal station of Huntdale to become the broad Nolichucky. Northwest through the Unaka Mountains into Tennessee the Nolichucky passes Erwin and turns due west and south, looping and curving like a limpid snake, receiving Little Limestone Creek in Washington County and Big Limestone in adjoining Greene, Little Chucky and Bent Creeks, and rich-bottomed Lick Creek.

From north and south the French Broad has now received all the headwaters of its basin, spanning Western North Carolina from just below its Virginia boundary to just above its South Carolina line. It has become a fat river flowing in a fruitful land. Nothing is left of the wild rapids of the gorge along its middle span. In fact,

it soon settles into a lake, the 31,600 acres of lake impounded by
the Tennessee Valley Authority's Douglas Dam, near the town of
Dandridge. Past the spillway of Douglas, the river winds on across
Sevier County, receives Greenbrier Creek and Little Pigeon River
from the Smokies high above Gatlinburg, enters Knox County,
passes islands and bluffs until, just at the city limits of Knoxville,
it joins with the Holston and they become the Tennessee.

Thus the barren outline of the river, meaningless until its place
names are fleshed with people and events, until the waters that
surge between its banks are gathered from streams and springs
that have somehow been brought alive. For the French Broad is,
above all, a region of life, with all the richness and paradox of life.
Water, forests, plants, animals, people: thronging here in rare and
wonderful variety.

The mountains on whose slopes the river begins are real an-
cients of the earth. Their balsam- and spruce- and rhododendron-
covered peaks rise taller than any east of the Mississippi River, with
four over 6,500 feet and some thirty over 6,000 feet. They were
old before the Rockies even began to be formed, as witnessed by
their rocks which belong to the Archeozoic or very oldest era of
geologic life, going back a thousand million years. They are part
of the Appalachian range, the oldest mountains in North America.
The story of nature's violence through the eras, of mighty pressures
exerting themselves into earthquake and upthrust, can still be read
in cross sections where rocks are exposed in distorted formations.
Born in colossal upheaval, how serene and steady, how green and
familiar, these mountains stand today. Rounded, tree-covered
Mitchell, whose own story follows later, but whose eminence rules
first and last over all of eastern America. The Black Brothers, the
Balsams, the Roan. Craggy Dome and Cattail Peak and the Devil's
Courthouse. The Great Smokies and the Unakas. Clingman's
Dome. Even the magic of their names can scarcely equal the maj-
esty of their age, the mystery of the million-featured life they
support.

First there are the forests, richer in variety of trees than the whole of Europe, for this is the area where Northern and Southern vegetation meet and mingle. Twenty-five thousand years ago, as a great icecap formed over Labrador and pushed slowly out across North America, animal and plant life fled before its crushing destruction. Seeds were distributed by wind and animals and insects in front of the creeping glacier, until at last all the northern United States was buried under ice, and trees and plants once native to Canada made their last stand on the heights of the Southern Appalachians. The glacier did not reach these mountains, and in them was preserved the plant life that gradually, as the ice receded, found its way back north. But these trees and shrubs and herbs also never deserted the mountain refuge they had found in Western North Carolina and Eastern Tennessee. Here are some of the largest stands of virgin spruce and balsam fir in the Eastern United States. Here are the great hardwood forests of America. Here, by climbing one mile up certain mountainsides you can travel, forestwise, more than a thousand miles north. The great stands of trees covering hills and coves were and are the most valuable natural heritage of the French Broad country. Not alone for quantity of board feet, nor for wide variety of species, but for the life they supported and their relation to the vast water resource of the region. For forests and water are as inseparable as the heart and its blood. If there is a water problem, there is a forest problem first.

The cold sweet springs of these mountains, the springs which feed with thousands of steady streams to make a river, have been valued for generations by the families they feed. If halfway up a hillside or deep in the heart of some remote cove you see a house and wonder why its people built there rather than on easier slopes, the answer is probably their water. Cupped in a clear steady pool under a thicket of blackberry vines and old shade trees, their spring bubbles from the earth like a rare gift for the taking.

When the buyers for the Great Smoky Park were appraising

some of the small landholdings on the Tennessee boundary, one old fellow would come down from his little farm each day. "When'll you be a-getting to my place?" he'd demand of the buyers.

"We'll be up there soon as we can," they'd reply.

"Well, I'm just aiming to make sure you see my spring. You'd have to see it afore you could know the worth of my place."

At last, after these urgings had interrupted work every morning for a week, one of the appraisers asked, "And what is it that's so special about this spring?"

"Everything," the old man retorted. "But mainly its cold. Year round, it stays the same: two degrees colder than ice!"

Springs influenced not only homesites, but the location of towns as well. After the General Assembly of North Carolina, in 1783, divided Washington County for the second time and created Greene County in later Tennessee, Robert Kerr, who had bought three hundred acres in the heart of this country, donated fifty of them for a county seat. More important than the acreage was the fact that they included the Big Spring, a supply of water so certain and abundant that it furnished the whole town of Greeneville until 1913—well over a century. And the old records of the entire region show consistently the influence of a bold spring on the location of church or school or camp-meeting ground.

But of all regions in the United States, this French Broad country is in the one most harried by a habit designed eventually to kill springs: the ferocious habit of woods burning. First resort of hand-to-mouth farmers and lazy lumbermen, the death brought by their fires is doubly fatal because it is also subtle. The greater part of the life of a forest takes place not above ground where we can see and readily measure it, but deep in the porous earth where roots penetrate far into the subsoil and as they decay leave a network of underground water channels. Sifting down through thick humus into this web of roots and veins, rain water is stored and finds its way with gradual steadiness into the springs and streams that water the countryside. Fire consumes not only the existing humus, but the trees and shrubs and plants that could create a new supply.

As nature's sponge is destroyed and becomes instead a hard-packed crust, rain cannot penetrate the earth. Instead of falling on plant leaves and splattering into a fine spray that soaks through mosses and mulch deep into the subsoil, the rain strikes hard ground trampled by cattle or crusted by unwise cultivation, and it runs off rapidly into the nearest stream, taking with it loose bits of soil. It is a much longer, more detailed story than this, the relation of the French Broad to its mountain forests and the tiny secret filaments of life that bring a giant river into being. The wonder and challenge of it can only be suggested here.

As the trees of the north fled before the icecap, so did plants and shrubs. Today the French Broad country is probably the richest area in the United States in botanical treasures. Like Shakespeare's Cleopatra, a great part of her beauty lies in her "infinite variety." From the explorations of French botanist André Michaux, 1785 through 1796, and the journeys of William Bartram in the same century, to the wild-flower pilgrimage led yesterday by a park ranger in the Great Smoky Park, this region has been a laboratory and a revelation for botanists of the highest professional caliber and most casual amateur status. Here is the rarest wild flower in America, the delicate shortia, discovered by Michaux, but lost for nearly a century afterward until rediscovered by the eminent Dr. Asa Gray. It is a relative of the handsome galax, whose leaves beautify these winter hills with their splendid bronze sheen. And there are no other relatives in this particular family. It has been said that "the little plant, *Shortia galacifolia,* found only in the mountains of Carolina, has caused more discussion, more searching, and has baffled botanists more than any other known plant."

Here are plants and shrubs of blazing beauty: the woods azalea that burns orange and yellow and crimson along the green hills, that has been called one of the purest examples "of the plant life of another age left in the world today." And the rhododendron (named from the Greek meaning "rose tree") that covers with a deep purple and pink and lavender blanket the heights of Roan and the Craggies. Over an area of some six hundred acres on the slopes of Craggy Dome and Pinnacle, the largest stand of purple rhododendron in the world blossoms each year.

In the mountains of the French Broad are found certain insects that occur nowhere else in the South; game animals, fish and birds, and every hollow tree, every rotting log, every rock slide and spring reveal such workings of common and uncommon types of smaller animals, amphibians and reptiles as to spark our curiosity and spur again our wonder. An ornithologist studying the forest litter of these Appalachians made us statistically aware of the multiplicity of the minute hidden lives around us: he found nearly a million and a quarter insects in the topsoil alone of every acre of forest litter. To these small unnoticed scrabblers also the forest owes its porousness, the water owes its storage powers, the river owes part of its existence.

Thus it is not such a startling marriage of opposites to shift from the smallest to what we call the highest form of life on the river—from its salamanders to its people. For the people too are richly varied, rare and worthy of attention. Who are they? What are they? And what has the river been to those who lived within the French Broad watershed?

To the earliest dwellers who have left us any mementoes of themselves, the ancient Mound Builders, the river was source of sustenance, spiritual power and pleasure. Along the lower reaches of the river they left the mounds that have become our Rosetta stones of knowledge concerning their existence.

A farmer on the river, who had one of these mysterious mounds in the middle of his wide flat cornfield, was shocked to learn that there were grown men who spent their time and muscle unearthing the secrets of the mounds. "Yup. They come up here from the University. A whole batch of 'em. Six or seven, I reckon. Know what tools they had? Teaspoons! I'd swear it true on a stack of Holy Bibles. Teaspoons and whisk brooms! They pitched in to that mountain down there, aiming to break it down with whisk brooms. Worked six months off and on. Then their funds run out, they said. I couldn't tell you what they ever found. Bits of bone and bowls, such as that, I reckon. But you can see they didn't make much of a dent on that there mound. I say a man ought to have a 'dozer to really get whatever's in there busted out."

To the Cherokee who roamed this country of the French Broad and had the legendary villages of Kanuga on the Big Pigeon and Kanasta on the French Broad, who hunted these forests and fished these waters, a river was part of their religion and livelihood, their commerce, their myth, and their recreation. From the solemn rites of purification when a boy entered manhood to the utilitarian pleasure of fishing for food, the river was a part of Cherokee life, and they gave it a name and a personification: Long Man, the River, fed by the tributaries of his Chattering Children, all the brooks and rivulets winding through the mountains. To the French Broad specifically they gave the name Agiqua, and for at least part of its length, the rapids below Asheville, they called it Tahkeyostee, meaning "Where they race." The Cherokees were right. This river needed several names to fit its several moods and natures.

The lower, more accessible Cherokee towns in Georgia and Southwest North Carolina saw the first approach of the white man. But Long Hunters were not long in climbing the mountains. From the coast of Carolina, they soon left behind them the fringes of civilization and penetrated wilderness. Discovering mountains, naming rivers, cataloguing for the first time the features of a new land, they were tough as whang-leather and literal as rain. They recorded the character of the country they found in the names they set upon its hills and rivers. Newfound Gap, Snakeden Top, Hawkbill, Bearwallow, Shinbone Rock, Humpback Mountain, Pretty Hollow. As their path led toward the upthrust Blue Ridge, the rivers must have impressed them by their width for they named

them First and Second and English Broad. And when at last a
party of these trail breakers climbed the Ridge and stood in a gap
facing toward the unknown western land under control of France
by way of the Mississippi, they looked at the new river they found
in the valley just beyond the Blue Ridge and called it the French
Broad. It flowed toward the lands and rivers owned by France;

when a Long Hunter had gulped from a spring on the far side of
the dividing mountains, he could say he had drunk of the French
waters. He had traveled a far piece west.

A strange beautiful river, this one the hunters found and settlers peopled and travelers described, but few knew intimately
and almost none knew in its entirety for many years to come.

To the treaty makers, part of its course served as a natural
dividing line between lands owned by Cherokees and whites. For
the soldiers of both peoples, white settlers and red owners, the one
seeking to have and the other to hold this land, the river was a
campsite and a route on their way to bring death to their enemy.
To the first surveyors, the French Broad was a handy and permanent boundary to set between land grants, counties, individual
farms. For explorers and later rail builders, its middle third set a
passage through the steep mountains that today divide North
Carolina and Tennessee. To some the river was inlet into the whole
challenging Territory South of the Ohio; for others it was outlet to

the great world of the Tennessee River and beyond. Thus William Faubion, near the site of Newport, Tennessee, built, in the early 1800's, a flatboat rigged with a paddle wheel on the rear end. He also took along a blind horse which could serve as a sort of land-locked tug when the boat was in shallow water or other difficulty. Loaded with flour, bacon, dried fruit, feathers and other farm goods, this little craft made its way down the French Broad to the Tennessee, up the Tennessee to the Ohio, from that river to the Mississippi, and at last to the metropolis of New Orleans. Here Faubion and his crew sold their boat as well as goods and made their way home by land. Flatboating to New Orleans from lower points along both the French Broad and Nolichucky rivers was fairly common at this early date.

Less common was use of the upper French Broad for naviga-tion, and totally unique was the saga of the *Mountain Lily*. Which came first, the idea for a company that could advertise itself as "the highest steamboat line in the world" (2200 feet above sea level), or the idea for improvement of the river channel, and whether or not the whole project was just a watered-down pork barrel, are all matters for debate today. It was, in fact, a matter of debate in 1876, when Robert B. Vance, Representative from the mountain district, succeeded in putting a bill through Con-gress appropriating $25,000 for the improvement of the upper French Broad "channel." It had first been necessary to have the French Broad declared a navigable stream, and to this even Rob-ert's brother, the famous ex-Civil War Governor and then Senator Zeb Vance, could not subscribe. Senator Allen Thurman of Ohio became so vehement in his opposition that he declared even a cat-fish couldn't navigate the French Broad River. Nevertheless, the $25,000 was appropriated, and became the first Federal under-taking for improvement of the French Broad. This particular proj-ect was also unusual because, as the government later reported, it was the only development on the whole Tennessee River system "that was not carried on with the expectation of contributing to navigation on the main stream as well as on the tributary. The lowest point to which the work extended was Asheville, separated by eighty miles from the head of navigation at Leadvale, Tenn. Between the two places the stream falls with such torrential force (an average of 13.4 feet per mile) that improvements to connect the two navigable sections would have been out of the question."

With this ditching, digging and blasting of shoals all going forward under direction of the U.S. Army Engineers, a steamboat company seemed the next logical step. Colonel S. V. Pickens, a man with wider vision than navigation experience, launched this enterprise. He became president of the French Broad Steamboat Company, authorized capitalization $25,000 (the currently popular figure apparently). A Captain Averill, experienced in boat building, was imported to supervise construction of the little sidewheel steamer equipped with two twelve-horsepower engines and accommodations for one hundred passengers and an equal burden of freight. Excitement mounted among the dwellers of the upper French Broad. River traffic would release them from their isolation; storekeepers figured carefully how much import and export by water would save them over wagon haulage. At last, bright as new money, the *Mountain Lily* was ready for her launching. Unfortunately, the French Broad was not so ready. The summer had been dry and the river had shrunk disastrously. Now the engineers decided that jetties were the answer to the navigation problems of this odd river. So large stones were hauled by sled and wagon from an old quarry near Davidson River Station and were anchored with cement, cables or logs, to banks where the channel was wide and shallow.

While this effort to make the French Broad wash a narrower, deeper channel for itself was going forward, short jaunts up and down the river provided ladies and gentlemen from nearby towns with a leisurely diversion. At last, when the full maiden voyage of the *Lily* was scheduled, a general holiday was declared in the upstream village of Brevard. In carriages and on foot they came to celebrate their steamboat. It took a rope and tackle and some heavy hauling to get her under way.

As to whether or not the *Lily*'s death came on this journey or her next, even eyewitnesses disagree. But it is certain her life was short and rugged, for either this first night or the following one a rainstorm struck in the headwaters of Transylvania County. The placid Dr. Jekyll of a river was suddenly transformed into a raging Mr. Hyde. Floodwaters swept debris down from the mountains and on the third day, the poor *Mountain Lily* yielded before their onslaught and swirled loose from her moorings. When the river quieted once more, the proud little packet was deep on a sandbank and the jetties were packed with mud washed down from the hills.

The conclusion to the whole affair was prolonged and indecisive failure. The government expenditure had grown from the appropriated $25,000 to $43,000. Its shoals were gone and its jetties worse than useless: now they were actually obstructing the course of the river. The *Mountain Lily* lay in stranded desolation for months before her final dismantling began. The boathouse at Johnson's bridge boasted the most appropriate ending: it became a meeting place for the Riverside Baptist Church.

If the French Broad seemed to reassure itself that there would be no traffic on its upper reaches, it invited, with characteristic paradox, traffic on its lower seventy miles. As early as 1793 Dandridge, forty-five miles up the river from its junction with the Holston, became Jefferson County's seat of justice because it was a general gathering place on the banks of the river. It was the head of regular steamboat navigation and the town grew as traffic increased. But even seventy-eight miles up the river, the capital of Cocke County, Tennessee, was located in 1797 at New Port on the French Broad because citizens believed it was destined to become a busy river city. A fleet of rafts went down from New Port each spring and many through the year, but a steamboat at the New Port was rare. And so, when the railroad went up the val-

ley along the Pigeon River, about three miles distant, the Newport contracted its name, packed its bags and moved from the water
to the rails. It was a very typical adjustment.

River traffic at Dandridge flourished, however. Federal improvements were made in the river channel and regular steamboat runs were scheduled. One of these boats, the *Lucille Borden,*
made ninety-six trips up river in 1891. The captains of these freight
and passenger boats became important personages in the region
they served, carrying news from the city of Knoxville—local affairs, market conditions, political opinions—upriver to the towns
and farms where in turn they learned the latest crop prospects to
relay to city merchants. Sometimes, as in the case of Captain John
Maples, they served not only as friends and newspapers but as
bankers too. Captain Maples was often entrusted to carry money
from merchants along the river to be deposited in city banks.
Once Captain Maples's boat sank in the French Broad. The thousand silver dollars he was carrying in a belt didn't make his rescue from drowning any easier. But Captain Maples escaped to
make many another trip up the river.

The old-time captains of the steamboats that plowed the
forty-five miles up to Dandridge, or the flatboats and rafts that
made the sixty-nine miles up to Leadvale, sometimes look at the
straight rails and roads of today and shake their heads. As one
old-timer among them said several years ago: "You'll see boats
going up the French Broad to Dandridge again sometime. 'Member all those tubs the French Broad Navigation Company used to
operate? My dad built most of them. Gee, but I'd like to see this
old river bearing up a good-sized tub, going full steam ahead with
her whistles singing."

They are nostalgic for something that is part of the past of
the river. So much has passed. Tribes of people have come and
gone along the French Broad. Mountains have shifted, plants have
emigrated. Ways of life have flourished and dissolved. In the scope
of our own small history, the light of army campfires has reflected

in its waters many times—always an independent personal army of soldiers who were merely aroused citizens. The army of Rutherford from North Carolina and Sevier from Tennessee going to attack or counterattack the Cherokees. The army of Overmountain Men crossing the high gaps along its headwaters to defeat with squirrel-hunter's techniques an English army of professionals under General Ferguson at the decisive battle of King's Mountain, just across the line in South Carolina. The armies in gray and in blue that chose sides so closely in this particular corner of a country racked by uncivil war.

Along the French Broad people have envisioned in small original plans, and in gigantic blueprinted finalities, the possibilities of power. On the upper river, some four miles below Asheville, North Carolina, in 1889, an individual undertaking completed a granite dam across the river and harnessed, for the first time in that area, power for electricity. William T. Weaver had been on his own to some extent ever since he was four years old and his father, a colonel in the North Carolina Sixtieth, had been killed during the Civil War. Store clerking, banking, construction of Asheville's first trolley line, he had succeeded in them all before he turned to this idea of power. Once it took hold of him he could talk anyone into anything, and he traveled from Boston, Massachusetts, to Augusta, Georgia, talking friends and strangers into investment in his Weaver Power Company. He secured the funds and built his dam and the electric age had arrived in Asheville. From this first experiment, he launched out in success to build other dams on the river: at Marshall, at the mouth of Ivy Creek, and a steam plant at Asheville.

If Weaver's success was prophetic of events to come, so were his problems. Especially the one involving Mary Brown against the Weaver Power Company, a case still cited frequently in the courts. Mary Brown owned three acres, more or less, of land buried under the water impounded by Weaver's dam. Also, she lived near the new lakesite and found the smell created by the lake offensive.

In final judgment on this case of "ponding and backing of river," Mary Brown was awarded $750 damage and $150 damage a year. Of the three submerged acres the verdict said: "The estimated rental value of the land showed great divergence of opinion."

Nearly half a century later, when the tremendous Federal undertaking of TVA proposed a dam on the lower French Broad, about thirty-two miles above its mouth, the "estimated rental value of the land" they would submerge showed another "great divergence of opinion." However, in this case, the differences of opinion arose not only from varying estimates of monetary value of the acreage, but also from divergent ideas on the purposes of TVA. This dam had been proposed before World War II, but, because of the rich and settled agricultural resources its construction would destroy, its building was postponed. Fifteen thousand acres of the best river-bottom land in East Tennessee and eighteen thousand less productive acres would go if Douglas came. Flood control for part of Tennessee was obviously not a sufficient reason for flooding some of the best land in another part of Tennessee. But when Pearl Harbor erupted in flames, power for victory entered the picture. Power and food had some partisan debates—it is difficult to say which was most right. But Douglas Dam was built and in record time. The President signed the law authorizing its construction on January 30, 1942. Construction began on February second. On February nineteenth of the following year, the dam was closed and the French Broad wore its most mammoth harness.

This twentieth century miracle of curved concrete and throbbing turbines, with all its attendant expenses, cost $41,800,000. In floods of 1946 and 1948 the dam is estimated to have saved Chattanooga alone $23,500,000. Costs and savings are tricky balances in any contest, however. As with so much in the French Broad valley, here again we need less concern with contest of opinion over parts of the picture and more desire for clear understanding of the whole. It is possible that land was a power TVA unduly disregarded in its construction of this particular dam on the French

Broad. It is possible that TVA electric power has improved the face of more French Broad land than facile critics might realize. Whatever the ultimate judgment as to its justification and merits, Douglas Dam has set a bold seal of the twentieth century on the French Broad River.

As for the TVA program as a whole, it has brought the French Broad dwellers of East Tennessee power of several kinds. Not only electric power to pump water up a steep hill leading from spring-house to kitchen, or to rotate the dasher in that washing machine decorating the front porch, or to run an engine irrigating drought-plagued pasture and crop land, but power to purchase those implements too, and the knowledge—which is power—of the best ways to use much of their land and many of their resources. In the matter of floods on the upper French Broad, neither TVA nor any other agency has been commissioned to meet the challenge.

Individualist even in catastrophe as in so much else, the region has most of its floods in late summer or early fall. The wide divergence of average rainfall readings—ranging from about 40 inches at Asheville to 70 inches and more at Rosman where the main forks of the newborn French Broad converge, to more than 100 inches in some years on the uppermost southern end of the basin—indicates the nature of the terrain and problem. The low but rugged mountains on the eastern boundary are the first high masses encountered by moist air moving inland from the Atlantic Ocean, and after this meeting and the consequent rains, the yet higher mountains on the western boundary cause still further rising of air and falling of moisture. Both heavy rainfall from Atlantic hurricanes and convergence-type storms that sweep up from the Gulf and in from the ocean simultaneously, have turned the French Broad, upon occasion, into a veritable tidal wave of death and devastation.

In 1791 a scarcely documented flood occurred in the whole area, which Davy Crockett, over on the Nolichucky, described as "the second epistle to Noah's fresh." From that date on, floods became more frequently mentioned and fully described, up to the dark peak of July, 1916. During that month two tropical cyclones synchronized so effectively that the French Broad and its tributaries seemed singled out to scatter destruction. Between the fifth and thirteenth of July, the waning force of a Gulf coast storm which had moved inland over the Mississippi coast, drenched the watershed of the French Broad. This rainfall by itself was not sufficient to cause large floods, but it saturated the soil and filled all streams to moderately high stages. When a second storm moved inland from the Atlantic coast on the morning of July 14, and reached those waiting mountains of Western North Carolina by the sixteenth, the drama of disaster was as swift as it was inevitable. Nineteen inches of rain in twenty-four hours, recorded at one station, had no place to go but down the already soaked and shifting mountainsides to join the already swollen current. Nowhere else in the area between the Atlantic and the Gulf were the effects of these storms as devastating as in the French Broad valley. Flood stage on the gage at Asheville is 4 feet. During that first, or Gulf, storm, on July 11, the river reached 8.8 feet, but by the morning of the fifteenth it had receded to exactly flood stage, 4 feet. That night the second, or Atlantic, storm struck. By 8 o'clock the next morning the French Broad was 13.5 feet. An hour later, at 9 A.M., it had risen to 18.6 feet. At 10 o'clock the bridge on which the gage was located washed away. The crest of that flood was 23.1 feet.

Farms and industries, homes and stores, crops and railroads, bridges, buildings and tons of loose earth: these and all other manner of natural and man-made permanances were swept away or inundated by the surging water. Most tragic of all were the lives lost. No accurate assertion of numbers is possible. There were the nurses drowned at the village of Biltmore seeking to serve their patients; there were those two men swept away while trying to carry food to guests marooned in a hotel near the railroad station; there were the unrecorded numbers of those overwhelmed trying to save property, livestock or family, and those who were trapped without warning by the sudden treacherous water. Certainly between forty and fifty, probably more, were killed in the brief time and relatively small area, of the great French Broad flood.

1916 stands as the year of the river's chief and unforgettable rampage. Those who felt its power then, remember something of the wild force that the combined elements of mountains and water can create in this special situation. And they remember its dark beauty too. A beauty perhaps more romantic, but no less real, than that of the dam built to protect man on the lower part of the basin.

The French Broad is a river and a watershed and a way of life where day-before-yesterday and day-after-tomorrow exist in odd and fascinating harmony. Beneath the deepest waters impounded by Douglas Dam lies buried the largest untouched Indian mound of the French Broad country. Our most ancient relic of man and our most recent trophy of his scientific skill rest practically side by side.

There is the same coexistence of past and present within the people. It helps explain how they may be at once so maddening and so charming, wrong about so many things and yet fundamentally right so often. This living past and present is my story of the French Broad. I should like to think that by some unmerited but longed-for magic I have spoken for a few of the anonymous dead along its banks and up its mountains. For the Negro baby drowned in the river when its mother tried to swim from slavery and bring it into freedom. For the sheriff who was shot in the back from a laurel-thicket ambush as he picked his way along a fog-blanketed early-morning trail. For the minister in a windowless log church who made foot washing a symbolic ceremony of humbleness and brotherhood. For the old taletellers around country stores and the urbane newcomers who seek but have not found as yet. For these and for the river itself, mountains, lowlands, woods, gullies, springs and ponds and brooks I should like to speak, to quicken understanding. For the French Broad is above all a live country. The Cherokees said, "We have set our names upon your waters and

you cannot wash them out." They were right—the Nolichucky
and the Swannanoa and the Estatoe—but they might also have
said, for all of us, "We have lived our lives along your rivers and
you cannot wash the memory of us out."

# 2

## Give Us the Wind

The twenty-seventh day of January, 1674, was a cold day at the little trading post of Abraham Wood. Wood was a Virginian, and his station was located at the Falls of the Appomattox in the southeastern part of that state, due north of the North Carolina line. He was one of the leading Virginia gentlemen enterprisers of the day. In 1668 Abraham Wood had been one of a "Company of Two Hundred Gent," including William Byrd I and Byrd's uncle, who had signed on for a projected journey to find the East India sea and any stray silver mines that might be overflowing along the way. The sea-and-silver search did not materialize, but Wood subsequently sent others out to explore beyond the Blue Ridge for him. These parties inevitably ran into those of the rival ubiquitous Byrd. But today Mr. Wood was awaiting news of a man who had penetrated for him a region untouched by other Virginians or Carolinians or any other Englishmen at all. Only last spring the man had brought Wood news of the land beyond the mountain ranges to the south and west, of the rich valleys and thick canebrakes, and now he was out there again—but where? There had been no word since autumn. The wait had grown long and filled with apprehension.

As he bartered or talked with the Indians who came and went around his post that day, Wood could not help but remember the

27

confident hopeful leavetaking which had occurred four months before in the bright warmth of September while the chill of winter was still only a vague threat riding the early morning air and oak and poplar and maple glowed on the colorful hills. On the twentieth of September he had stood in the clearing before this post and watched a little procession of twelve Indians, led by a single white man on horseback, set out from his headquarters and turn their faces southwest. Many hopes rode with that group. Its leader's name was James Needham. He had been returned only nine days from the first English journey, of which there is any record, into the country of the French Broad. Financed by Wood, with eight Indians, four horses and an indentured servant of Wood's named Gabriel Arthur, Needham since the previous April had followed buffalo paths and a maze of interlacing Indian trails which webbed North Carolina, Virginia and Tennessee, and found rivers for which he knew no name. The one that was probably the French Broad he described with slight exaggeration to his employer Wood as "half a mile broad all sandy bottoms, with peble stones, all foardable and all empties themselves north west."

Leaving Gabriel Arthur in one of the Indian towns, Needham had returned to report his findings to Wood. With fresh provisions and encouraged by his first success, he set forth again after only nine days' rest into the land of unexplored mountains and waters. And the wilderness seemed to have swallowed him. After a message from a village called Eno, some five or six days' journey from Wood's post—silence. Weeks had accumulated into months, and Wood's anxiety had increased with each turn of the calendar. He had wondered about the hazardous mountains, the untried rivers with sucks and whirlpools and sudden depths; he wondered about Indian John, "a fatt thick bluff faced fellow" who had helped guide James Needham on the first trip and been well paid, but had asked for half his pay in advance before this second journey. It was a danger-ridden expedition, and no news was not good news—but more likely a tongue and hand forever stilled.

Now, this chilly January day, Wood put his familiar questions to the Indians who straggled by. Their response was usually a dark and secretive silence, but today he had some luck. A new group arrived, withdrawn and taciturn at first, but gradually giving forth their news. Needham and Arthur, they said, were dead at the hands of the Tomahitans, a branch of the Cherokees. It seemed a dark frozen day indeed to Mr. Wood.

In the weeks that followed, there was confirmation of a general misfortune, but no details. The Indians, fearful of becoming involved in the murder, were uncommunicative. A trader who had seen Needham and his party in one of the Indian towns told Wood that the travelers had not been well received there and that Indian John had had Needham's pistols and gun in his hands.

And what of Gabriel Arthur, the servant turned explorer? Practically a prisoner in a land never yet seen by Englishmen, wasn't he, in all likelihood, dead at the hands of red men too?

Spring came, and Abraham Wood looked at the greening hills and wondered if his countrymen would ever be able to penetrate those barriers in search of land or silver or whatever lay behind them. Then, on the eighteenth of June, Gabriel Arthur staggered into the house of his employer and master. With him he brought only a Spanish-Indian boy—and the story of James Needham's death as he had learned it from the Indians accompanying Needham.

Journeying southwest, probably along an eastern branch of the old Catawba Trail that eventually runs north and south through the heart of the French Broad country, Needham's party came to a river, and in process of crossing one of the Indians let his pack slip into the water. Whether it was intentional or an accident, part of a well-laid plot or simply the spark for a sudden explosion, no one ever knew. Needham, tired and doubtless overwrought, spoke sharply to the carrier for his negligence. The man replied in kind, as did Indian John, who seized upon the opportunity for quarreling at Needham through the rest of the day. When they had stopped to make camp for the night, the bad humor persisted. In the gathering darkness, among a strange people, confronted by ill will, Needham picked up a hatchet which lay near him and threw it on the ground beside his guide and protector. The Indians remembered that he asked, "What, John! Are you minded to kill me?"

For a moment, only the quivering hatchet on the ground, then like an arrow Indian John's arm shot out and clutched his hunting rifle. A report, the smell of powder, the sudden movement among the other Indians to restrain John, and Needham dead on the new-found earth. While his fellow red men stood aghast, crying what should they do now that the Englishman was dead and they would be cut off by the others of his countrymen, John took out his hunting knife and ripped open the body of his victim. Holding Needham's heart high in one hand, he shook it in the direction of the plantations and cried that he did not value "all ye English." After he had ransacked the packs, he sent word by the other Indians of the party to the town where Gabriel Arthur was held, to put their prisoner to death. His messengers carried the news of Needham's murder and the instructions for Arthur's death with equal fidelity. With details of his friend's betrayal ringing in his ears, Arthur was tied to the stake and piles of dry cane were heaped around him. In a rescue of authentic melodrama, he was saved just before the first torch was lit by the king of the village who had taken a liking to their visitor. Thus he had narrowly escaped Indian John's vengeance and been allowed to return to his master's trading post.

The expedition had been a failure. No more had been learned of the vast green wilderness of the five rivers Needham and Arthur had seen on their summer journey. James Needham had been the first of many, red and white, who would give their lives to know and hold this land. And when Abraham Wood sat down on August twenty-second to write an account of his venture to a friend in London, he gave voice to two features which would character-

ize the Western exploration and settlement to follow: the spirit of
pure adventure balanced by the drive for personal gain. He said,
"Soe died this heroyick English man whose fame shall never die
if my penn were able to eternize it which had adventured where
never any English man had dared to atempt before and with him
died one hundred forty-foure pounds starling of my adventure with
him. I wish I could have saved his life with ten times ye vallue."

Even the regional histories have recorded little about this hired
explorer and the indentured servant, but they were the first Englishmen on record into the land of the Nolichucky-French Broad-
Big Pigeon. They had opened a crack in the domain of the Cherokees, covering a vast area in Georgia, Alabama, Tennessee and
North and South Carolina, and set into motion a surge of territorial engulfment that would only end in 1838 with nothing less
than complete dispossession of the Cherokees and the Trail of Tears
westward, only a small government-controlled "reservation" left
to them in their mountains of the Great Smokes. It was a hundred-
years' struggle played out on a thousand small stages, with the
actors staking their lives on the outcome of the conflict—a conflict
of intimate savagery and hate such as can only arise from homes
devastated, children kidnaped and families slaughtered in hand-
to-hand combat, be the homes and children and families Indian
or English. For a while it almost seemed that the irresistible force
had met the immovable object, but gradually the force was victorious, eating away and away and away until both land and spirit
of the opposing Cherokees were at last reduced to meagerness.

From the first treaty the Cherokees ever made with the English, in 1721, through the treaty of 1798 when the last of their lands
on French Broad headwaters was ceded to the young United States,
the area, especially in Tennessee, bounded on the north by the
French Broad, was constantly and hotly disputed between settlers
and governments of both nations. There were few Cherokee villages
in the immediate vicinity of the river at this time, and those were
small and unimportant compared to the ancient populous Kanuga

and Kanasta it had once boasted, but the region was a rich hunting and fishing ground, and many parties in search of food and
sport frequented its virgin forests and streams. Extensive hunting
grounds were essential to Cherokee existence, and these lands had
been theirs as long as mind could remember or legend relate. Likewise, fertile farmlands and new settlements were essential to the tide
of homesteaders constantly pushing back the natural boundaries
of wilderness and the artificial boundaries of treaties. Conflict between those who owned but did not till these inviting acres and
those who did not own but needed to cultivate them was inevitable.

At the treaty of Paris in 1763, France relinquished to England
the whole western territory which had given the French Broad its
name, and a great conference was called at which the governors
of Virginia, North and South Carolina and Georgia and Captain
John Stuart as British superintendent of the Southern tribes explained the situation to the chiefs of all the Southern Indians. Now
the English push for settlement began to gather energy. Boundary
lines were set and broken and reset. Individual whites treated with
individual Cherokees—there was, for instance, Jacob Brown's lease
from the Cherokees of a large tract of land along the Nolichucky
River, for which he gave a horseload of goods and became the
first settler of that fertile region. As such independent transactions
had been forbidden by royal proclamation, the situation was anything but firm for all concerned.

Since the royal government had seemed to be the only protection standing between their national survival and complete engulfment by the settlers, and since familiarity had unfortunately
often bred contempt between American and Indian, whereas the
English officials were sufficiently removed to maintain respect and
dignity, the Cherokee sympathies were already pledged when the
Revolutionary War came. They hoped by helping the Tory cause
to diminish the American encroachment on their homelands.

Now came the time of terror and bloodshed for all. Up and
down and across the French Broad, warriors and settlers attacked

and counterattacked. Everyone was a soldier and a potential victim. It was not long after war began until the states realized that they must deal with the enemy in the rear before they could fight effectively the foe at their front. As a consequence, the first American army to march over the Blue Ridge by way of the French Broad watershed, and the largest expedition ever sent against the Cherokees, crossed the mountains at Swannanoa Gap in August, 1776. Commanded by General Griffith Rutherford, Irish-born and about forty-five years old, there were 2,400 North Carolinians in the expedition which was to co-operate with three other armies from Virginia, South Carolina and Georgia in one vast pincer movement. These four were to attack from different points the main towns of the Cherokee nation and decimate the population as quickly and completely as possible.

At Old Fort, North Carolina—then called Davidson's Fort for the family who built it—the North Carolina Blue Ridge raises its mighty barrier between the lowlands and the mountain inland of that state. This barrier was to hold back settlement, discourage railroad building and influence the routes of later war, but it was not too hazardous for Rutherford's army, who followed ancient trail and trace up the eastern slope, through the Swannanoa Gap and kept on the course of that little river till its junction with the French Broad. A short distance down the French Broad, at Warrior Ford, the army crossed to the south bank and up into the hills again. They penetrated some of the steepest country of Western North Carolina, crossed the Pigeon River, picked their way through the headwater country of both Pigeon and Oconalufty rivers, and finally after many "a blind path through a very mountainous bad way," as one of the soldiers recorded it, reached the country of the Overhill towns.

En route there had been cursory fighting. While crossing the mountains on one occasion, the marchers approached a house where an Indian trader lived and, when they caught sight of someone fleeing through the door, their chaplain, the Reverend James

Hall, shot the man, believing him to be an Indian. When they came to the body they saw the man was a Negro slave of the trader's. He remains an anonymous victim of the trigger-happy fury of the times. But when the towns were reached, all destruction was really loosed. The participants themselves left accounts of the merciless deeds of this border warfare. Not only was the usual devastation of war carried out in the killings, the burning of towns, the leveling of fruitful fields, but every Indian warrior was scalped, if time allowed, women were put to death as ruthlessly as warriors, and such prisoners as were taken were sold at immediate auction into slavery. Every house of every town Rutherford's army passed through was burned, its fields of corn were trampled, and its survivors were left to roam the woods and live as best they could. This was a scorched earth policy such as even General Sherman of Civil War fame could not equal almost a hundred years later.

The French Broad saw other marches and encounters besides those of Rutherford and the North Carolina men, however. When the army of Virginia, coming a little after Rutherford, reached the War Ford of the French Broad, they found a detachment of Cherokees waiting to prevent their passage. An English trader who was with the Indians came to visit Colonel William Christian and his two thousand men as soon as they reached the vicinity of the river. Knowing he had an impressively superior force, the colonel took his guest through the whole camp and sent him back to his friends with the word that there was no possibility of truce until the Indian towns were become ashes. Then he proceeded to the ford where his army made camp, built great fires and gave general signs of a lengthy stay. As soon as it was dark, however, Christian took half his men and went down river seeking a place where they might make a crossing and come around to the rear of the Indian camp in a surprise attack. With its characteristic unpredictability, the French Broad became deeper and swifter downstream of the ford and the crossing was difficult. The men went four abreast to battle the heavy current. In spite of the water's depth they managed to keep the powder for their rifles dry, and when they had all reached the riverbank they set forth on a stealthy encirclement of the camp. Only there was no camp. Just the remains of old fires and the trampled earth that suggested a hasty departure by the Cherokees in the face of the numerous and well-prepared army. Christian and his men were too late on this occasion, but there would be an abundance of opportunities to come when a victor's vengeance could be indulged. It was part of the tragedy and irony of the frontier that Colonel Christian in years to come would be burned at the stake somewhere on the Ohio by another tribe he had gone to conquer.

Four years later, in December 1780, the most spectacular leader in the Tennessee territory won a battle on the French Broad that was considered by contemporary historians the best-fought battle of the border wars. This was no tremendous distinction, considering the disorganized character of most of these struggles, but it displayed the quality that made John Sevier the epitome of the frontiersman and the idol of his followers.

"Nolichucky Jack" Sevier was a romantic figure. Of French origin, with a gracious polished manner when the occasion demanded and a fierce resourcefulness when the need arose, he was to become the founder of the state of Franklin which later gave way to the larger state of Tennessee, whose first governor he became. At this time, Sevier was only approaching the peak of a career which earned him a reputation as the greatest Indian fighter in the Southwest.

On the seventh of October in that year of 1780, Colonel Sevier had been one of four leaders who took a thousand backwoodsmen in hunting shirts and skin caps and, with no orders from the military, no authorization by Congress, and no supplies or equipment of any kind except their own hunting rifles, marched across the Blue Ridge into South Carolina. Here they engaged an invading portion of Cornwallis's army under Colonel Ferguson and defeated it so decisively at a place and battle called King's Mountain that the whole British campaign in the South was altered. Then they shouldered their rifles and returned home. When they reached home they learned that the Cherokees, recuperated during the years since Rutherford's campaign, had been attacking all along the outer boundary of settlements. Everyone who received warning in time had taken refuge in one of the many community forts strung across the frontier; others were murdered amidst general havoc.

The first of the upper East Tennessee leaders to rally his men and march for the Cherokee towns was Nolichucky Jack. With something between two and three hundred men, he started south, following the great Indian War Trail. On his second night out he sent scouts, as usual, on the trail ahead. As these scouts mounted one of the hills along the way, they came suddenly upon an encampment of Cherokees. After firing into the Indians' midst with more daring than prudence, the advance spurred their horses back to camp. Sevier prepared against attack, but nearly at dawn he received reinforcements rather than bullets.

On the next day's march they passed through the deserted enemy encampment, decided it had been a large party, and pursued as fast as they could. They crossed the French Broad and made camp. The following morning the men in the advance march discovered fires where the Indian camp had been. Ashes were still warm and ends of sticks were still smoking. Above the mouth of a creek, now called Boyd's Creek, where it empties into the French Broad, Sevier arranged his frontiersmen in a half-moon and directed his advance guard to overtake the Indians, open fire and then retreat toward camp. In about three quarters of a mile the scouts were shot at from ambush. They promptly returned the fire and commenced their strategic retreat. As hoped, the Cherokees followed and were sucked into Sevier's trap. Hemmed in from three sides, with the two outer columns rapidly closing, the Indians had no time to fight, only to escape. They left their dead and much of their "plunder" behind them. Sevier's victory was complete and decisive and credited with staving off a major conflagration along the border. At its conclusion he took his men back to the French Broad where they made camp on the Big Island, which was later to be called Sevier's Island, and waited until other companies joined them. Then, seven hundred strong and all mounted, they swept down on the towns of the Overhill Cherokees along the Tellico and Little Tennessee rivers, leaving—at the end of their raid—less than half-a-dozen villages not demolished.

This was the beginning of a long bloody series of forays against the Cherokees. The very next summer when some new settlements near the junction of the Pigeon and French Broad rivers were attacked, Sevier again led his men in a successful raid on the enemy. When, in 1783, the Revolution ended and British power in America was broken, the Indians sued for peace also, and so came about the treaty of Hopewell made in 1785, called "the turning point in the history of the Cherokee" because it was the first agreement signed with the newly created United States. Its phrases and purposes were typical of many a document to follow. Commencing with "peace to the Cherokees" and receiving them "into favor and protection," concluding with "the hatchet to be forever buried between the United States and Cherokees," the heart of the matter lay in the middle provisions wherein almost four million acres of Indian lands were ceded to the United States.

Because of a series of unsettled points, however, chief of which was some three thousand white settlers on unceded land between the French Broad and Holston rivers, the treaty did not bring peace. By the following year, 1786, Tennessee settlers were assuring the Cherokees that North Carolina had given them all the land north of the Tennessee River and west to the Cumberland Mountains. Since the Federal government had guaranteed them this land by the Hopewell Treaty only twelve months before, the Indians were disbelieving. And rightly so, for in 1783 North Carolina had reserved the area south of the French Broad and Big Pigeon and east of the Tennessee to the Cherokees and many of these later land grants were illegal. What the Indians did not grasp was the fundamental issue that was already raising discord in the infant republic—the conflict between States' rights and the central government. It was an issue that was to influence the steady defeat of the Cherokee cause, that was to flare into prominence during the debate of 1836 on removal to Oklahoma, and was finally to bring civil war upon the country. During the whole long process of dealing with the Cherokees, the Federal authority worked by one standard and made one set of promises, while state authorities followed other goals and made altogether different pledges. In the end, state interests—or more accurately, the necessities and greeds of local people—won every time. Those three thousand people between the French Broad and Holston, those unestimated numbers on unceded land south of the French Broad, most of whom had moved in under authority of the state of Franklin, were not of a mind to move. They built their forts and stations and fled to them when need came; the Indians resorted to every method of warfare to drive the poachers away; Sevier raided and fought and private parties went out on retaliatory thrusts, a man sometimes getting killed and leaving his name on the stream or cove as lone memorial to the event.

In August, 1790, President Washington pointed out to Congress that some five hundred families had settled on Cherokee lands since the treaty of Hopewell, not counting the illegal settlers who had been there previously. He also pointed out that either the 1785 boundary should be enforced or else a new one should be arranged and paid for. Typically it was decided that a new treaty should be drawn; it seemed almost as if the people created their own laws and then the government came along and made them legal. Consequently, on July 2, 1791, 2,500,000 additional acres were enfolded in the widening embrace of United States boundaries and they consisted of a North Carolina-Tennessee triangle which included most of the French Broad River and the sites of the present cities of Knoxville, Asheville and Greeneville. Perpetual peace was,

of course, declared, and the United States "solemnly" guaranteed
to the Cherokees "all their lands not herein ceded."

The gulf was already beyond spanning. Indian disillusion
about the white treaties was fairly complete, and border cynicism
in dealing with the Cherokees was fairly constant. The Cherokees
said they had signed this last treaty under threats and pressures
and they did not feel bound to respect it. Consequently, the terrible tale of massacre and pillage repeated itself once more. Up
and down the French Broad men and women and children in
lonely cabins were scalped; the border army forded the river and
struck at the Indian nation; settlers were shot as they plowed in
the field. A Moravian missionary traveling through the French
Broad territory found that most of the settlers he met "would rather
like to extirpate them [the Cherokees] altogether, and take their
land themselves; they scarce look upon them as human creatures."
Wounds of the sword bred further wounds.

In addition, another complication arose. It was discovered—
or perhaps only alleged—that North Carolina had given grants
for lands lying inside the Cherokee borders to some of her sons
who had fought in the Revolution. The Federal government now
proposed to remove such settlers. A ground swell of protest arose.
The settlers said they had come to these acres in lawful good faith
and they did not propose to be dispossessed by a "cruel, tyrannical
and oppressive" law. The government said it was trying to fulfill
a contract it had duly signed with the Indians. Governor Sevier,
putting his state to the forefront as usual, and the senators and
representatives from Tennessee—among them young Andrew Jack-
son—all urged a new treaty. At first they were defeated, then, in the
summer of 1798, negotiations were opened for the writing of a new
agreement. On October second, thirty-nine chiefs from the Cherokee Nation ceded another million acres to the United States. These
included the headwaters of the French Broad and its tributaries,
Big and Little Pigeon rivers. Now they had relinquished possession of all that vast woodland and bottom land feeding and fed

by Tahkeyostee, the Racing Waters. From that first English exploration by James Needham and Gabriel Arthur in 1674 and the first treaty signed in 1721, until this cession of 1798, the territory of the Cherokees had shrunk like a hand atrophying or a pool of water drying up under desert sun. The process was to go on until 1838 with the removal to Oklahoma along the tragic Trail of Tears, when one fourth of the driven fell by the roadside, starved, ill or frozen. And the remnant that remained in the Great Smoky Mountains were permitted to do so only by the martyrdom of Old Tsali and his sons and brother. Thus came the final guarantee of peace and protection from further plunder of land. But by the turn of the eighteenth century, the French Broad and its tributaries, heart of all the old wild hunting grounds, was forever lost to the owners, including Dragging Canoe, the bitter unyielding chief, and Sequoyah, the mellow linguist, who had cherished it "time out of mind."

Before going on a hunt, the Cherokees had a brief prayer they offered to their gods of nature. "O great Kanati, I come where you repose. Let your bosom be covered with bloodstained leaves. And you, O Ancient Red . . . let my hunting be good. Give me the wind." It beseeched the Inscrutable Spirit to send the wind from the right direction so the hunter's prey would not scent him and so be warned to escape. But as the Cherokees knew, there were four winds. The South wind was white and brought peace; the North wind was blue and meant defeat; the West wind was black and brought death. The wind from the East was red. It brought power, and war. The gods had given the Cherokees a wind from the East.

# 3

# The Western Waters

They did not know they were the forces of empire. Frequently they were the pawns of land speculators and political connivers, and they didn't know that either. Individually they were people in search of homes and farms; raw, brawny, penniless people, some of them; quiet, weather-toughened, people of spirit, others of them. They fought the Indians and gave them Bibles; traded with them and broke the pacts they made with them; they saw the great empty green acres of Cherokee land and believed it was meant to be settled and planted and harvested—by civilized folk, by white folk: by themselves.

This part of the French Broad story, then, is about three of these settlers, three of the first and the best. Their plain solid names are Jacob Brown, William Moore, and Samuel Davidson. A merchant turned speculator, a soldier turned settler, a homesteader who instigated a migration. They were not particularly extraordinary men and that is why they are here, because there were many others like them. They were like all the Americans, these three: they could not hear of the country beyond, the country on the western waters, without wanting to see it. They were full of curiosity and courage.

Jacob Brown came first. Like the course of a river which seeks the route of least resistance, so early settlers followed valleys first and only overcame the mountains later when there were no other new paths to try. Because of this, the French Broad watershed was first settled, not from due east as might have been expected, but along its northern boundaries. This was the result of a lengthy process beginning in the middle of the eighteenth century when German and Scotch-Irish Pennsylvanians emigrated from that state to North Carolina. In their advance westward, they had been halted by the Alleghenies and had begun to flow south. When they reached the valleys of Maryland, Virginia and Carolina, they found them comparatively unsettled because movement from the coast had not yet reached the mountains. To make these areas more attractive, land, at this early date, cost much less in Virginia and North Carolina than in Pennsylvania. So, over a period of two or three generations, the Pennsylvanians moved farther and farther south and then, with the restlessness and energy characterizing the pioneers, helped in the push over the mountains of North Carolina and Tennessee. The greater number of these were Scotch-Irish, although some were of German or "low Dutch" origin. While most of the direct settlers from Pennsylvania paused in North and South Carolina and only reached Western North Carolina and Eastern Tennessee by the next generation—or right after the Revolution— it was still this Scotch-Irish heritage that predominated in early settlement.

The Scotch-Irish were always roamers and adventurers, and the ones who continued on to middle and upper Carolina were especially strong in wanderlust and sense of individuality, for they left behind in Pennsylvania the ones who were content with rich farms and full barns and deep roots. The second and third generation, who finally reached the valleys and mountains of the French Broad, could therefore be called the essence of Scotch-Irishness. They had pushed on beyond the most forbidding barrier, discovered the most rugged country and settled under most isolated conditions a country where individual liberty was the prize, with loneliness and privation the cost. In this general ebb and flow, it was inevitable that some of the Watauga settlers from upper North Carolina should move on south, discovering new country.

Jacob Brown was a merchant and a trader. Originally from South Carolina he had, more than likely, made trips to the Upper or Overhill Cherokee towns with his burdened horses and their tinkling bells breaking the stillness of long forest paths. After moving to the Watauga settlement, he may have even followed some of the Indian paths (the Great Indian Trail was very near) to those same towns. It was in such a way that many of the first settlers found their homesites and gave up the life of trading.

At any rate, Jacob Brown saw the Nolichucky River, a wide beautiful body of water rising in some of the highest mountains of Eastern Appalachia, depositing along its broad bottom lands silt as rich and real as gold. These bottoms, when Brown saw them, were dense with luxuriant green growth of cane. Near such canebrakes there was bound to be game and to spare. This was land for hunter, cattleman or farmer: cane was succulent feed for stock, or it was much easier cleared from the land than timber. In 1771 or 1772, Brown pitched his tent on the north bank of the Nolichucky. Not knowing whether the land was in Virginia or North Carolina (he later said he believed it to be in Virginia), he entered into a private trade with the Cherokees. In exchange for the goods from one pack horse, he secured the lease to land on both sides of the river. Just what the exact acreage was, we don't know. Perhaps Brown himself didn't know. But it would be safe to assume he was not niggardly in dealing out the miles to himself—as many as the Indians would allow.

After his settlement with the Cherokees, Jacob Brown set about bringing others to his land. He sold them the rights to certain portions of his lease until its date of termination. Several other settlers came down from North Carolina and joined Brown. This was a fairly common way for the original investor to recover some of his initial payment and make a profit as well.

The legality of either the lease or these subleases did not trouble Brown or his friends very much. Law in that precarious time and place consisted principally, for the actual settlers, in keeping their powder dry and their scalps in place. Documents of conveyance were simple and straightforward. "For value received of eighty-five pounds, I do hereby assign all my right, claim and interest of the within deed, unto —— , as witness my hand and seal." Thus were hundreds of acres on the Nonachunheh, as Brown had learned the name Nolichucky from the Indians and as it appeared in all his early leases, transferred and laid claim to by the first settlers in the French Broad watershed.

Meanwhile, North Carolina pointed out to these people that they were on Cherokee land. After threat and persuasion, Brown returned as far as Watauga, but following the great treaty at Sycamore Shoals on March 17, 1775, Jacob Brown made another treaty of his own. The merchant-trader-landholder met with Oconostota, chief warrior and head prince (who had just made the most eloquent speech of his career against the encroaching white man who melted whole nations before him "like balls of snow melting before the sun"). With Oconostota were the Tenesay Warrior, Attakullakulla and Chenesley and the Bread Slave Catcher. In consideration of ten shillings, these Cherokee chiefs sold Jacob Brown land on both sides of the Nolichucky "and as far west as the mouth of Big Limestone Creek." It was not a homestead, it was a principality embracing the best part of what, at present, are the two rich East Tennessee counties of Washington and Greene.

Jacob Brown remained on his land ten years. Then, judging by the crude sandstone marker still weathering in a green antique cemetery in this Nolichucky valley, he died the twenty-fifth of January, 1785. Fifteen years later, about the turn of the century, his grandson built a brick farmhouse which also still stands on the original acres staked out by Jacob. The giant oak under which he traded with Oconostota and the other Cherokee chiefs, the grandson's house of handmade brick, the small marked plot of earth:

perhaps these were all Jacob Brown had bargained for in settling here anyway. His tombstone in a sociable churchyard and a heritage of land he could pass on to others of his name.

William Moore didn't mind a fight. He was from Ulster Province, Ireland, and when, after removing to America, the Revolution came, he was glad to join in on the side of revolt. In 1776 his wife's brother, General Griffith Rutherford, was assigned to make an expedition against the Cherokees who were coming to Britain's aid and massacring colonists all along the border. Moore became a captain of one of the companies under Rutherford and marched with him over the Swannanoa Gap, down the French Broad and along the route already described in chapter two as Rutherford's Trace. Being at war neither blinded nor bewildered young Captain Moore. He saw the untouched, and—better—unclaimed, fertility of the land he passed through. Perhaps he responded to its green beauty too, seeing something of the fresh landscape of Ireland in these tree-covered mountains, thick canebrakes, grassy balds. The next year following the Indian expedition, in 1777, Captain Moore came back over the Blue Ridge to the French Broad River, not in war but in peace. A few miles west of the present city of Asheville, he built a small log-cabin fort, but before he could bring his family and begin their new life there, the Continental Army demanded his services once more.

Six years later, in 1783, the General Assembly of North Carolina opened a tract of the lands west of the Blue Ridge for settlement, and with a grant of six hundred and forty acres from Governor Richard Caswell, ex-Captain Moore returned, in 1784, to the French Broad and his "land on Hominy Creek" near its junction with the river. With wife and slaves, three daughters and three sons, he forgot soldiering and became a homesteader, one of a typical pattern for much of the river's settlement as it came: hunter, trader, soldier, speculator, they saw and stayed to conquer or be conquered. William Moore's grave is also in a public ground, near one of the North Carolina county schools. There lies a fragment of history on the classroom step, if teacher and pupils can lift their heads from the textbook monotony men have made of their own living past to sense for a moment one day or one night of the fear, satisfaction, drudgery, determination in the life of this first lone settler of their vast region. The stone says simply: "William Moore, died Nov. 11, 1812, AE 86 y's." But where, in what book, are the complexity and wealth of those years?

When Samuel Davidson first saw the French Broad, or why he decided to settle there, or if he even saw it before he decided, no one has bothered to record. His is the only pathetic one of these three brief chronicles. It also contains a measure of irony such as only the processes of history can perfect.

After the defeat of the Cherokees in 1776, North Carolina had an understanding

with the nation's chiefs that as soon as North Carolina could get sufficient goods on hand she would buy the territory now called Buncombe County. Accordingly, in 1783, by the Act that had also sent Captain William Moore back across the Blue Ridge as land-holder, North Carolina opened all the land east of the Big Pigeon River to settlement.

Hunters who had ranged over the area returned to Old Fort, the last outpost at the eastern foot of the Blue Ridge, and told the people there of the rivers and their valleys waiting to be claimed. Samuel Davidson was one who listened to their reports. He had had a brother murdered by the Cherokees in 1776, and the deci-sion to go to Indian country must have been a hard one to make, because his brother's wife and children had been killed too—and Samuel had a wife and baby daughter to take with him. But the call of new land proved more urgent than whispers of safety. Some-time in the autumn of 1784—surely early autumn, to be settled under a roof with a bit of food laid by before winter came—Sam-uel Davidson came over the mountains with three females: wife and baby and his wife's Negro slave.

They found a place near the Swannanoa River, a little dis-tance above its entrance into the French Broad, and they built a small, crude cabin that must, nevertheless, have seemed a cozy human thing in the midst of so much wildness.

Grass and cane and pea vine were thick along the river and slopes, and each night Samuel hung a bell around his horse's neck and turned him out to pasture at will among such abundance. One morning soon after the cabin was finished, he heard the bell on a hill a little distance from the house and went to fetch his horse for the day's work. Through the still woods, up the mountain wrapped in early autumn wisps of fog, he hurried to begin the morning, fol-lowing the steady tinkle of the bell. Probably he never saw the In-dians who shot him. Lying behind a tree, or half concealed in the tall grass, the Cherokees had tolled him on to the ambush near one of their chief trails.

Back at their cabin, the sounds of those rifleshots must have sounded like the crack of doom. With her baby and servant, the wife of Samuel Davidson fled the house, which seemed now more like a trap than a haven. Through that unknown country, with no guide but her own determination, she brought herself and two dependents up the mountains, through the gap and across the Blue Ridge back to Old Fort. Bedraggled and grief-stricken, she told their family and friends of Samuel's almost certain death, and then, although they had not accompanied him in life, a party, mostly relatives, set out to avenge him in death. They found his scalped body on the mountain, where she had said. They gave it proper burial and followed the nearby trail until they encountered a hunting party they supposed to be the murderers. After a skirmish, the Indians fled, leaving one or two dead behind.

If the Cherokees had killed Samuel as a warning to other settlers, in an effort to keep white men beyond the bounds of land they still clung to as their own, exactly the opposite result was forthcoming. On their avenging journey, the men who saw this land decided to return. A few months later Major William Davidson, a twin brother of the dead Samuel, and their sister Rachel with her husband Alexander, and a party of other relatives and friends came over the mountains to the Swannanoa River and established permanent settlement. Samuel had been able to bring them to this country of the upper French Broad only by being scalped. His death had served as spur rather than barrier, and if the Cherokees could have read this token right they would have known that no hardships of life or death would stop the surge toward the western waters. Trader or soldier or farmer, they saw the land of the Nolichucky or Big Pigeon or French Broad and they could not let it go. It was too fertile, too beautiful, too free. Jacob Brown, William Moore, Samuel Davidson had found it so and had known that there would be many to follow in that first path they unfolded, where they stood their first tent or chinked the first cabin.

# 4

# *Every Home*
## *Its Own Community*

Over the mountains, through the gaps, down the watersheds they came, Scotch-Irish, English, German, low Dutch and occasionally French Huguenot, overcoming the Blue Ridge barrier in their search and settlement of what they called the Southwest. No wilderness they found was more isolated than the valley of the French Broad and its tributaries. Because of its barriers against the outside world and the "money" poverty of the people, it came to be called "the land of do without." More accurately, it was the land of "make do." To a large extent it remains so today. From the passage of the first thin trickle of settlers, on through the growing stream before the Civil War, to the most recent phases of development, the people of the French Broad have been, for the most part, thrifty, ingenious, skillful and imaginative in using what lay close at hand to make many of the necessities and some of the pretties of life.

By any standard, most of the early families were poor. Many a man came into the new country on foot, carrying his clothes on his back, hunting knife and ax at his belt, rifle over one arm or shoulder, and powder, flint and bullets and cook pot and hooks, perhaps, on the other. Some came on horseback, but where there was a family, it was rare that all could ride, although a few necessities were added—on the pack horse—to those above: bedding, maybe, blankets and empty ticks which could be filled with leaves or, later, straw and feathers—a froe, an extra skillet of iron, eating utensils, hoes and plowpoints and an auger. Those who came next, in wagons, hauling slowly up the steep mountains, creaking down rutted inclines and over rocky creekbeds, could add still more of the necessities, even seeds and plants, sometimes the tools of a trade, and a spinning wheel.

Tired and eager, they found their place, each his own cove or mountain slope or river field, and faced their first tremendous task: that of destroying the most precious resource on the continent. With all the vigor and recklessness of necessity which had been behind their forward push to this very place, they attacked the forests of primeval pine and poplar, walnut and oak, chestnut and maple. With ax and fire they laid the giants low. The bitterest irony of all the years of settlement is in this process by which a people so frugal they utilized every element of nature, animal, vegetable and mineral, to its least portion, made every scrap count, scraped and pinched and survived only by the closest economy, could waste, with prodigal abandon, the vast harvest of centuries as if it were not only useless but actually an enemy.

Their complete self-dependence lent an immediacy to pioneer lives that closed out all foresight into the long future and made unimaginable the possibility of a day when these vast stands of trees would have disappeared. The forest, despite all it gave, was enemy. Even while the logs for a home were being felled and cracked, shingles split and laid, puncheon floor scraped and fitted, and fields encased in rail fences, by far the greater number of trees were being "deadened" on hillsides or melted to ashes on huge pyres. It is at once a tribute and a heartbreak that so few, with such crude implements, could have wrought so large a destruction in such a shortness of time.

The first cabins were simply logs notched on top of one another, covered by a roof of boards split with the froe and held in place, since there were no nails, by weight poles laid across their length. A door and one or two openings for windows were cut in the logs. The door and the wooden shutters used at the windows in cold or rain were hung on wooden or leather hinges held by pegs. There was a fireplace, usually stone chinked with clay, and it served as means of heat and light and cooking.

The fireplace was the heart of the family's life, for in its wide opening swung the crane on which pots of venison or wild turkey, squirrel or rabbit or bear stewed to savory tenderness. It was the only sterilizer, by heat or boiling water, which was at hand in times of childbirth or accident. Against its warmth chilled hands and feet thawed in winter; where there was a cow, the crock of cream sat on the hearth turning to clabber for churning; by its light a man or boy could sharpen tools and whittle utensils of a long cold night, while the woman or girls spun on the wheel that stood ready in the chimney corner. And when the mountain winter had closed in, a person could sit before roaring logs of hickory or oak, watching them crumble into heaps of clear red coals, listening to the dash of wind or whisper of snow outside, and think long thoughts about this hard compelling abundant region of hills and river that had become home.

In the far corners of the room from the fireplace, beds were built against the logs. A table was made near the center of the room, pegs for hanging clothes or split-oak baskets or rifle were scattered around the walls and rafters, and backless stools and benches served for chairs. Uncomfortable they might be, but there wasn't much time for sitting anyway. The floor remained the hard-packed earth, or, if there was time, puncheons were laid. These were logs split, smoothed on the flat side and laid face up to make a tight, if irregular, protection from damp and cold.

In a few years, after the farm had been cleared and planted, some of the fields fenced in long solid queues of rails, and stock was thriving, this cabin might be turned into a barn or storehouse and a better house built. Usually the surrounding countryside had become more peopled and this could be the occasion for a log-rolling or house-raising. With distances long and mountains lonely, any undertaking seemed a social affair if there were other people to help. To exchange news and eat with others and be reassured that he was not altogether alone in these hidden coves along these silent rivers was ample repayment to any man for his day's work.

This finer house might have two rooms, perhaps a breezeway or dogtrot between them, and a loft overhead reached by ladder or steep stairway. Instead of boards, sometimes called "shakes," there would be shingles for this roof. They might be made of poplar, chestnut, white oak or white pine. If they were oak, it was believed they could not be laid when the moon was light or they would "cup," that is, curl up at the exposed end. But the shingle maker began where the board maker left off. Beginning with a board one-half inch thick at the butt, he used a drawing knife and shaved the other end to a smooth finish which tapered evenly in the whole lot without varying over one-sixteenth of an inch. The edges, too, had to be even. Because white pine was soft and light and had an easy grain to work with, and because the virgin pine was extremely durable, this was the most popular of all woods for shingle making along the French Broad. And as shingles were an advance over the old boards, so making them was more of a craft, a small example of the steady daily advances in the ways of life from wilderness to village.

When a family settled on the frontier, and much of the French Broad region remained frontier until a late period, they became their own community. They raised their own food or found it in

the forest. Salt was the greatest necessity they imported. Its price, because of the mountains over which it must be hauled, put it in the luxury class. Brought at first from Atlanta and Richmond by pack horse, it cost ten dollars a bushel in the overmountain region. Later, by wagon, it cost around five dollars, still enough to make the salt gourd one of the best-guarded possessions in the kitchen.

Clothes were as crude and utilitarian as the cabins and simple as the food. The wool was raised at home, sheared, cleaned, carded, spun, dyed and finally sewed into hunting shirts, dresses, socks and coats. The deerskin breeches worn for everyday by most of the men gave birth to a song called "Leather Breeches," and it began:

> Hey! my little boy, who made your breeches?
> Daddy cut them out and mammy sewed the stitches.

Sunbonnets were the only beauty aids mountain women allowed themselves: to be white as bolted corn meal was considered the ideal complexion. The everyday processes of eating and staying clothed and well were constant and pressing. They overrode even the high drama of war. In 1863 when a Tennessee man sat down to write his sister a letter, he went into detail on the essentials of their existence, and more of it concerned the spinning of cloth than the spinning of history which was taking place all around him. He wrote:

> Dear Sister, After rather a protracted delay I attempt a reply to your last but as I have misplaced it I have forgotten the date.
>
> I don't remember any question you asked except what I gave for my wool. It cost me $4.00 per pound. We have all picked except what we want to color. I have been out to day getting walnut bark to color with. I bought eleven pounds of wool. Harriet wants to make my suit gray—something like the Confederate uniform but I don't know how she will succeed.

We have a piece in the loom now. She had me two pairs of pants flax jeans—that is flax filled on cotton chain the balance she filling out with cotton—making very nice drilling. . . . When did you hear from Brother Campbell? I have not heard a word from him only through you since he left. I heard last night that Fain's Regt is at Knoxville. Bragg has fell back to Chattanooga. Vicksburg still ours at last account. A heavy fight at Gettysburg Run a few days ago. Confederates claim victory. Loss heavy on both sides. All well. . . . Rain in abundance. My wheat nearly a failure. Write soon. Love to all.

Wool and wheat and Gettysburg were equal realities in the toil for food and life and victory.

Iron, for tools and utensils, was brought at first from east of the mountains. However, the price was so dear that its use was curtailed. Sometime near 1800 three forges came into existence in Buncombe County, North Carolina, all on tributaries of the French Broad: one each on Hominy Creek, Reems Creek and Mills River. An early foundry was also located at Pigeon Forge on the Little Pigeon River, near Sevierville, Tennessee. Primitive and exhausting methods forged iron into the necessities of life: axes, hatchets, knives, horseshoes, nails, bolts, chisels, augers.

A man's gun was often his life. During the days when French Broad land was disputed by the Cherokees, the handiness and accuracy of his rifle determined whether a man would live or die. Firearms were needed for protection, for food, and sometimes as a source of amusement at the shooting matches, when all the men gathered for a day to prove who was champion of the mountains. Such a match is still held once a year high on old Fie Top Mountain near the Tennessee-North Carolina line, when the old-timers bring their family rifles and vie for a beef from the Cataloochee Ranch. Many times the outcome used to depend on who had made the "rifle-gun" as much as who fired it. There were certain men who became renowned through the region for their precision and distinction in manufacturing rifles. Such an artisan was one Gillespie who lived near the headwaters of the French Broad River. For many years, through the Civil War and after, a Gillespie rifle was a prized possession. So true was the aim of these rifles and so sure their reputation that when a famous Cataloochee Creek character, old Neddy McFalls, had a good square shot at a buck one day with a Gillespie gun and missed, he was sure his rifle had been bewitched. He made the tortuous journey out of the beautiful but remote Cataloochee cove and visited a woman who had reputed success at lifting "spells." When the curse had been removed and his Gillespie rifle returned to its pristine state of utility, Neddy went home again, satisfied that the next buck to cross his trail was as good as dead.

The mill was an important center of every settlement. At the very first session of the Buncombe County, North Carolina, Court, in 1792, William Davidson was given liberty "to build a grist mill on Swannanoa" and the following January a grant was given to build a grist mill on a branch of the French Broad near where it emptied into the river. Across the state line in Tennessee, one of the first mills on the river was built by a French Huguenot family named Faubion who, in addition to being millwrights, were blacksmiths and wagonmakers.

Building a mill was no easy job, for, besides the construction of the house itself, there had to be dammed up a sufficient head of water to turn the heavy stones, the millrace had to be accurately and durably built, and the stones themselves had to be made and set in place. For corn, a set of native stones chipped into form by hand with a hammer and cold chisel was adequate. Water power gave a slow steady grinding that kept grain from becoming heated and losing flavor, and many a mountain man to this day will go many extra miles to find water-ground meal, for if there is one food of which he is a connoisseur it is the corn bread he has at least once every day. For wheat the grinding was different, however; the best stones were from a kind of granite or feldspar found

only in France. It was still a newsworthy item when, in the early
1870's, a set of French wheat-grinding millstones was imported
and set up at the little town of Clyde on the Big Pigeon River.
Bringing those great stones over the rocky and precipitous mountain roads of that decade must have been a man-sized undertak-
taking.

It was no inconsequential matter to get a month's supply of
meal or flour ground. After picking, husking and shelling the corn,
it was cleaned of all bits of trash and poured into a sack. Then,
slung across the horse's back behind the saddle, it jogged perhaps
twenty or thirty miles to mill. Some mills were open only certain
days for grinding, and then there would be a long line and a wait
during which news of neighborhood and nation could be exchanged. Sometimes arguments flared as to the heaviness of the
"tolls"—the miller's fee in kind for grinding the grain. Sometimes
it took as much as twenty-four hours to go and come with a bushel
of meal, and as meal was the staple food in every mountain home,
a bushel would not last very long. But the slow rhythm of the great
wheel creaking around and around and around, the clear splash
of water against its water-slick sides, the unhurried crushing of the
corn and the rich smell of its dust, the leisurely talk and cool twilight dusk of the tree-shaded millrace and shed: these made a journey "to mill" more of an outing than a labor.

As settlers increased, it was inevitable that someone should
turn merchant, and often the most prosperous or most advanta-
geously located farmer simply set up a store in part of his house or
a small nearby building. Such was the case with Peter Fine, first settler on the old site of the town called New Port, when it was still
on the French Broad River and a port for goods rafted down from
the mountains to the town of Knoxville every spring. In 1797 Fine
was keeping accounts by pence and shillings and pounds for customers with classical unusual names: John Gilliland, Evin Murgin,
Theophelaus Paget, Amos Exley and Uriah Rector. His customers
charged such items as one spoon of ginger, cloth for leggins, four

yards of gimp, one fine hat, two pewter dishes, one ounce of turkey red, one Bible, five gimlets, one quart of whiskey, one quire of paper and one pair of candle molds. In payment merchant Fine gave credit for almost any farm product, with such entries as: cow and calf, by hauling one day of corn, three large Bantams, brandy and bearskins, seven bushels of oats, by smith work, beeswax, whiskey, feathers, thirty-one prime deerskins, by the making of forty axes.

When towns grew and merchants became more plentiful, one old-timer in North Carolina still remembered it as a singular fact that "old settlers in the country each had his merchant in Asheville, not only to supply his wants, but in whom he confided as a trusted friend." It was before the days of cut-rate prices and comparative shoppers, and a storekeeper made a profession out of his trade. Sometimes, even in later years, travelers were shocked at the jumble of articles which accumulated in these stores over a long period of barter. In the London *Daily News* of August 8, 1874, there appeared an account by an Englishwoman who had lived for two years in the mountain village of Asheville, of the habits, people and climate of that part of the world. The lady from Leamington went into a lengthy discussion of the food situation in North Carolina, and although she found the food there plentiful and inexpensive, she added:

> All the shops are general shops. I have gone to buy a bit of ribbon, and have seen horrible raw hides, barrels of nails, meat, groceries, and every imagineable thing for sale, including, perhaps, masses of mica, which is found in the neighborhood, and the roads sparkle with it everywhere.

The yellowed leather-bound account books from these old stores give an oddly factual picture of the times and people. There are stories buried, too, in these entries. For instance, in one ledger, under April, 1861, there were these expenses listed to one man:

| 1 ribbed dress patter | 5.00 |
| 1 pr. silk mits | .50 |
| 1 pr. Moracco shoes and cotton hose | 2.25 |
| 1 silk handkerchief | .85 |
| 1 paper pins | .10 |

and this chilling revelation as the final entry:

| 6 artificial wreaths | 1.25 |

Was it wife or mother or daughter who had fallen prey to the end-of-winter and, in the fresh greening April of Western North Carolina, died? Probably she had never in life received so many new clothes as were now to glorify her funeral, crowned by the splendor of half-a-dozen artificial wreaths!

In these accounts, the necessities and fripperies and realities of life mingle as naturally as the people themselves mingled in mutual need and pleasure. Here are axes and knives, trace chains, 1 rifle-gun at $18, jeans cloth and wool hats and one ready made vest; castor oil and Pain Killer, vermifuge and Mustang Liniment; Ladies Kid Boots, hoop skirts, sheepshears, Arithmetic book, brass-bound trunk, half-dozen coffin screws, a lead pencil, one log chain, a scrub broom and one dozen Guilt (sic) buttons.

Would it be more accurate to observe that there were fewer specialists and more well-rounded people among the pioneers, or that there were more people who specialized in many fields? Sixteen miles from Asheville, at the head of Hominy Creek, lived a man named John C. Smathers who impressed travelers from other parts of the country with the versatility of his offices and accomplishments. He was considered a representative countryman, and the place he occupied in his small local settlement was best illustrated by the story of a cross-examination which he underwent one day.

"Mr. Smathers," a stranger stopping at his tavern inquired, "you're the proprietor of this hotel?"

"Yes, sir."

"And who is the postmaster here?"

"I am, sir."

"Who keeps the store?"

"I do."

"And who runs the blacksmith shop?"

"I do."

"How about the mill?"

"Why it's mine, of course."

"Is there anything else you do, Mr. Smathers?"

"Well, I'm a farmer."

"What about your social life?"

"I'm a pillar in the Methodist church, the father of thirteen children, and my sons and sons-in-law just about run the neighboring county seat."

As late as 1912, when he was eighty-six years old, John Smathers was still called "a good rock and brick mason, carpenter, shoemaker, tinner, painter, blacksmith, plumber, harness and saddle maker, candle maker, farmer, hunter, storekeeper, bee raiser, glazier, butcher, fruit grower, hotel-keeper, merchant, physician, poulterer, lawyer, rail-splitter, politician, cook, school master, gardener, Bible scholar and stable man. . . . He can still run a foot race and 'throw' most men in a wrestle 'catch as catch can'."

He was no doubt the last such pioneer in the French Broad country. Deep in the heart of the Smokies the Walker sisters still live in their hundred-year-old cabin with the loom on the porch where the linsey skirts they wear in winter were woven, the turkey-wing fan above the clay-chinked fireplace, five beds and a trundle bed around the walls of the sitting room, and seed beans drying in little white and brown and purple and speckled heaps beside the door. Some of the seeds have been saved for over sixty years from season to season. But this little island of self-sufficiency has become almost a museum in itself, where one of the sisters writes poems to sell to tourists who occasionally find their way along the tree-roofed road to the Walker fastness.

There are still many artisans left in the area. It is good to talk with such people and watch them work with quiet independence and satisfaction. Yet even these are specialists and stick to their own craft. Perhaps it is better so, for their product can be more professional, more handsome, more perfect. But there was a time when every person was his own manufacturer and consumer, when every home was its own community.

The tide of settlement had crossed the mountains, claimed the French Broad country from magnificent wilderness to an uncertain but man-made future. All these early people asked was to be let alone to work and play, become saints or sinners as they wished. But history was not to leave them in isolation. Not far away, national issues were smoldering. Presently they would explode into open flames. That fire would mark the end of a nation divided, and it would mark, more subtly, the end of the period of self-sufficiency.

Even without war, the isolation of the mountains and their people was being gradually broken by adventurers restless for greener fields and by explorers thirsty for facts and eager for first-hand knowledge. One of the strongest local legends of this isolation and self-sufficiency and its contact with the outer factual world concerns an occurrence just before the War Between the States. It unfolds like a pastoral prelude before a shattering holocaust.

# 5

# The Professor
## and the Hunter

The farm was only a minute human patch laid at the foot of the great wooded mountains in the midst of hundreds of acres of unexplored wilderness. There was a house—two rooms and a kitchen with a porch across the front and a loft above—and clustered nearby were the open-air barn and squat springhouse, all the color of weather: wind and sun and rain.

On a July afternoon in 1857, Big Tom Wilson sat on his porch and enjoyed the fresh breeze that occasionally drifted down from the heights around him. Chickens wallowed lazily in the dust near the barn, and out in the pasture between the blackberry vines the sound of the cowbell was slow and long. His bear dogs had long since stretched out in the cool shadows under the house. At one end of the porch a loom stood with a half-finished piece of cloth in its intricate maze; fish rods leaned limp against the wall. From inside the house there was the sound of children.

The lethargy of late afternoon was broken by two visitors. As the men came up to the porch from the narrow rough trail, children clustered in the open doorway and the dogs bristled till they heard their owner's voice. "Howdy, John Stepp."

"How are you, Tom? This here's Charley Mitchell, the Professor's boy."

With good-natured manners, the tall sinewy mountain man shook the young stranger's hand.

"My father," Charles Mitchell said, "has my father been here, Mr. Wilson? Have you seen him in the last four days?"

"No. I ain't seen him since his last exploring trip up here." And Big Tom looked at John Stepp.

"Last Saturday, the twenty-seventh I reckon it was, the boy here parted company with his father at the Patton House, over on the south side of the Black Mountain. They'd come up from Swannanoa and the Professor wanted to go back up to the peak where you'd taken him nigh thirteen year ago."

Big Tom nodded. He remembered Dr. Mitchell, with all his learning and his measuring apparatus, as clear as he did that bear track he'd found this morning down in the cornfield among his tender roasting ears.

"Well," John Stepp went on, "he started on up the mountain alone about noontime last Saturday. Nobody's laid eyes on him since. Monday Charley and me was supposed to meet him up on the Elizabeth Rock where he was going to do some more surveying and measuring. We went up to the rock Monday but he never did come."

"We can't find a trace of him," Charles Mitchell said.

Big Tom looked up toward the Black Mountain and the Black Brothers that ranged there beyond it, looked at the cap of giant fir and balsam that had given the peaks their name. There were vast stretches in there that had never been explored by white men. Clear rushing Cane River that wound through his farm here drew its waters from a dozen streams webbed like crooked veins up into the hidden recesses of those mountains, and no man had traced them to their source. Bear and "painters" and lesser varmints roamed undisputed in this tangled domain. It was a wild dark region. He'd better tell it to the boy plain out.

"If the Professor ain't been here, and if he ain't come back to where he was supposed to have met you, then he's dead on those mountains."

Nobody said anything for a little bit, while the sound of Cane River and the cowbell took over. Then Charley Mitchell asked, "Would you help us look for him?"

Big Tom Wilson said he would help. It was not in the nature of mountain men to refuse a person in need. And within two days, in that sparsely settled region which had no system of communication, one hundred and fifty men had answered the call for searchers. Twice that many were eventually to volunteer. They could not be just any men, either, for the job they offered to undertake would demand the last ounce of their physical strength. It was not only that the mountains were steep and trailless, or that the contours of every slope shaped a unique ruggedness, but the thick mazes of twisted laurel made every climb and descent a battle with tough interlocking limbs and roots. Nevertheless they came as gladly and freely as one who said, "When I heard that Professor Mitchell was lost on the mountain somewhere, I was plowing, but I dropped my plow and took out to find him."

Who was this lost stranger they went in search of?

Elisha Mitchell was about as different from these men as could easily be imagined. He was as different from Big Tom Wilson as a Doberman is from a bear dog, but there is one virtue common to both and that is intelligence. Developed along different lines, with unlike methods and varying uses, the intellects of these two men were drawn together because of mutual need. Each represented a sort of mind that seems peculiarly American, and without either the development of the country would have been far different and much less interesting.

One more thing that the professor and the hunter had in common, the factor that gave them ground for understanding: interest in the natural world around them. Keen curiosity to know about creatures and inanimate creation as well, quickness to see what was to be seen, alertness to make judgments and draw conclusions from observations. The curious interweaving of Wilson's and Mitchell's life and death seems a parable of each man's worth in his own particular sensibility.

Born in Connecticut, a graduate of Yale University, Elisha Mitchell had received an education for the ministry from a New England seminary before he came to the University of North Carolina as a professor of mathematics. His variety of interests and abilities soon became legendary. In addition to mathematics, he taught natural history, chemistry, botany, surveying, agriculture, geology, and geography; his university students called him "the walking encyclopedia." Besides writing books for his students to study, he taught his own family of five children. Almost every Sunday he preached either at the Chapel Hill village church or in the college chapel. He was also the college bursar, a justice of the peace, a farmer, a commissioner for the village and at times its magistrate of police. It is self-evident that he was a man who, as one of his friends said, "enjoyed being busy. Neither laziness nor idleness entered into his composition, so that he always had something which he was doing heartily." There was nothing he did more heartily than study the birds and animals, the trees and plants, the rocks and sands and clays of North Carolina. He had said once in a sermon that God is a part of nature and nature a part of God.

While on an exploration in the Western mountains years before this trip with his son, he had measured the Black Mountain and discovered that it was higher than Mount Washington in New Hampshire, at that time considered the highest peak in the East. A few years later he and Thomas Clingman, also an avid explorer of this region, made a trip together through the Balsam and Black Mountains as well as the Great Smokies, measuring and making scientific studies. But when Clingman issued the news that he had discovered a peak higher than Dr. Mitchell's Black—a peak called the Smoky Dome which would later be renamed for its discoverer —a scientific feud flared between the two men. Each published his findings and made his claims and the public was left to wonder about the "accuracy" of science.

But not for long. Dr. Mitchell was not one to let such a controversy run on without verification of his own figures. It was this necessity to establish, without doubt or falsification, the claim he made for his mighty Black that had sent him on this last journey into the mountains. When he had struck off alone toward its summit, he had gone to find the marked balsam under which he had stood years before and made his first exciting measurement. Somewhere between that pinnacle and the overnight hiker's cabin on one side of the range and Big Tom Wilson's farm on the other side, the Professor had become lost or injured.

As the party of volunteer searchers increased and was organized, a natural division separated them into two groups: the Men of Buncombe and the Men of Yancey they called themselves, men from the two westernmost North Carolina counties whose boundaries were among these mountains. The Buncombe Men were led by two of their famous old bear hunters, Eldridge and Frederick Burnett. The Burnetts directed the early part of the search, mostly on the south side of the mountain.

For days they toiled and looked. One party followed the east fork of the Cane River and another took the west. More scenic, more difficult terrain would be hard to imagine. Through the July heat they combed the undergrowth, working higher and higher, across the gaps, and finally late one afternoon, hungry and exhausted, they met at the Patton House on the Buncombe road from the pinnacle. They looked at one another and shook their heads and there was no need for comment or explanation. They were bone-tired and there was nothing for them to eat.

Zeb Vance, who in a few years would become the famous Civil War governor of North Carolina, was one of the searchers. When he arrived at the house and saw the situation, he promptly directed some of the men to drive up a fat heifer that was grazing in one of the mountain pastures nearby. A skilled marksman named Ephraim Glass put a bullet through her head, and the sharp hunting knives soon had the meat divided and roasting on long sticks over an open fire. A few of the men were too famished to wait, and they ate the chunks raw, without even the savor of salt. Vance had also started a party down toward the settlement of Swannanoa to get flour, salt and a little "extract of corn."

When they returned, far up in the night by the light of pine torches, the jug of "corn extract" made the rounds from one thirsty mouth to another. The older hunters began to compare details of the day's search and plan the next day's route, and finally they launched into a few tales of past hunts and hardships. There was no one who could equal Big Tom in telling about the woods and bears and the ways of both. The men listened, reassured, as his calm, low voice recounted dangers he had overcome, not once or twice but many times. He described bears individually, like people, familiar with their habits and oddities, and he called his dogs, past and present, by apt affectionate names. The bear who turned, finally, and stood his ground tenaciously against assault by pack and hunter, the dog who hung on to the trail no matter how many days it took to bring their bear to bay, these were victim and victor Big Tom admired. The men shared their experiences and knowledge of the woods. They slept, at last, by the chunky coals of the fire that felt good at night in this high altitude.

Monday was another hard fruitless day and that night the pessimism in the camp was so solid it seemed almost tangible. After eating a chunk of crude bread made of the flour brought up the night before, and some of the leftovers of beef, they discussed plans for tomorrow. When someone suggested the hunt be postponed for three or four days until birds of prey might begin to gather and point out the location of the corpse, there was almost unanimous agreement. The size of the area to be combed, its dense tangle and generally unknown terrain, made the task of finding one small man

seem hourly more hopeless. But young Charley Mitchell could not abandon his father so completely, even for a few days. He pleaded with these worn realistic mountain men to continue for even a little longer.

Then Big Tom took over. Soft as rain on moss but firm as granite, he explained: "Now I've talked with the men who gave Professor Mitchell his directions regarding the way to my house, and I've talked with William Wilson who guided the Professor the first time he ever visited that peak. Turning what both these fellers have told me in my mind, I'm certain that if any trace of the Professor is ever found, it'll be somewhere between a little garden patch that opens out just before you get to the top of the peak, and my house."

He paused but there was no comment.

"Now, Mr. Vance," the tall rawboned mild-mannered man went on, "up to this time I've been letting the old men and you men from Buncombe search. Now I'm going to search. Any of you men want to come with me, that's all right too. I'm going up to the cabin on the mountain tonight. From there we can get a soon start in the morning."

He stood up and four of the Yancey men joined him, four of the keenest who had trailed many a mile in these woods: Adoniram and James Allen, Berton Austin and Bryson McMahan. They took scanty rations from what was left of the flour and beef. That night they climbed to the cabin—jumping-off-place for any exploration of the Black.

Big Tom Wilson who had always walked quietly beside the Professor's learning and scientific instruments, who had stood aside a little awed at the university air that clung to the older man, open and friendly though he was—this Wilson now became the leader, putting *his* learning to the test. That learning was a mixture of reading the lost man's mind, observing every detail in the woods he searched, judging distances and possibilities and correlating small separate facts to a significant whole.

Several years later, Big Tom gave his own account of the following eventful day. Tuesday, the seventh of July, ten days after the Professor was last seen alive by his son, the last intensive search began.

We Ate our breakfast at Day break consisting of some Beef and Biscuit and took enough along for our dinner and started off in the direction that we Supposed Dr Mitchel would have gon from the top of the peak to my house and had only gon som 2 or 3 hundred yards When Mr. A.D. Allin Said, 'Come here Big Tom I believe I have found his track. calling all the party together We followed the impressions in the moss resembleing the foot prints of a man Some 200 yards and found the marks of a Shoe heel on a small balsam root and was Satisfied then that we were on the track As we could See the print of the tacks on the root then we held a hurried consultation and agreed to return and backtrack to where he had left the top of the mountain and give the whole force Notice of our success doing so and finding a complete track under a fallen Balsam which formed a Shelter for the foot print in the Soft loos earth beneath . . . then Big Tom over anksose to spread the good tiding Whooped long and loud makeing the mountain wring for miles away with the echoes of his Stentorious voice then retraceing our Stepps the New recruits consisting of Mr. Westall Robert Patton and a young Mr. Burgin accompanying us we proceeded to the tracks and then without hesitation or delay traced the tracks to the heel print on the rock thence we must follow the dim foot prints of the lone man after the laps of 10 days Big Tom Said come gentlemen it is dinner time we then took dinner and resumed the Search sending two men back to the top to let all the force know. . . . Big Tom leads the way and Said com on boys here hes went Mr Bob Patton said how can you say here hes went when we could not track a horse here for the laurel! Come Said Tom and I will show you how at the Same tim pulling off a branch of Laurel Said do you see the top of the leaf is dark green and the underside is white look now I can see the white side of the leaf up turned for 20 yds go ahead Said Patton you are better than any old hound that ever Jumped on a track So I did goe a head only looseing the track one time then it was found by Bob patton and all stood stock still and called the old hound Big Tom and set him on the track as you would your fox hound.

The "hound" remained steady at his tracking throughout the afternoon. When he stopped at one place and said this was where night had overtaken the Professor, his companions demanded once more "how he could tell." His explanation was as simple and logical as any of the best of Sherlock Holmes—and just as neglected by the less observing eyes of those around him.

"Don't you see," Big Tom said, "back there among the laurels the doctor picked the best ways and crept through the open places, and here he ran up against a bush and there he fell over a rock. Don't you see where he slid down and this shows he couldn't see his way any longer?"

When they came to a creek soon afterward, Tom went down in the creek bed and found scratches on the jutting rocks made by those same tacks in the heels of the Professor's shoes. They crossed, as he had done, to the opposite side of the creek, certain now that he had decided to follow this water route down the mountain and to some eventual settlement. But Big Tom had already seen the signs and heard whispers of the menace that lay just ahead. As he joined the others he said, "There's a high fall in the creek just below. I wouldn't be surprised if he's found right there."

Only a short distance farther they came to the precipice over which the stream plunges forty feet. Crawling to its edge, Big Tom looked over into the pool. The dark water was impenetrable, but on a driftwood log lodged at one side lay a familiar soft fur hat. Crumpled and water-soaked, it lay like a black period marking the end of a search and a life.

"I've found the hat. Come and see," Big Tom called to his companions.

At the base of the falls was a pool fifteen feet deep, and at one side a rock ledge shelved over part of it, deadening some of the sound of the falls. This had probably helped deceive the Professor as to the height of the falls. When he worked his way around the slippery rocks in the darkness, he had turned too soon back to the channel of the stream he was trying to follow, while he was still above the pool. Tom crawled and clung and slipped around the falls and back up to the pool. Now he could make out the body, caught by a log about halfway between the bottom of the water and the top, floating face down with outstretched arms. The watch he wore had stopped at nineteen minutes past eight o'clock. Big Tom's estimate of where night had overtaken the Professor was correct.

All the other parties were called back now. The search was ended. Charley Mitchell was with Zeb Vance and a group of the Buncombe men deep in another valley when they heard a horn blasting in the distance to tell them there was news. As Vance later described it, "About one o'clock in the night, while we were resting . . . they came and told us the body was found. Sitting around the camp fire on the trunks of the fallen firs, in the light of a glorious full moon . . . we heard the tale."

Confronted with the problem of getting the Professor's corpse out of this chasm that had never, as far as any of these mountaineers knew or had heard, been seen by white men before, they responded as concretely as ever. The body was wrapped in stout sacking and a pole was run between the body and cloth. Only two men at a time could shoulder their heavy burden that weighed almost two hundred and fifty pounds. There were ten men in all, making five relays, but each could go only a short distance in the tangled laurel. When the two bearers came to a place that seemed impossible, the rest of the group made a chain by clasping hands, with the uppermost man gripping a tree, and by will power and muscle and shouts of encouragement, they heaved their burden along. After hours of this toil they reached the top of the mountain.

"There," Big Tom later said, "we were met by a large crowd from Buncombe, who said that a public meeting had been held in Asheville on receipt of the news of the finding of the body, and the meeting resolved that the body should be brought to Asheville and buried there.

"That made me and my men mad and we asked them that if the Asheville people were going to say where the body should be buried why hadn't they come and searched for the body and found it; that we were the ones that had found the body and were the ones to say where it should be buried. For a few minutes things looked lively and very much like there would be a fight.

"Finally Zeb Vance called me aside and told me that Professor Mitchell's children requested that the body be turned over to him."

So, as Zeb Vance said, the Yancey men yielded and the Buncombe men proceeded to bring the body "slowly down the valley of the Swannanoa" to Asheville.

In the end, however, the Yancey men were victorious, for after a church funeral and burial, the Professor's body was brought back, a year later, by ox-drawn sled, to his mountain. Mount Mitchell, highest point east of the Mississippi.

Big Tom Wilson lived on to become a legend in his own lifetime. The many visitors who came to visit Mount Mitchell, once its supremacy was established, hired him as guide and helped furnish support for the ten children born to him and his wife Niagara Ray. He was a fine sampling of the finest sort of mountain person —the six-feet-two, spare, sinewy, bearded man whose naïveté often overshadowed for strangers the shrewd wisdom that kept him alive. The Professor had been given degrees attesting to his learning, yet Tom Wilson knew something that meant the difference between living and dying in this mountain country, and that was respect for the unmeasured power of any adversary, mountain or bear or stream or even the darkness of night. If the splendid old man could have been, for that one night of June twenty-seventh, only a little less busy and zealous. If that once he could have assumed some of the mountain leisureliness that is supposed to be laziness but often masks caution and awareness, if he could simply have let the mountain and the night have their time and waited until daylight to break his hazardous path, the steep little falls would never have had their victim.

The falls are still there, at the head of Cane River before it becomes the Nolichucky before it becomes the French Broad. The falls and the wonderful dark pool, cold and hidden, under a mountain thick with pathless undergrowth and pungent with the smell of ancient leaf mold. The cupped stones where constant water has swirled and rounded their contours and hewn them into a basin holding the still water that does not reveal its bottom but seems only quiet and waiting, like some ancient sacrificial well, the ferns in the ledges along the perpendicular sides of the falls, the nervous water bugs and the resilient moss, all are still there.

The Wilsons are there too. A grandson of Big Tom's talks to you in a voice so mild it is difficult to hear above the sound of the water—and he carries a mammoth pistol on the belt at his hip. He wears a neat businessman's tie with his crisp brown Game Warden's shirt—and tells you that last week he saw twenty-one places back on the mountain where bear had just crossed the path. His house is small and unpainted, but it sits at the edge of sixteen thousand acres of Wilson land. His grandfather killed 114 bears during his lifetime. He's killed only fifty-seven. There are still remnants of the "differences" between the Yancey Wilsons and the Buncombe Burnetts. You tell this man that you talked with a Burnett a few months ago who'd choked a bear to death. He gives you a quick blue-eyed glance. "I'm not that husky," he chuckles quietly and winks. "The moon's got to be just right for that sort of hunting."

A new highway now runs almost to the summit of Mount Mitchell. The doctor lies there among the frequent clouds and constant evergreens of 6,684 feet. Nearby, and only 126 feet less than its mighty brother, is the peak called Big Tom. So the professor who could be bound by no classroom and the hunter who was learned in his own way have in death what they had in life: a common earth and an uncommon awareness of all its marvels.

# 6

# Enemy in the House

The year 1861 came as inevitably to the headwaters and lowlands of the French Broad as it did to the plantations of Georgia and the government in Washington. It came filled with tensions drawn near to breaking, with deep unease, and most of all with differences beyond reconciliation. The Civil War has been called a brother's war until the term is tired and usually not precise, for actually the number of families so divided as to send soldiers into the opposing armies was negligible: in Vermont few brothers decided to fight with the Confederacy, and in South Carolina very few cast their strength with the Union. But in Eastern Tennessee and Western North Carolina, the phrase of brother's war was bloodily, tragically true.

To understand why this region, located almost exactly in the heart of the Confederacy with aristocratic Virginia to the north, patrician South Carolina and Georgia to the southeast, the gentry of Alabama and Mississippi to the southwest and the planters of middle Tennessee to the west, should give birth to the "little rebellion inside the big rebellion," it is necessary to understand differences as fundamental as the differences between the Mississippi and French Broad rivers. In fact, the geography of these rivers influenced the men along them, their economics, their politics, their philosophies, far more than the brief human events ever influenced

76

the rivers. On the western boundary of Tennessee, the Mississippi spread great level miles of loam for the mass production of a single crop and the growth of far-flung acres to a single holding. Then it added ease of commerce to its bounty and brought into being a way of life.

Four hundred miles distant, crossing the eastern boundary into Tennessee, the French Broad cut its way through rugged mountains, deposited fertile silt at random along a scattered chain of river bottoms and provided, for at least half its length, no possibility of transportation. So its farms were small, independent, multicrop, and lonely. A man and his family worked their whole acreage. And the same difference that existed in Tennessee held true in North Carolina. The western mountains and the French Broad headwaters had a way of life widely separated from that of the eastern Piedmont and the Atlantic coastal plain. In both states the very instinct which had caused its people to settle in this scenic but poorer, varied but more isolated region led them naturally to be at economic and political odds with the other parts of their states. Thus, when secession came and war began, inborn prejudices of nature and belief flared into the open and the little-known rebellion against rebellion began. Began and did not end until the war ended, in fact has never yet come to an end but lives in the memory of the old woman on her hewn-log porch back in the Tennessee hills who tells strangers on a summer day, "Right in yonder by that chimney a Democrat shot a Republican during the War. Shot him as he set there by the fire"; or the recollection of the beard-stubbled old man with the rheumy eyes who leaves off feeding his cattle up one of the North Carolina coves and comes through the thick-falling snowflakes of late November to lean against the traveler's car and say, "The other side of that hill yonder the Confederate soldiers caught up with a bunch of renegades and killed thirteen of them dead then and there"; lives on in the votes cast in ballot boxes at the county seats where the towns are Democratic and the counties are Republican in the same divi-

sion that grandfathers and great-grandfathers established in 1861.
In November, 1952, Sevier County, on a French Broad tributary
in this heart of the South, voted 87 percent Republican.

This region of Western North Carolina and Eastern Tennessee was one of the most constantly and bitterly contested areas of
the whole South. The bitterness was as deep as friendship and
trust turned into fear and hate. There is no wound like uprooted
love, and the Confederates did not despise the Yankee armies as
thoroughly as they did their friends or family who were "Lincoln-
ites"; the Union men did not dislike the plantation aristocrats as
heartily as they did local "secessionists." The constancy of the
struggle grew from the fact that the enemies were intimates,
neighbor to neighbor, cousin to cousin, door by door, and such
proximity did not allow forgetfulness even for a day. At first, Union
supporters surrounded by Confederate authority, and later Confederate sympathizers living in Federal-controlled territory, each
side knew the harshness of war, civilian as well as military, for
the natural daily intercourse of families and neighbors kindled
sparks that frequently flamed into conflict and death. Beyond this
was the constant realization on the part of the two governments
as to a certain importance invested in this area. As early as July 6,
1861, Landon C. Haynes wrote L. P. Walker, then Secretary of
War of the Confederate States of America: "I regard the peril of
Civil War in East Tennessee as imminent. . . . *The New York Times,*
in a lengthy article, says that East Tennessee is a vital point to
the Lincoln government; urges the Union men to seize Knoxville,
and hold it till Lincoln can give aid." Two years later the Confederate Assistant Secretary of War declared that the condition of
things in the mountains was as great a menace to the Confederacy
as either of the armies of the United States.

In a strict military sense, only the lower third of the French
Broad area was strategic. First, it was a crossroads between the
two governments and their armies in the field. Second, the valley
of East Tennessee was the second richest grain producer in the

whole Confederacy, superseded only by the valley of Virginia, and of this valley, the fields along the French Broad, from Newport to Knoxville, yielded an abundant share of wheat and corn. In addition it provided hay for army mules and horses, and beef and bacon for men. When the Richmond *Enquirer* called this section the "Keystone of the Southern Arch," the bacon and meal staples of the soldiers' diet undoubtedly were in mind.

It was in a more oblique and perhaps effective way that the river basin as a whole was influential. That a large proportion of the people located near the very core of the Confederacy would reject that government, refuse to support it with arms or goods, actively rise against it and leave native state to join the opposing Federal forces, weakened to a certain extent the morale of the Confederate government and in like proportion strengthened the Union. Closer by, Union sympathizers along the French Broad and all its feeders influenced the people in adjoining counties and states to a similar viewpoint, or at least to an attitude of neutrality. East Tennessee seemed to be the center of such sympathies and various Confederate county and state officials of North Carolina made complaint to their government about "infection" of treason from their sister state.

Beyond its moral support to the Union, the region gave an astonishing amount of concrete affirmation. The quota of soldiers set by the Federal government as expected from Tennessee and North Carolina was 1,560 apiece. North Carolina furnished officially twice as many as her quota—3,156—and in addition, 5,035 who were not accredited on the quota but were recruited by the government, a total of 8,191. As for Tennessee, she sent 31,092 Union soldiers to the War plus 20,133 recruited by the government but not counted on the state quota. The amazing total is over 50,000 soldiers, the large majority of whom came from the Eastern mountainous region. On her official count alone, Tennessee provided more Federal soldiers than Rhode Island or Delaware or Minnesota and almost as many as New Hampshire or Vermont.

It is interesting that part of the reason for so large a number of recruits not accredited to their states can be found in the difficulty of enlisting in the Union army in a seceded state. Men from these mountains had to escape from their own homes, their local communities and usually their native states before they could join the Northern army. No doubt the Federal occupation of Knoxville, at the mouth of the French Broad, accounts in part for the large Union enlistment from Tennessee, for it meant accessibility to Federal headquarters that otherwise were reached only by long and wary flights to Kentucky or beyond.

To prevent such wholesale exodus and to keep as tight a grip as possible on this recalcitrant region, the Confederacy was forced to keep from five to ten thousand soldiers here all during the war. This was another of the oblique, but no less real, effects which the region had on the war: simply keeping so large and constant a number of men out of the mainstream of battle was no mean strategy.

Because the mountain people of Tennessee and North Carolina were cruelly divided in their loyalties, and because the extent and depth of Union sentiment here has been so little realized abroad, it would be easy and misleading to minimize Confederate support. Beginning with the French Broad at its headwaters and following it and its largest tributaries, the Nolichucky and Big Pigeon, the Union men were usually the mountain men par excellence, the mountaineers among mountaineers, owners of small farms, advocates of strong central government, and the Confederates were the town people or the owners of farms down in the lowlands where the river became more like a river and less like a pent-in brawling cataract.

Asheville, county seat of Buncombe County in North Carolina, sent one of the state's first Confederate companies to Raleigh and on to Bethel, mustered in as the First Volunteer Infantry Regiment North Carolina, and throughout the war Asheville was the mountain center for Confederate activity.

At Knoxville, the differences between town and county were evident from the first vote on Secession. On the night of November 26, 1860, Union sympathizers at a public meeting in the city, knowing they were outnumbered heavily at that night meeting and fearful of immediate call for a Southern conference which would counsel general secession, felt they had gained "everything" by delaying the vote until December eighth and a daytime meeting. The day meeting would allow country people to attend and most of them were staunchly Union. These upcreek people did turn out at the December meeting and one of the resolutions they passed was against, rather than for, secession. And at final vote on Secession, in 1861, when Knoxville had 400 more votes for secession than Union, the county around it still had a majority of 2,390 Union votes. Bitterness in the town against the county was harsh and prolonged. It exists today in numerous towns along the river where the township is Democratic and the county is Republican.

With dissension in these upland parts of their state, North Carolina became next to the last state, and Tennessee the last state, to secede. They may have begun as the reluctant rebels, but they nevertheless contributed past all proportion to the Confederate cause. With only one ninth of the population of the Confederacy, North Carolina furnished, over the whole period of the war, one fifth of its army and one fourth of its "killed in action." More than 40,000 North Carolinians fell in battle, and a disproportionately large number of those were from these very disputed mountain counties. When the Confederate muskets were stacked away at Appomattox, one half of them were from North Carolina. Tennessee gave fuller meaning to her new title of Volunteer State. She furnished more than 115,000 men to the Confederate army; many counties furnished more soldiers than they had voters.

And so, while the larger part of each state turned a united front toward the war, felt its ebb and flow and frequently followed its shifts of fortune from afar, along the French Broad the war was civil and daily, and every man looked to his own conscience and his own musket. The soldiers were neighbors, and the betrayer might be in a man's own family. Food and lack of it were weapons sure as guns, and age or youth knew no mercy, for this was fratricide in both the larger and the more specific meaning.

The rugged path of the French Broad led out of the mountains to the armies in the field, and many took that road out to wear a uniform, blue or gray, and never returned. The path of the river also led in. Colonel Thomas with his company of Cherokee Indians loyal to the Confederacy maneuvered here. Colonel Kirk with a company of mountaineers willing to die for union came from upper Tennessee and Kentucky and raided here. Generals Longstreet and Burnside, one within and one without Knoxville, looked at those mountains and wished they could overcome their obstacles. And up the coves and through the hills, recruiting officers went their useless rounds, searching for men they could make fight against their will and finding it a weary impossibility. This then is the story of the French Broad people—those who had lived there all their lives and wanted only the isolation of their own small fields apart from any government at all, those who came to conquer and stayed to hold, those who died there in uniform and in homespun—during four dramatic terrible years of war.

Causes for the wide division among the people of the French Broad region were deep-rooted and ripely aged. Some of them, the geographic and economic, have already been named. Among a people whose spirit is as strong as these, however, the ethical and religious certainties claimed on both sides are perhaps the most apparent, most cherished causes. Those who joined the rest of their state in resisting forced union gave the familiar Protestant cries of freedom, anger at the invasion of sovereign states by soldiers from other sections. In the choice between mother state and mother country, they clung to the more familiar, the particular opposed to the whole. As a young visitor from New York to Knoxville observed in a letter written April 23, 1861 to a Tennessee friend:

I am struck with the fact that at the South the loyal feeling goes to the State, while at the North it goes to the General Government. The radical difference of belief concerning the relations of the separate States to the Nation, is a principal cause in the whole trouble.

Those who defied community, state and region and cast their lives with the Union in 1861 also worked from a tradition. As early as 1808 Methodists in East Tennessee had taken a vocal stand against slavery. Under the further influence of Quaker and Covenanter Presbyterian belief, the oldest newspaper in the United States advocating emancipation was published. Begun in 1819 as *The Manumission Intelligencer,* its message seeped from the village of Jonesborough and later Greeneville, where it was called *The Genius of Universal Emancipation,* into the neighboring counties and state. And at the Lost Cause Meeting House in Jefferson County on a chilly twenty-fifth of February, 1815, the Tennessee Manumission Society was organized. When war erupted it was from groups such as these, who had wrestled on hewn-log benches with straight backs, in sharp winter cold or warm summer drowsiness, wrestled with their consciences and struggled, faintly or firmly, to understand man's duty of brotherhood to man, that the first Union volunteers came. Compelled by no conscription, favored by no foresight into the fortunes of war, they were the core and the spirit of the little rebellion.

Representing Unionism's pure economic appeal, Knoxville's famous "Parson" Brownlow—onetime carpenter and saddlebag preacher now turned politician-editor—stated, more briefly but as oratorically as usual, in his Knoxville *Whig* for January 26, 1861:

> We can never live in a Southern Confederacy and be made hewers of wood and drawers of water for a set of aristocrats and overbearing tyrants. . . . We have no interest in common with the Cotton States. We are a grain-growing and stock

raising people, and we can conduct a cheap government, inhabiting the Switzerland of America.

As opinions solidified, the breach grew wider, nourishing the fears and suspicions that give rise to war. Small occurrences gathered large meaning. Such as the journey of an Ohio visitor from Asheville, North Carolina, down the French Broad to Knoxville. He carried a bundle of fruit tree scions with him, a traveling Johnny Apple-twig, but the temperament of the times made Knoxvillians suspect his salesmanship as a front for devious abolition activities. Despite the protests of the man with whom he lodged, a group of aroused citizens visited the stranger and hauled him off to prison. There, at a public meeting before a citizens' committee selected to determine his guilt, the rumors were reported, argument broke out among the audience and the prisoner decided to take his fruit scions back to Ohio, which he promptly did. Emotion—both for and against slavery and secession—had succeeded reasonableness, and the land was ripe for battle.

Fort Sumter was fired upon, the President's call for soldiers came, and the states voted. East Tennessee threatened to secede from Tennessee, in a convention at Greeneville on June seventeenth asked the state legislature to consent to the formation of a new state, and North Carolina threatened to secede from the Confederacy. One of the large ironies of the Civil War began to unfold: the new government which had come into being for the express purpose of guarding and enlarging its citizens' freedom, when it felt the bite of States' rights threatening its own success, curbed that freedom and suspended the writ of habeas corpus. North Carolina alone among the Confederate States of America refused to suspend the writ of habeas corpus. Significantly enough this was accomplished by a leader born in the mountains on one of the little creeks that feeds the French Broad. Zebulon Vance he was called, a large man with a mind to match. And there was nothing small about Vance's courage. Pledged to support the Confederate cause to the last dust of corn meal and the final ounce of strength, this governor nevertheless kept an untiring, often unpopular (with the government) vigilance over the freedom and morale of his state. He was jealous of its rights and articulate when they were challenged. In letter after letter he grappled with the Confederate officials, explaining his people (especially his fellow mountaineers), demanding redress for injuries, seeking explanation.

Under Governor Vance's leadership and his understanding of these folks, the authorities in North Carolina were considerably more tolerant toward Union sympathizers in the western part of their state along the upper half of the French Broad than was the Tennessee government toward its Union people in the east along the lower French Broad. This was perhaps one of the strongest reasons, the temperament of mountain men being what it is, for the much larger exodus from Eastern Tennessee than from the neighboring counties of Western North Carolina, and for the ranker bitterness that followed. Zeb Vance knew what Richmond never learned: You can lead a man into battle but you can't drive him there.

But in April, 1861, such problems were still tiny shadows on a bright landscape. On Saturday, the sixteenth of April, an order came from the Governor of North Carolina, and by Monday noon a company had been formed in the little village of Asheville, a company made up of volunteers from the mountains around, and at four o'clock in the afternoon they marched off to join the Confederate Army. They were eager to meet their comrades and they marched three days to reach the nearest railroad. Two days later they came to the state capital at Raleigh and were organized and mustered in as the First Volunteer Infantry Regiment of North Carolina. Its members had enlisted for only six months. The war would be over by then.

For those who wished to join the Union Army, there were no such public gatherings. They must leave home secretly, travel by night through little-known gaps and trails and enlist in Kentucky

or some more distant state. In the very beginning, such hardships discouraged many men from following their sympathies, and they simply remained at home, seeking to withdraw into a self-sufficient shell of neutrality. Besides, they believed that the Federal army under General Buell was about to enter East Tennessee and secure it under the protection of the government. General McClellan and President Lincoln asked Buell to consider the moral as well as the military help which their followers in this area deserved and needed and which could best come by a decisive winning of the region by early use of arms. Buell was in the field, however, and knew the dangers of overextension, especially away from supplies. To the despair of the Union leaders in these remote mountains, the general disregarded his superiors' advice and made no move, although Confederate officers wrote numerous letters to Richmond warning that attack was imminent.

Upon advice from Washington and in hopes that drastic action on their part would call forth a corresponding move from the army, a group of Union leaders planned a concerted destruction of seven railroad bridges which were vital to Confederate communications in the Southeast. The night of November eighth a small band of men in the vicinity attacked and attempted to burn their assigned objective. Only four of the bridges were actually destroyed, and although none of these was across the French Broad, one was on the tributary of Lick Creek, and the effects of this first overt violence swept immediately over the entire area. Men who had tried to be neutral were driven to a decision; people all over the country became aware of disunity existing in at least one corner of the Confederacy; and—most important—Confederate leaders, political and military alike, were seized with sudden fear of this internal dissension whose size they could not estimate but whose power, however small, was inadmissible. Alarms and demands for armed assistance flooded Richmond.

Rumors were plentiful of large armed uprising all over the area. The force with which the Richmond government felt the impact of the bridge-burning demonstrations was recorded most sharply in Secretary Benjamin's order to Confederate Colonel Wood at Knoxville:

First, all such as can be identified as having been engaged in bridge burning are to be tried summarily by drum-head court-martial, and if found guilty, executed on the spot by hanging. It would be well to leave their bodies hanging in the vicinity of the burned bridges. Second, all such as have not been so engaged to be treated as prisoners of war, and sent with an armed guard to Tuscaloosa, Alabama, there to be kept imprisoned. . . . In no case is one of the men known to have been up in arms against the government to be released on any pledge or oath of allegiance. The time for such measures is past.

The military was not more alarmed than the citizenry. Suggestions were plentiful, such as the one to President Jefferson Davis from an aroused East Tennessee Confederate who demanded that all local enemies be exported, bag and baggage, for the peace of mind of soldiers' families left at home.

Alarm spread into North Carolina as well. A member of the state government at Raleigh wrote the Secretary of War pleading for arms, but the reply he received introduced a specter that was to haunt the Confederacy up to its very end: lack of adequate supplies. The pressing need for arms was born at Bethel and did not diminish until Appomattox. Even in the village of Asheville, where the armory already mentioned was established, the newspaper as early as September 19, 1861, had run the following notice:

> To the Patriots of the Mountains!
>
> The subscriber having been appointed agent of the Government of the Confederate States of America, to collect, alter and fabricate Guns for the Army, Begs to announce that Messrs. Ephraim Clayton and George W. Whitson have been engaged to conduct this important service. . . . In a very short time, if the patriotism of the country is not over estimated, the thousands of Domestic Guns now idly reposing in the racks of their owners, will be handed over to the Government for the purpose of being changed and put in proper condition for service in the field. . . . In short, all arms of every description are needed in this our country's emergency.

The searching finger of necessity was probing along the remote French Broad as well as along more commercial waterways.

In the same category, decidedly less important, but somehow much more pathetic and even slightly humorous in its civic enthusiasm, was a news item in the same paper:

Hurrah for Buncombe!

Some weeks since we noticed the fact that Drums of an excellent quality were being manufactured here; and now we are gratified at being able to state that we have examined, and heard tested, a lot of Fifes, manufactured by our ingenious townsman, Mr. John Hilderbrand, Jr. for the 25th Regiment. They are pronounced . . . equal to the best. We repeat, Hurrah for Buncombe! We are cutting, one by one, and in rapid succession, the fetters which bound us down in galling dependence upon the North. It is eminently right and proper that as our gallant soldiers march to meet the enemy to the tune of *Dixie,* the music should be extracted from Southern made instruments. Buncombe can supply orders for any number of Drums and Fifes, warranted equal to any in the world.

If the Unionist bridge burnings of East Tennessee had been meant to consolidate opinion and arrest attention, then, they did just that—in exactly the opposite way intended. Attention of all Confederates in the area was galvanized into action, and opinion which had been fluid or noncommittal was solidified against any relative or acquaintance who did not take an immediate outright stand for the Confederacy. Men suspected of taking part in the bridge conspiracy were summarily arrested; in the French Broad watershed, at Greeneville, Tennessee, three men were tried by drumhead court-martial and sentenced to be hanged, two of whom were thus put to death and left hanging by the railroad for four days as a lesson to travelers, perhaps; the other was imprisoned. Persons known or suspected to have Union sympathies were frantically arrested. One of the more vocal of these was that same "Parson" Brownlow whose Knoxville *Whig* had led the campaign against secession. In his diary, Brownlow recorded the rapid filling of the jail with his fellow thinkers:

Dec. 7, 1861–This morning 31 others arrived . . . from Cocke, Greene and Jefferson Counties. They bring us tales of woe from their respective counties as to the treatment of Union men and Union families, by the . . . cavalry in the rebellion. They are taking all the fine horses they can find and appropriating them to their own use; they are entering houses, breaking open drawers and chests, seizing money, blankets and whatever they can use.

Sunday, Dec. 22–Brought in old man Wamplar, a Dutchman seventy years of age, from Greene County, charged with being an "Andrew Johnson man and talking Union talk."

Feeling ran strong in all parts of the state. In Memphis, two Confederate officers put the following advertisement in the November 16, 1861, issue of the Memphis *Appeal:*

We, the undersigned, will pay five dollars per pair for fifty pairs of well-bred hounds, and fifty dollars for one pair of thorough-bred bloodhounds that will take the track of a man. The purpose for which these dogs are wanted is to chase the infernal, cowardly Lincoln bushwhackers of East Tennessee and Kentucky.

Through the winter and spring of 1861–62, official and unofficial awareness of the mountain dilemma grew. In March, 1862, General Kirby Smith wrote from his headquarters at Knoxville to Richmond that he had found East Tennessee soldiers held too strong Union proclivities to be allowed to remain in that area and should be removed to more distant fields.

On the sixteenth of April the Confederate government passed the first of three laws that alienated the mountain people more completely than any act or attitude yet encountered. In fact, if it had been designed deliberately to play into the hands of the opposition, it could hardly have been more effective. This was the first Conscription Act. A government born in the enthusiasm and surge that surrounded the Confederacy necessarily lost some of its prestige for spontaneous support when it was forced to pass a law compelling Southern men to join its ranks. To hill men, peculiarly jealous of individual freedom, the Act was most galling. For those who wished to join the army anyway, this was like an insult. For those who had no mind to fight, law could not make them and turned them rather to open resistance.

Dissatisfaction was deepened by exemptions for any conscript who could send a substitute and for any owner of twenty or more Negroes. A slogan sprang into being: "A rich man's war and a poor man's fight." In North Carolina the courts honored the writs of habeas corpus and were upheld by Governor Vance in thus allowing evasion of this law. Conscription officers carried on activities through the western counties, however, and especially across the line in the eastern border of Tennessee. With no writs of habeas corpus to support them, East Tennesseans began wholesale flight into Kentucky and the North. Not only were a few single stragglers making their way along this new "underground railroad" through the mountains, but numerous large parties were seeping through to join the Union Army. For example, in April, 1862, seven hundred Union men en route for Kentucky were attacked by a Confederate company and four hundred were taken prisoner.

Of those who did, at the point of guns, pledge allegiance to the Confederate States of America and join her army, many were still uncertain converts and their desertions grew more numerous. As one said, he took the oath only "from the teeth out."

Two other laws which brought the war forcibly home to the region were the tax-in-kind and impressment acts. The first was a tithe to the government under which farmers were compelled to give one tenth of all their produce for distribution by the authorities at Richmond. It was the first real tax which the lower middle class of the South had been conscious of paying and was held in as much affection as most taxes. Since the middlemen who took no production risks of land and weather, as well as the speculators and many manufacturers, were not included in the tax-in-kind law, it seemed particularly unfair to small marginal farmers.

The second law gave specified committees the right to take livestock, slaves, provisions, and wagons for use by the Confederate Army, and to set the price which should be paid for them. Since this was always well below the inflated market price, resentment on the part of farmers was natural. When corn was selling for $5 a bushel, the commissioners of valuation set the impressment price at $1.85 and $2 a bushel. Many of those who were known to be Union sympathizers said that their property was taken without any compensation whatsoever, not even the form of a certificate such as was issued to Confederate citizens for the goods received. Impressment of livestock, especially mules and horses, was resented most of all, because without these to turn the land and tend the crops farmers were practically helpless. It was difficult—more, next to impossible—to make a farmer believe armies needed his live-stock for supply trains as desperately as he needed it for the grow-ing of food when hunger was plentiful and increasing all around him.

This same spring saw the beginning of a new select group of men: the pilots who knew the remote parts of the mountains and the little-traveled trails and could lead parties of Union men out of the grasp of tightening conscription laws to the army of their choice. Stations of rest, or for the gathering of other parties, were established at sympathetic homes along the way. Stories of some of the more daring and resourceful of these pilots were to grow into legends during years after the war.

Although these laws of 1862 turned latent discontent into open resentment and sent many soldiers into the enemy lines, a hard core of belief for states' sovereignty continued to recruit men from all the French Broad region into the Confederate Army. An excellent example of their experiences and character is the Sixtieth North Carolina Infantry which was made up almost entirely of men living along this river or its tributaries. Formed of six companies from Asheville, it left there on May 1, 1862, and followed the rocky gorge of the French Broad down through the mountains. They went ten miles that first day and stopped at a famous old tavern called Alexander's. With beds and a bountiful table spread for them, fire warm on the hearth, in the first excitement of new companionship and experience, going to war must have seemed a fine undertaking that first night.

The next day's march went on down the river to the village of Marshall and then Warm Springs, full of the fresh spring sweetness which makes May unlike any other month in the mountains, the trees thickening with new green leaves, fern fronds unfolding under damp hidden pockets of moss, birds busy with nests and young, and the swirling icy torrent of the river carrying away the melted snow and rain of winter. Two miles below Warm Springs on an island in the French Broad, they made camp and were joined by a company from East Tennessee, most of whom were from the farms along the river or one of its large tributaries called Big Creek. Its captain, James T. Huff, had already been in the war, but had asked to come home and form his own company when he could not get along with his commanding officer. With these two groups, from Buncombe County in North Carolina and Cocke County in Tennessee, the North Carolina Sixtieth went into its island encampment of drill and instruction. Here most of the boys had their first try at cooking, simple, indigestible items of flapjacks, bacon—meaning hunks of pork streaked with lean—sometimes biscuits, and molasses, "but mostly," as one old veteran recalled it, "mostly flapjacks and molasses."

From that beginning they went on to the Battle of Stone River (where they wakened the next morning of January 1, 1863, to find themselves surrounded by Federal corpses, where they had all lain together, dead and live alike, during the night), into the winter quarters at Tullahoma where rain, sleet and snow made the camp one big mud slush, and disease was an enemy more to be dreaded than Yankee armies; on to Mississippi with the opening of spring in time for the fall of Vicksburg; and in the autumn, Chickamauga —where these boys from the mountains penetrated farther into the enemy lines than any troops in battle—and then Lookout Mountain and Missionary Ridge. When they gathered at that island in the French Broad in May of '62, they may have been untried volunteers, but by November of '63 they were veterans. They knew the war of day-to-day attrition and its sudden fierce explosions into battle where history was made but men died wholesale.

The Confederates who stayed at home organized too. The boys too young to enlist formed Junior Reserves. They were called "the seed-corn of the Confederacy." At Asheville the men who had been too old for the army formed groups for protection called "the silver-grays."

In Knoxville, the thorny problem of how to deal with that majority of Union sympathizers continued to vex Confederate authorities. Upon promise that he would leave the country, Parson Brownlow and many of his friends were released from prison. When he was asked to quit East Tennessee, Brownlow said that he replied to his captors: "Good! We will strike a bargain; give me your passport and a military escort and I promise you in return to do more for the Southern Confederacy than the devil has ever done—I will quit the country." The depth of his feeling and the height of his oratory on the whole matter was displayed in the first of many speeches he delivered in New York City in early summer of 1862, soon after his release from Knoxville jail. Among other things, he said: "If I owed the devil a debt to be discharged, and it was to be discharged by the rendering up to him of a dozen of the meanest, most revolting, and God-forsaken wretches that ever could be culled from the ranks of depraved human society, and I wanted to pay that debt and get a premium upon the payment, I would make a tender to his Satanic Majesty of twelve Northern men who sympathized with this infernal rebellion."

To paint for his metropolitan audience a picture of what life was like in the region he had just quitted, he said, "Hanging is going on all over East Tennessee. They shoot Union men down in the fields; they whip them . . . they actually lacerate with switches the bodies of females, wives and daughters of Union men." Little wonder that before the war was over a fund for the Relief of East Tennessee was raised in the Northern cities of Philadelphia, New York and Boston amounting to more than $160,000.

By the middle of the year, General Smith wrote Confederate Headquarters that he was in the midst of people enlisted against him and faced a force of at least four to one, more efficient and better equipped than himself. Such a situation did not deter General John Morgan, the famous raider who was determined to carry some of the war onto Northern soil. On the fourth of July he left Knoxville with nine hundred men, moved swiftly into Kentucky, through towns and villages, and came close to realizing his goal which was Richmond, Kentucky, with hopes of holding it until all Southern sympathizers in the state could rally to his ranks, but superior opposing numbers forced his retreat. He returned to Tennessee with twelve hundred men, three hundred more than he had taken, such was his personal magnetism and reputation. However, he had captured public imagination more than military supplies.

Winter came. One of the Confederate soldiers from the French Broad wrote in his diary:

> I have finished reading "Dollars and Cents." I shall commence "The Mysteries of Udolpho" next. . . . How unpleasant sitting in a leaky tent, wind and rain blowing in at the door, chimney smoking. [And later,] The weather is very changeable, raining, snowing, sleeting. . . . Drew no beef today and have nothing to eat but corn-bread. . . . What a luxury a feather-bed and fireplace is.

Back home not everyone was enjoying a feather bed and fireplace, however. Food was growing scarcer, especially among back-country Unionists, and salt was one of the most serious shortages. Passports for wagon and driver to the saltworks were frequently denied Federal supporters, and Confederate storekeepers were not quick to sell from their small hordes. Early in January, 1863, a group of angry men defied local authority, broke into several stores in Marshall, North Carolina, plundered and stole what they needed and fled back to their separate homes. Such a bold, forthright move brought to the Southern authorities a vision of things to come.

Immediate reaction was harsh. General Davis, at Headquarters of the Confederate Provisional Forces at Warm Springs, was convinced that the attack on Marshall was made by a band of about fifty citizens and he placed Major Garrett, Sixty-fourth North Carolina Volunteers, in charge of a force of about two hundred, one company of cavalry and thirty Indians, to proceed to Laurel Creek. Major Garrett was ordered to pursue and arrest every man in the mountains of known bad character, whether engaged in the recent outrages or not. He was to be aided by six companies of cavalry scouring the mountains in Tennessee, and Colonel W. H. Thomas, with two hundred whites and Indians of his legion, was also in Madison with orders to arrest all deserters and tories who were engaged in unlawful practices on the Tennessee line of mountains. General Davis also wrote Governor Vance that he believed North Carolina would be safer if "rid of such a population as that inhabiting the Laurel region," and he proposed to allow all who were not implicated in any crime to leave the state and to aid them in crossing into Kentucky.

Governor Vance, perhaps more knowledgeable in the devious ways of men and consistently guarding the delicate balance of justice, issued a plea against letting "our excited people deal too harshly with these misguided men. Please have the captured delivered to the proper authorities for trial." Zeb Vance—struggling to keep alive and stout the spirit and letter of law in the midst of barbarous war.

In February the cruelty of the mountain struggle reached a

dark pinnacle. A lieutenant colonel, still leading the Confederate search for those who had broken into Marshall stores, had at least thirteen of the prisoners he had taken on Laurel River shot to death under the most cold-blooded circumstances. Most of them had been arrested at their homes one Friday, and none of them had offered any resistance to the officers; perhaps a few had run out the door, seeking cover in a nearby laurel thicket, a field full of dead winter weeds or blackberry bushes, but they had been caught easily enough. The following Monday they were lined up by the soldiers, marched to a secluded place in the woods and forced to kneel. There is no record as to what was said or thought or felt, by either the victims or the soldiers, before the shots rang out and the thirteen prisoners were dead. A trench was dug and they were put into a common grave.

News of the killings boiled through the mountains and down to the capital at Raleigh. Governor Vance asked A. S. Merrimon, State's Attorney for this Judicial District, to investigate and make as full a report as possible. A Confederate stalwart, Merrimon was nevertheless able to make an angry and unbiased report. After describing the event, he wrote:

> I learned that probably eight of the thirteen killed were not in the company that robbed Marshall and other places. I suppose they were shot on suspicion. I cannot learn the names of the soldiers who shot them. Some of them shrank from the barbarous and brutal transaction at first, but were compelled to act. [He then went on to list the names of those killed, with pertinent remarks concerning each. Their youth is the first surprising characteristic.] Elison King (desperate man); Jo Woods (desperate man); Will Shelton, 20 years old (of Pifus); Aronnata Shelton, 14 years old (was not at Marshall); James Shelton (old Jim), about 56 years old; James Shelton, jr., 17 years old; David Shelton, 13 years old (was not in the raid); James Madcap, 40 years old; Rod Shelton (Stob Rod); David

Shelton, (brother of Stob Rod); Joseph Cleandon, 15 or 16 years old; Helen Moore, 25 or 30 years old; Wade Moore, 20 or 25 years old. It is said that those whose names I have so marked did not go to Marshall. . . . Several women were severely whipped and ropes were tied around their necks. . . . Four prisoners are now in jail. . . . One thing is certain, thirteen prisoners were shot without trial or any hearing whatever and in the most cruel manner. I have no means of compelling witnesses to disclose facts to me, and I do not know that I shall be able to make a fuller report.

Much has been written of the large battles and decisive deaths of the War Between the States, but nowhere is there a microcosm more chill and revealing than this episode of war at its heart and core.

Governor Vance wrote Secretary Seddon at Richmond demanding the colonel's dismissal. Trying to deal justly with both the government above him and the people under him, aware of the balance between personal freedom and collective duty, he issued a little later that year a proclamation to all North Carolinians which he closed with a plea for unity. He asked if they would seek to cure the evils of one revolution by plunging the country into another and begged them not to add the horrors of internal strife and entire destruction of civil law and authority. Earlier in the year he had promised to share the last bushel of meal and pound of meat in the state with the wives and families of men who were in the Confederate Army.

This spring of 1863 had been a tense violent season throughout the French Broad country. The enemy was in the house, and it would take a great deal more blood to end the conflict and generations of tears to wash away the bitterness brought by the season past and the summer to come.

# 7

# A Dark and Bitter Time

The long summer of 1863 saw a growing defiance to the conscription laws of the Confederacy among the mountain people of Western North Carolina and East Tennessee. Desertions became more frequent, especially among troops stationed in East Tennessee close to their homes. General Buckner, commanding at Knoxville, wrote that desertions were numerous and arrests infrequent because "of the difficult country to which they can retreat." He stated that he would rather have a thousand troops from distant states than the whole twenty-four hundred from the East Tennessee and Western North Carolina regiments.

The roads through the mountain region were frequented with travelers defying the Army's laws, and since they carried guns and accoutrements with them and often went together in groups of from half a dozen to fifteen or twenty, they were untroubled by citizens and local authorities alike. When they were confronted by enrolling officers and asked for their furloughs or the authority by which they were absent from their commands, they would look squarely at their questioner, let one hand slip down to pat the gun beside them and say with slow deliberation, "This is my furlough." By August of '63 there were 106 men absent without leave from the Sixty-fourth North Carolina Regiment, and the commanding officer was reluctant to send men in pursuit because of the open persuasion to desert, from citizens along the route.

Untutored in the devious ways of war, ready to fight and then go home, the mountain boys could not reconcile themselves to the tedium of camp, the stagnation of strategy. Bold, daring, hot-headed, they had joined the army to kill or be killed. And when, drilling in camp, lying under the damp tents of winter or the smothering canvas of summer, they thought about home, about the clear rocky water of its streams and river, about the mountains changing with the seasons and the little fields waiting to be tended, it took only the smallest spur to make them leave what seemed a useless waiting. The spur often was a letter from home, like the one Martha Revis sat down and wrote her husband one rich summer day the last of July, from Marshall in Madison County, while neighbor men cut ripe oats out in the bee-loud fields and dinner cooked in the heavy black iron kettle swung over the fire on the rough stone hearth.

Dear Husband: I seat myself to drop you a few lines to let you know that me and Sally is well as common, and I hope these few lines will come to hand and find you well and doing well. I have no news to write you at this, only I am done laying by my corn. I worked it all four times. My wheat is good; my oats is good. I haven't got my wheat stacked yet. My oats I have got a part of them cut, and Tom Hunter and John Roberts is cutting today. They will git them cut today.

I got the first letter yesterday that I have received from you since you left. I got five from you yesterday; they all come together. This is the first one I have wrote, for I didn't know where to write to you. You said you hadn't anything to eat. I wish you was here to get some beans for dinner. I have plenty to eat as yet. I haven't saw any of your pap's folks since you left home. The people is generally well hereat. The people is all turning to Union here since the Yankees has got Vicksburg. I want you to come home as soon as you can after you git this letter. Jane Elkins is living with me yet. That is all I can think of, only I want you to come home the worst that I ever did. The conscripts is all at home yet, and I don't know what they will do with them. The folks is leaving here, and going North as fast as they can, so I will close.

Your wife, till death,

Martha Revis

And one of the men came in from the oat field to add a postscript:

I pen a line, sir. I am well, and is right strait out for the Union, and I am never going in the service any more, for I am for the Union for ever and ever, amen. I am doing my work. There was 800 left to go to the North, so will tell you all about it in the next letter; so I will close.

Your brother till death. Hurrah for the Union! Hurrah for the Union, Union! Thomas Hunter.

This was powerful psychological warfare. Through the countryside people were writing such letters, thinking such thoughts. In Knoxville, Confederate occupation brought a military flavor into everyday life, influencing politics, finances, social activity. Through the winter and spring of '62–'63, soldiers were on the streets, sick, dying and wounded soldiers filled the hospitals. News of victories and defeats and rumors of military movements and skirmishes were the main food for conversation. As one occupant of the city described the financial maneuvering of the time:

Men bought and sold, Confederate notes and bonds went down in value, and gold went up. Purchases of different commodities in trade and of real estate, were made in sums of money nominally large and really small. Some men seemed to prosper, in like manner with the speculator, of whom an admiring friend said, "He is rich—that is to say, he is not rich, but he has all the sensations."

So, while some left home to take up arms in defense of beliefs as dear as life, others stayed behind and speculated on the rise and fall in price of land and commodities and read about the siege of Vicksburg, the battle at Gettysburg, the movement of armies toward Chattanooga.

Late in August of 1863, General Buckner took his troops from Knoxville and moved west. The vacancy they left invited small bands of thieves who had begun to prowl the countryside to venture inside the town. The horses that were stolen during the night, the suspicious skulking of single marauders was the prelude of pestilence to come through all the surrounding country during years to follow.

On the second of September, loiterers in the streets of Knoxville rubbed their eyes at the sight of blue uniforms coming swiftly, steadily through the city. While Rosecrans marched to engage Bragg at Chattanooga, Burnside moved into East Tennessee. His cavalry came in first, and the next day General Burnside led his army into the capital of East Tennessee. He was greeted enthusiastically, undoubtedly surprised to find so many supporters in a South he had found heretofore solid, and after his headquarters were established in one of the old downtown mansions, supporters gathered to demonstrate their feelings long subdued by rule of a Confederate government.

Now the tide was reversed, and Southern citizens who had previously enjoyed the privileges of power gave way to the Union people who flocked to drape a stars and stripes before the headquarters and welcome Federal occupation with all the spirit of which mountain people are capable. After an expedition the following week to secure Cumberland Gap, main gateway between training camps of the Federal army and the mountain region of

East Tennessee and Western North Carolina, Burnside settled in Knoxville.

Rumors from an opposite viewpoint now became frequent. Attack by various Southern armies was daily gossip, part of Lee's army was on its way to dislodge Burnside, eager but usually ill-informed partisans came and went at headquarters. After one particularly annoying report, when an excited citizen had electrified headquarters with news that a group of Confederate soldiers was approaching only seventeen miles away and a body of cavalry had been hastily dispatched only to find the alarm false and their ride needless, General Burnside on the following day greeted his would-be helper and informer, "Sir, you bring me a great deal of news. Now, I don't want you to bring me any more, for *the average is bad!*"

The inflation from which Confederate currency was suffering became immediately apparent in drop of prices when quoted in regular government money. For instance, ferry rates which had been, in July, $1.25 for a horse and team became, after Federal occupation, 60¢. Man-and-horse fare went from 25¢ to 10¢, hogs and sheep per head from 6¢ to 1½¢.

With Knoxville as its center, Federal authority reached over a large part of the region, up into North Carolina where a regiment of North Carolina troops, organized in Knoxville from those who had fled Confederate conscription, captured Warm Springs and took possession of Paint Rock Gap. By November thirteenth, General Burnside was able to tell authorities in Washington that he was in possession of all the important points in East Tennessee and was in the midst of friends.

This Federal establishment in a vital area had to be dislodged, if at all possible, by Confederate forces, but that that strategy should have been begun right after Chickamauga, while Grant still remained in Bragg's vicinity and was receiving reinforcements, seems incredible. It was no time for Bragg to divide his strength, but that is just what he and President Davis decided to do. Longstreet,

with Wheeler's cavalry in support, was ordered toward Knoxville.

On the rainy Wednesday night of November fifth, amidst the
noisy confusion and interruption of striking camp and packing,
Longstreet sat down beside an empty flour barrel and using its
head for a desk, wrote to General Buckner, stating his feeling on
the matter, repeating his resentment of Bragg, and concluding
with this request: "Have you any maps that you can give or lend
me [of the Knoxville region]? I shall need everything of the kind.
Do you know any reliable people, living near and east of Knoxville, from whom I might get information of the condition, strength,
etc. of the enemy?" His plea was more important than he realized.
Such maps as he did receive were inaccurate and one of those in-
accuracies proved fatal to his purpose. On such delicate threads
as the slip of a map maker's pen sometimes depend pivotal events.

The night of November fifth Longstreet left Bragg and began his advance, with some twenty thousand men and Wheeler's
five thousand cavalry, against Burnside and East Tennessee. On
the fourteenth, Burnside moved from Knoxville out to meet his
new opponent. Following a plan previously devised, and approved
by Grant, Burnside hoped to draw Longstreet on to Knoxville,
separating him as far as possible from Chattanooga. In cold rain
the armies met and maneuvered, retreated and followed, urging
horses and mules through thick clay muck, slipping and sliding
and often losing their own pitiful shoes in the wet suck of mud,
shouldering ropes to pull the artillery out of deepening ruts. Probably few of the men struggling on either side could appreciate
what some strategists were later to call a display of real general-
ship where "every motion, every evolution, was made with the
precision and regularity of the precision on a chess-board."

As Burnside fell back to Knoxville and fortified its boundaries,
Longstreet began a siege which has since been criticized, but whose
purpose was meant to be starvation of the enemy shut up inside
the city. What Longstreet did not understand was that along the

French Broad lived a population largely dedicated to the Union and that the river was beginning to play its most important part in the history of the war.

When the siege of Knoxville began, supplies were already limited. All the cattle and hogs in the pens were immediately killed and salted down. Quarter rations were issued to the army for several days, then they were cut off altogether; patients in the hospital received the last food supplies and civilians living in the town had to manage as they could. Since Federal occupation, the population of Knoxville had been swollen by the stream of Union people fleeing from the mountains and the constant pursuit by conscription officers. This unsettled group added further strain on larders that had long been bare of the luxury of coffee and sugar, but now faced empty meat shelves and flour barrels. The army, at least twenty thousand hearty appetites, and the animals with them were near destitution. But, because of a map maker's error, the Confederate Army did not seal off the French Broad River, and by means of flatboats, rafts, all sorts of devised vehicles, the people on the river and its near tributaries sent food into the besieged city.

Longstreet's strategy of starvation might have been speedily realized—except for that error on the map. Unfamiliar with the country around him and without any engineers, at least in the beginning, who knew the landscape, Longstreet was forced to rely on an official map for information of the terrain. The map from which he worked showed the French Broad joining with the Holston River below Knoxville, rather than above. The Little River was probably mistaken for the French Broad. When he gained control of the north side of the Holston, Longstreet believed he controlled the water entrance to Knoxville. However, the French Broad in its entire length was left open to navigation.

Several Confederate residents in and around Knoxville, seeing that Burnside's army was receiving food by the unobstructed French Broad route, tried to tell General Longstreet that his holding of

the Holston was purposeless because the richer area of the French
Broad was still open to the Federals, but for some unaccountable
reason the general trusted his map instead. The boats and rafts
floated on down the river, and the Union army owed its survival
to loyal citizens along its banks and tributaries. A few foraging
parties even ventured out into Knox County and nearby Sevier
County and brought back corn and wheat. All along the river the
harvest had been abundant that year, and bread made of a mixture of meal and bran soon came to be the basic ration.

Longstreet and Wheeler also had to feed their more than
twenty-five thousand men. Orders concerning the capture of hogs
became as important as those dealing with capture of enemy prisoners. Details were given as to when and where such forage should
be driven and, in the case of difficulties, how it should be distributed for safekeeping till it could be brought into camp.

Meanwhile, however, suspicion of the maps and realization of
the importance of the French Broad to Burnside and his army
seemed to be dawning at Confederate headquarters. Word was
sent to General Martin: "It is said that he [the enemy] draws supplies by his wagons and flat-boats on the French Broad. . . . Keep
the enemy closely confined to his lines, if possible, and endeavor
to cut off his means of supplies."

To cut off this main artery of supply, a detachment was sent
up to Boyd's Ferry on the river, where it began building a raft
large and heavy enough to destroy the bridge used by the Federals
as well as the checks devised along the river to catch the rafts and
boats of food as they floated downstream. As Longstreet's men
worked, however, the felling of timber and building of the wreck-
ing raft attracted local attention, and one woman made her way
through the Confederate lines to warn Burnside and his men of
their enemy's intentions. Union soldiers immediately stretched a
big boom across the river in order to catch and hold the raft above
the bridge and the smaller booms they had previously used. By
this, their source of supply was saved, and the corn and wheat and

meat from river bottoms and mountain patches continued to enter the city. Longstreet's cherished plan—that his enemy might be starved into submission before the deep of winter—was rendered futile.

November twenty-ninth, news of Bragg's defeat at Chattanooga and his withdrawal to Dalton reached Longstreet. Orders to march to Bragg's relief had previously been received, but now he knew what he had surmised ever since he began this unwanted expedition: His greatest help to Bragg would come through trying to divide the Union forces. Besides, he bore no love for Bragg; he had come on this expedition unasked, and he was not eager to ask his men to return to Bragg's unpopular service. That day he wrote: "Our forces here must capture the army at Knoxville, or force the enemy to relieve it by a strong detachment from his main force."

The morning of the twenty-ninth, he chose a picked command and made his major assault of the siege. Fort Sanders, standing at a strategic point above the rest of the town and strongest fortified point of the defense, was the place chosen for attack. Unknown to the Confederates, a moat had been dug around the fort and well meshed with wire. In the first rush of attack, they fell and floundered, tripped others behind them and, when some of the soldiers finally managed to cross the trench under a barrage of fire and began to climb the earthen side of the fort, they found it a mass of slippery mud. Grape and canister, lighted grenades, rained on those in the trench struggling toward the base of the fort. The slaughter was wholesale. The dead, the dying and the living were piled on top of one another in the moat. After their third desperate dash across the wire-tangled, body-filled moat in the face of the cannon and musket fire directed down on them, Longstreet withdrew his men. Pollard, a contemporary Southern historian, said of the assault: "In this terrible ditch the dead were piled eight or ten deep. . . . Never, excepting at Gettysburg, was there in the history of the war, a disaster adorned with the glory of such devout courage as Longstreet's repulse at Knoxville."

The Union report summarized that the Confederates were completely repulsed with a loss of 1,000 men, of whom 250 were killed. General Burnside lost 45 killed and wounded. Longstreet's entire force was estimated at 38,000 men. Longstreet's report of the battle to General Bragg was short and direct, with figures varying slightly from General Foster's: "I made an assault upon the enemy's works upon the 29th ultimo, and was repulsed with a loss of 800 in killed, wounded and missing."

General Sherman was sent from Chattanooga to help Burnside. Grant at this time was of a mind to push Confederate forces completely out of East Tennessee. With his conception of "total war" that was a forerunner of what we have seen develop in modern tactics, General Sherman sensed the trap which this part of the state could become. At seven o'clock the morning of December first, he wrote to Grant:

> Recollect that East Tennessee is my horror. That any military man should send a force into East Tennessee puzzles me. Burnside is there and must be relieved, but when relieved I want to get out, and he should come out too. I think, of course, its railroads should be absolutely destroyed, its provisions eaten up or carried away, and all troops brought out.

Sherman did not linger long in Knoxville but left General Granger with his Fourth Army Corps as aid to Burnside.

Longstreet faced the morass Sherman meant to avoid. His official communiqués had been tersely informative, but behind them lay the dark dread of winter approaching an army which lacked provisions, clothing and—most miserable—shoes. There was the bitterness of defeat, the misery of official ignorance of the situation, the slowly accumulating sense of Confederate loss. December third and fourth he began his eastward withdrawal. Sherman received the news from General Granger: "I have captured a number of prisoners, from whom I learn that Longstreet . . . has ske-

daddled by the mountains in Western North Carolina." Longstreet's move was neither as fast nor as complete as General
Granger's note suggested. North Carolina, lying behind the hazy
mountains which framed the eastern horizon, must have seemed
far distant indeed to a leader who could not even ask his armies
to "skedaddle" as far as Bean's Station, a little crossroads thirty
miles from Knoxville, to make winter camp, because of the poor
condition of clothing and transportation facilities. Gradually his
tired, threadbare army moved toward Morristown.

Meanwhile, the request for resignation which General Burnside had sent President Lincoln in September was now officially
accepted, and on the twelfth of December General Foster replaced
Burnside in command of Union forces in Knoxville. A common
enemy now faced both armies: winter. Distant from any source of
help from their fellow soldiers, largely cut off from outside supplies,
in a region unfamiliar to the majority of the soldiers, each was
forced to resort to living off the surrounding countryside. Foraging
became the principal occupation and the prime headache of Federal and Confederate forces alike. General Granger's men in their
improvised camp just outside Knoxville had come there by forced
marches, living upon the country, and were now without shoes,
blankets, overcoats, shirts or shelter. Their only clothing was the
light blouse and pantaloon of summer wear. Their animals had
been so starved at Chattanooga that now they were scarcely able
to haul empty wagons. General Granger implored to be returned
to his camp at Chattanooga, but was denied.

On December fourth another officer of the Fourth Army Corps
said that if they were left much longer in this exposed, unprotected,
and unprovided condition, the ordinary military commanders
would soon be relieved of the further care of many of the men, for
they would be replaced by Generals Rheumatism, Diarrhea, Pneumonia, and Typhoid Fever who would muster them beyond the
reach of further human care.

The army in Knoxville sent its wagons out into the countryside collecting food and firewood. Search for the latter frequently caused much discontent among the citizens who complained that all their fences were being torn down and hauled away by the army and that a hardship would be worked on them when time for spring planting arrived. And although the people up the French Broad helped with provisions and foraging went on daily, an army of twenty thousand, plus the swollen city, was a large number of appetites to satisfy.

Longstreet's army was hounded even closer by hunger and cold. That they were aware of the country around them at all, in more than the utilitarian sense, is surprising. In his memoirs of that time, Longstreet wrote, years later:

> Before Christmas [we] were in our camps along the railroad, near Morristown. Blankets and clothes were very scarce, shoes more so, but all knew how to enjoy the beautiful country in which we found ourselves. . . . Stock and grain were on all farms. . . . The country about the French Broad had hardly been touched by the hands of foragers. Our wagons immediately on entering the fields were loaded to overflowing. Pumpkins were on the ground in places like apples under a tree. Cattle, sheep, and swine, poultry, vegetables, maple-sugar, honey, were all abundant for immediate wants of the troops. . . . The enemy were almost as much in want of the beautiful foraging lands as we, but we were in advance of them, and left little for them. . . . For shoes we were obliged to resort to the raw hides of beef cattle as temporary protection from the frozen ground.

Life along the French Broad, for soldiers and citizens alike, was weary with apprehension, work, enmity and loss during that winter of 1863–64. Its cold was the severest of any winter during the war and on New Year's Day the temperature fell below zero. Such cold is infrequent in this region, but much more unusual was

its prolongation for two weeks. Mud in camp and on roads froze
as hard and sharp as stones. Its jagged edges were cruel to the unprotected feet of most of the soldiers, and their footprints often held
splotches of blood.

Reconnaissance between the two armies was more constant
than reliable. A few horsemen of Wheeler's cavalry in any vicinity
could birth rumors in Knoxville of a march on the city; gossip of
Federal reinforcement from Grant ran like leaf fires through the
Confederate encampment, flaring easily and dying quickly. The
little town of Dandridge, on the banks of the French Broad about
thirty miles above Knoxville, was the center for rumor and foraging. It was here that Longstreet and Granger fought the last real
engagement of Longstreet's East Tennessee campaign. January 14
and 15, 1864, the Federal army marched out from Knoxville
through Dandridge as a flanking measure toward running the Confederate army out of East Tennessee. Longstreet decided to make
a short march and settle the issue at that place. His cavalry moved
first, followed by the infantry still able to make jokes about "the

graybacks," as they called the ever-present lice, singing perhaps "Juanita" or "Arkansas Traveler," speculating on when they might get the pay that was decreasing in value daily as goods purchased with Confederate paper doubled and tripled in price. One of the soldiers caught a chicken that ran across their line of march and popped it in his haversack without ever losing step or changing face. Inconsequential, memorable tidbits that stuck in the minds of the marchers long after important generals' names had faded.

The cavalry forces met and the Federal cavalry withdrew, followed soon after by General Granger and his infantry. Just when he should have pursued most fiercely, the weather broke and Longstreet's men and animals mired down in thawing mud. There is no ground softer than that melting from a rigid freeze and snow. When, after dark, slow rain began, the horses sank up to their fetlocks in mud and, following the hard service and lean foraging they had experienced during fall and winter, they were barely able to keep their footing. The pursuit was called off, and each army went back to its private sufferings, the Confederates unable to dislodge their enemy and the Federals unable to clear the region of theirs. Each attempted to secure the foraging area along the French Broad. One of the Federal officers reported: "The foregoing disposition of troops was made with a view to holding the fords, securing the supplies in the rich Dutch and Irish bottoms of the French Broad and Chucky Rivers—in the vicinity of which two forage trains of the rebels were captured." As General Granger said, "Nothing has pained me so much as being compelled to strip the country; friend and foe must fare alike, or the army must starve."

Soldier or citizen, the problem for each that winter and spring was food and clothing. Women, children, old men, streamed from the mountains into Knoxville where they hoped to find shelter for their bodies and sympathy for their beliefs.

To the difficulties brought on by Union soldiers and Confederate conscription officers were now added the depredations of de-

serters, from both sides, who banded together to take advantage
of the weakened condition of the whole region. Southern sympathizers said these bands were made up of Yankee bushwhackers;
Union patriots said they were Rebel renegades. As usual, each was
wrong and each was right. Bushwhackers and renegades they all
were, with belief in no "side" but their own skins, and serving no
command but their own lawlessness. Their hideouts were caves
along the river or in shaley mountainsides far from the settlements.
Horses and food were their prime necessities and these they stole
frequently. Then their thefts turned to valuables and the large summer homes around Flat Rock, North Carolina, some twenty-five
miles from Asheville, were ransacked. Old quarrels were renewed
and ancient blood debts repaid under the mask of war. A man
whose son might have sometime disagreed with one of the outlaws
would be called to his door on a moonless night and, without a
word, murdered. Lonely trails became traps of theft and death,
and nothing in the mountains was safe—corn in the crib, a gold
piece in the cupboard, or breath in the lungs. A name was given
these bands: "the Outliers." They were the men both parties to
the war should have hated most, had they not already pledged
their emotions as well as their lives and possessions to hating each
other, for this was the ancient everlasting enemy—greed. Nowhere
in the United States was a group like the outliers more bold or
destructive than in the divided section along the French Broad.

Beyond this behind-the-lines warfare, the maneuvering of
army detachments took place. On the eighth of January, '64, after
the severe cold had eased a little, Confederate General Vance—
brother of Governor Zeb Vance—took three hundred men with
their horses from his command and left Asheville, North Carolina,
for a march across the jagged mountains. On the thirteenth, five
days later, he reached the vicinity of Sevierville, a stronghold of
Union loyalty on the Little Pigeon River some ten miles before it
comes to the French Broad. That evening General Vance and his
men entered the town and captured a train of either twenty-three

wagons (according to his report) or eighteen wagons (according to Federal reports). With this prize, he began a quick march back to North Carolina. Colonel Palmer, of the Fifteenth Pennsylvania Cavalry, heard of the raid that same night in his camp on the French Broad, four miles from Dandridge. Choosing detachments from his own Fifteenth Pennsylvania and the Tenth Ohio, he started in pursuit. All morning they rode, and into the afternoon, until at three o'clock they came to a wild mountain stream thick with laurel and rhododendron, spruce and poplar—Cosby Creek, near the Great Smoky Mountains, twenty-five miles from Sevierville. At this creek the tired Confederates had paused to feed and water their horses before taking the road down to the village of Newport on the Big Pigeon. Either through carelessness or over-confidence in the speed of their flight, they had failed to post pickets for their brief pause. Colonel Palmer arranged his men in column of fours and immediately charged the unsuspecting camp. Surprise, consternation and wholesale flight were the disorder of the day. Horses for the most part abandoned, they ran afoot, throwing away guns, blankets, saddlebags. Prisoners were plentiful, fifty-two in all, including General Vance, his adjutant general and his inspector general. The rest took refuge in the difficult hills.

Besides the prisoners and the recaptured wagons, an ambulance with medical stores, one hundred and fifty saddle horses, one hundred stand of arms, and a quantity of bacon, salt and meal were captured. On the number of men Colonel Palmer had with him, the official reports are at even greater variance. The Federal colonel said he had "in all less than two hundred men." The Confederate report estimated he had at least four hundred. Apparently even mathematical judgments could be colored by the light of humiliation or vanity. With this rout of the Confederate forces from North Carolina, the area of East Tennessee seemed secured to the Union.

Longstreet's continued presence in the region caused much Northern discontent, however. The last of February General Grant sent General Schofield, who had succeeded General Foster in command of the Army of the Ohio, this message: "Farmers in East Tennessee should be encouraged to cultivate all the grain they can the coming season. Quartermasters may sell them what can be spared for seed purposes, and seed of all kinds will be permitted to pass over the roads." Grant was of a mind to make one of the last major moves of the war in East Tennessee, and he felt that Longstreet should be driven out completely.

Grant had visited Knoxville the latter part of December and quizzed one of its old citizens:

> . . . [Grant] asked me a great many questions as to the feasibility of sending an army up the pass through the mountains, along the French Broad River, into North Carolina . . . it was evident from the questions asked that an expedition up the French Broad into North Carolina was one of the near probabilities, if not certainties. It was evidently in contemplation by General Grant at that time to send an army up that river with a view of penetrating the interior into North Carolina, seizing the railroads, reaching the coast and cutting the Confederacy into two parts. . . . Doubtless the difficulty of keeping up, or securing on the way, supplies for a large army constituted the main and a sufficient reason [for abandonment of the plan].

Another reason was advice of Generals Foster and Schofield. They urged that, as far as Federal forces were concerned, Longstreet should remain just where he was. They painted a dark and accurate picture of the exhaustion of both animals and supplies in the area. Sherman had sized up the situation months before.

Grant decided to leave Longstreet where he was and prepare for a major drive elsewhere. That it was a wise move he would have known immediately if he could have intercepted a note which

Longstreet was sending to General Robert E. Lee, a message marked "Confidential." Its brevity heightened its pathos. " . . . There is nothing between this [Greeneville] and Knoxville to feed man or horse. Our supplies are getting very short, too. Here nothing but extraordinary exertions will save us, and the sooner we get to work and make them the better it will be for us. . . ." The man who had ordered Pickett to make his charge, who had struggled against the immovable incompetence of Bragg, had further hard orders to give and struggles to meet.

On April seventh, he was ordered back to service with Lee on the Rapidan. He and his army, with the strips of rawhide and homemade shoes on their feet, left the crude huts where they had waited and suffered, hoped and despaired, hungered for home and fed, at the beginning, on the rich forage of the French Broad fields, played chuck-a-luck, cursed Bragg's bodyguard (the lice), and heard the mounting toll of defeat following defeat. In the fresh expectancy of spring they marched out of one valley into another.

They left behind an area almost destitute, where more than fifty thousand men and their animals had ravaged fields and storehouses alike in their constant search for food, and where war raged hotter and more personal than ever. April eleventh, Governor Vance sent Secretary of War Seddon a strong plea:

> I beg again to call your earnest attention to the importance of suspending the execution of the conscript law in the mountain counties of North Carolina. They are filled with tories and deserters, burning, robbing, and murdering. They have been robbed and eaten out by Longstreet's command, and have lost their crops by being in the field nearly all the time trying to drive back the enemy. Now that Longstreet's command is removed, their condition will be altogether wretched, and hundreds will go to the enemy for protection and bread.

Even as he was writing a band of some seventy-five men came into the county seat of Burnsville in rugged Yancey County at the remote northern headwaters of the French Broad and surprised the local home guard. After breaking open the magazine and capturing all the arms and ammunition—some one hundred State guns—they went on to a local store, broke in its door and carried off most of the contents. Last, they went to the room of Captain Lyons, local enrolling officer, during a short struggle wounded him in the arm, after which he escaped. From the Home Guard Commissary they took the greatest prize: five hundred pounds of bacon —perhaps some of it impressed from smokehouses well-known to the attackers.

The men were not alone in demonstrations. In the same locality, fifty women assembled and carried off an estimated sixty bushels of wheat. These were direct, impetuous hill men and women who could not see the logic of hunger while wheat and bacon lay stored in warehouses.

This accumulating anarchy caused North Carolina General McElroy commanding the First Brigade of Home Guards to write the Governor:

> The county [Yancey] is gone up. It has got to be impossible to get any man out there unless he is dragged out, with but very few exceptions. . . . I have one hundred men at this place to guard against Kirk, of Laurel, and cannot reduce the force. . . .

Kirk, to whom the writer referred, was a Union colonel, whose headquarters were in Greeneville, Tennessee, from which he kept a sharp eye and frequently sharper attack on Eastern Tennessee and Western North Carolina. Among Confederates he was called a bushwhacker, among the Federals he was known as a man who could conduct the guerilla war necessary in these mountains. On the thirteenth of June, '64, he made one of his most spectacular raids.

Setting out from Morristown, Tennessee, with 130 men, he marched through Greeneville and Crab Orchard to Camp Vance, within six miles of Morganton, North Carolina. At Camp Vance he routed the Confederates, who lost eleven men killed and many more wounded, and then destroyed much of the enemy property. This included a locomotive, three railroad cars, the depot and commissary buildings, twelve hundred small arms with ammunition, and three thousand bushels of grain. The main purpose of his expedition had been to destroy the railroad bridge across the Yadkin River, but he found this impossible. Making arrangements for its burning after his departure, Kirk captured 277 prisoners and took 132 of these back to Federal headquarters at Knoxville. He also brought thirty-two Negroes, forty-eight horses and mules, and forty recruits who had joined his regiment. The whole swift expedition, done with as much surprise to Federal as to Confederate commanding officers, cost Kirk one man killed, one severely wounded and five slight wounds, including one to himself.

While some Union reactions to Colonel Kirk's march were markedly admiring, realistic Sherman urged that the colonel should spend more time organizing the Union sympathizers rather than in undertaking hazardous expeditions.

The Southern report from the Western North Carolina Headquarters in Asheville to Richmond tried to explain why Kirk had not been detected on his march to Camp Vance. "It appears that in going to Camp Vance, Kirk, with a small band of Indians, negroes and deserters . . . traveled in the night avoiding all roads." That Colonel Kirk's command was made up of regular enlisted men, although they were from the mountains, their Southern neighbors would never concede. They should not, however, have been scornful of Indian troops, for one of the main companies supporting the Confederate States of America in the mountains was Colonel W. H. Thomas's Sixty-ninth North Carolina Infantry composed

chiefly of Cherokee Indians. Most of the decimated tribe, still dwelling in the inaccessible parts of the Great Smokies, remained loyal
to the states during the war, those very states which had confiscated their land and caused the reluctant Federal government to
remove the majority of their Nation to Western territory. Colonel
Thomas was the white trader who had helped bring about permission for a small group of the Cherokees to remain in their native hills, and for this he had become an unquestioned leader
among them. His main duty with the Sixty-ninth was to control
the Smoky Mountains passes and those up the French Broad.

Each side thought it was bearing most of the depredations
and each company thought it deserved more of the over-all rations.
Looting done by outliers was laid to the enemy of either side, so
that to read Confederate letters and accounts of the situation would
make it seem that the Union controlled the mountain region, while
Union reports make it seem as if Confederate officers were engaged
only in terrorization of Federal sympathizers.

Death piled on death. On the stormy, rain-swept night of
September third, General Morgan, who had led his rebel raiders
on so many attacks and retreats into the North and over the South,
returned to an old friend's house, Mrs. Williams's, in Greeneville.
He and his staff ate supper and retired. In the night a detachment
of Federal soldiers rode into Greeneville, avoided the pickets with
precision and rode into the Williams yard. Skirmishing followed.
Morgan and his adjutant general ran into the yard, the pouring
rain, and, by the glare of a vivid streak of lightning, a private
named Andrew Campbell took aim at the proud erratic general.
"Oh my God!" Morgan cried, as the shot mingled with the noise
of other shots, stamping horses, confused soldiers. He died instantly.
Amidst curious circumstances which hinted at betrayal—but by
whom? soldier or lady friend?—one of the Confederacy's glamor-
ized careers came to an abrupt close.

The Confederates continued raids from North Carolina into
East Tennessee. With eight hundred men and three pieces of ar-

tillery, Colonel John B. Palmer (no kin to Colonel Palmer of the Fifteenth Pennsylvania Cavalry) went from Warm Springs, North Carolina, over Paint Mountain into Cocke County, Tennessee. In November he reported:

> I brought everything out that I took to Tennessee with me excepting the mountain howitzer. . . . I likewise brought out some cattle and hogs, my train loaded with wheat and commissary stores, and some captured horses, mules, and intrenching tools.

The Union soldiers made raids from East Tennessee into Western North Carolina. Colonel Kirk came into Yancey County, but was turned back by a company of soldiers from Asheville under Colonel Love. On a return march he went up the Big Pigeon River into Haywood County.

Followers of both armies continued to kill innocent victims. In North Carolina an old man called "Uncle Billy" was murdered on his doorstep because his son, a Confederate captain, had helped run down deserters. In Tennessee, an old Union man shucking corn on his farm was sighted in the field by a group of Confederates riding by. They shot at him and, with presence of mind, he fell among the shucks and lay as if dead. When his attackers made no closer investigation, he was saved. Others were less fortunate, as the woman who was made to come and watch her "Lincolnite son" being hanged. The notorious Jim Ferguson spread horror wherever he moved. His sole aim in life seemed to be the cold-blooded murder of Southern sympathizers. He sought to kill his own brother because he was in the Confederate Army.

Secret societies for the Union had been growing through the whole mountain area, and by fall of '64 the Confederate government had grown enough concerned over them to send spies for information. One spy became a society member and wrote to President Jefferson Davis that he had learned the well-guarded signs

and passwords. Members of the group were bound by rigid oath
to encourage desertion from the army, to harbor all deserters or escaped prisoners and give them passage, to give information to the
Union of troop movements or plans made by Confederate troops,
and to help the Union army in either advance or retreat. This was
called the Order of Heroes of America, and in North Carolina
members often wore red strings in their coat lapels, which led them
to be called "Red Strings." The password was:

> Question: These are gloomy times.
> Answer: Yes, but we are looking for better.
> Question: What are you looking for?
> Answer: A red and white cord.
> Question: Why a cord?
> Answer: Because it is safe for us and our families.

There was also a society which was a truly underground organization. There were no regular times or places of meeting, and
no organized "lodges." The league was nameless but was generally
called the Peace Society. No records were kept. Each initiate was
"an independent, dissevered link in a perfect chain."

The divided nature of the mountain region had brought another interesting and varied group of men into being. Already mentioned, these were the guides, or pilots, who personally directed
Union men through Confederate territory to the army camps in
Kentucky. One of the most popular of these terminals was Camp
Dick Robinson, near Lexington. It required a special sort of man
to be a pilot. He must first of all know the country—the back
roads, the unused gaps in mountains, the less-traveled valleys, the
river crossings—and he must be an expert woodsman. He had to
have daring and cool calculation, must trust the right people many
times, but never the wrong person once.

Such men were William Reynolds, Frank Hodge, Charlie
Davis (really Robert Boone, a great-grandson of Daniel Boone),

and Daniel Ellis. Ellis was called "Old Red Fox" because of the many times he closely escaped capture or death by Confederate guns, and from his first trip into Kentucky on April 1, 1862, to his resignation as a pilot in March, 1865, he claimed he had taken ten thousand men to the Union Army in Kentucky or East Tennessee. Through rain and mud, snow and ice, heat and dust, he had crossed many streams with hoarded breath fearful lest enemy pickets should hear a sudden splash, had struggled through overgrown paths and waited in laurel thickets to avoid unexpected encounter with the enemy. It was such loyalty to the Union that split the region to its core and made reconciliation long and difficult.

The year 1864 came to an end, and with it the hopes of the Confederate States of America. Oh, Colonel Stringfield still went out from Asheville and struggled down Spring Creek in an eighteen-inch snow with mountains so steep he and his men often had to hang on to bushes along the banks of the stream, holding off a feared Union invasion through Tennessee. The little town of Asheville was thrown into confusion by the approach of nine hundred Federal soldiers from the Hundred-and-first Ohio Infantry encamped near Greeneville. Kirk and Stoneman raided, were engaged. But it was all decided. On wider, distant fields, between larger armies, perhaps even at a time in the past when the evolutionary processes of history were forming and reforming—the victory and the defeat had been decided.

But war had brought something at once dark and bright to the country along the French Broad. It was the darkness of hate for one's fellow man and the brightness of belief so closely cherished that it could claim life or death. Here the war, despite Burnside's large army of occupation and Longstreet's army of attack, was minor in scale but always major in intensity. It was "war waged with unspeakable bitterness, sometimes with inhuman cruelty. Fought by men in single combat, in squads, in companies, in regiments, in the fields, in fortified towns and in ambush, under the stars and stripes, under the stars and bars, and under the black flag."

Grief for a Union father or a Confederate son dead in battle, fear of neighbors who had stood with "the enemy," agony over lives and treasure lost to the outlier gangs from both armies: This grief and fear and agony was not as easily stacked away as a gun. A truce was signed April 9, 1865, but it was days before some of the North Carolina soldiers heard about it and ceased fighting, months before some of the Tennessee companies disbanded, years before some of the defeated could return with ease to their homes, and generations before the smell of spilled blood could be diluted in memory. Just as the river of mountain water rushes on, however, and eventually carries off the debris great storms leave behind, so time in human affairs is no less sure. As soon as the first soldier turned home toward the mountains and left war behind him, so soon began another cycle of human renewal in this part of the South. The pieces were smashed, the pattern was lost, but the processes of life were as sure as time, sure as the river.

# 8

# The Broken Pieces

As they made their way back to the rich farms along the river, back up the narrow paths to hidden coves and hollows, back to the familiar streets of small mountain villages, whether they wore blue or gray or an undecipherable bundle of prison rags, they carried a new thing with them: a horizon enlarged by new places and people. Boys who had seldom visited their own county seats had gone to other states, seen regions and ways of life far different from the mountain scenes. Their knowledge had been enriched and their curiosity stimulated.

If the war sent people out, it also brought others in. As much as a year before the close of the war, in March, 1864, a report published by two visitors from Philadelphia to East Tennessee struck the major chord for a chant that was to rise for many decades to come—through our own day—all over the South. The Pennsylvanians wrote that the existing war was clearly destined to introduce Northern men, Northern ideas and Northern enterprise into the border states, and, as Northern military lines advanced, throughout the whole South. East Tennessee, they said, with its fertile lands and valuable water power, presented a fine field for the application of Northern labor and capital. When the calamity of war should be past, and a direct railroad communication with the North secured, they felt sure East Tennessee would prosper as never before.

Such cool foresight was possible, at that moment, only in a brace of strangers, however, for most families were still stinging under loss of a smokehouse robbed of hams and side meat, barns emptied of cows, horses, any livestock. And the plans of the soldiers themselves were as usual personal and immediate. Twenty days after the peace had been signed, while he was waiting in Nashville to be mustered out, one young East Tennessee boy wrote back to a girlish cousin some of his very typical speculations and hopes:

> April 29, 1865 . . . The Regt. is mustard out all but the recruits and tha are still here at this plase. I have a bout six months yet to surve yet. I dont no what tha will do with us yet but from all accounts I dont think that tha will bee much use of a grate many solgirs much longar for I think the war is a bout plaid out. You stated in your lettar that tha third Tenn boys had got home and tha talk of reinlisting and that you thought tha hadant much respect for the Girls. You musint think that for all that a Solgier thinks of is a nice young Girl and the happy years that has past and for evear gone.

While some rushed home eager to flush a bride, others hurried to reunite with wives and children already theirs. One husband—with the Federal cavalry—wrote ahead for his wife to change their baby's name from Mary L. to Mary U. Then he explained that the U. stood for Ulysses. Did he give this smallest symbol of his partisanship an extra hug when he came home in '65?

In a dozen designs, the first days after peace unfolded. Areas where tension and conflict had been sharpest during the war became, with the return of soldiers from both sides, tense again.

Bloody conflict sometimes seemed to belie the fact that peace was supposed to have arrived. For instance, in Knoxville in 1865, while some of the first men from each army were returning, a recent dischargee from the Confederate forces, named Abner Baker, and William Hall, the son of a well-known local Union man, plunged into a fight. Hall had struck Baker with a stick. Before their struggle was over, Hall lay dead, killed by Baker. Abner Baker was arrested and put in the Knoxville jail, but that night a mob of Federal soldiers broke into the jail, captured their victim and hanged him from a nearby tree.

Humorous things happened, too. During the latter part of the war an elderly lady at the mouth of Ivy River in North Carolina had had a piece of cloth stolen from her loom by bushwhackers. Now, at a Church Association meeting, when representatives from churches all over the locality were gathered on denominational business, a woman on the bench next to our lady weaver's happened to pull her skirt a little high as she moved to make more room on the seat. A good weaver could tell her own work anywhere. The Ivy lady snatched her startled adversary's skirts up over her lap, exposing the hidden petticoat made of the telltale stolen cloth. Because of his part in this raid, the luckless woman's husband-thief was always afterward known as "Petticoat Jim."

On the public political level, the pendulum was swinging wide. In Tennessee, only four days before the armistice, on April 5, '65, Parson Brownlow had been given another title: that of governor of the state. And in July, only three months after Appomattox, he led Tennessee back into the Union.

The following year an old issue was revived. Once more a movement gained ground to make East Tennessee into a separate state. Because of differences in economy, way of life, and politics, the Eastern counties had tried to break away from the rest of Tennessee at the very beginning of the Civil War, but the Confederate government had put down that plan. Now, on May 3, 1866, delegates from twenty-two counties, including those of the French Broad,

Pigeon and Nolichucky rivers, gathered in Knoxville to draw up a petition asking the legislature for permission to form a new state. This time the other two thirds of the state, middle and West Tennessee, suppressed the petition. It appeared that East Tennessee, like it or not, was going to have to remain with her mother state.

Elections throughout the area were frequently bloody events. Negroes, in the few localities where there was any considerable Negro population, were urged on one hand to use their new-won vote and on the other were menaced with violence if they did vote. Politics settled into a normal chaos following the total disruption of war. And the whole economy of the French Broad people was reduced to pristine poverty. Nowhere are the individual problems, the typical harrassments of a people divided in war and frustrated in peace, more interestingly revealed than in letters penned during the very press of the events on which we can now turn such comfortable perspective. Labor was a fundamental problem of the region. During the war, white people as well as Negroes had gone North seeking higher wages.

The summer of '65 a leading citizen of Asheville wrote a friend in Pennsylvania, asking if there was a possibility of receiving any labor force from among the German population of Philadelphia for help in his city. Pennsylvania Germans were not the only people this man was trying to lure to his part of the state. He wrote to a friend in London, too, describing the unsettled state of affairs in Buncombe County, inquiring about possible English or Scottish immigrants. His friend was grieved to hear of Buncombe's present condition and equally sad to describe his lack of hope about her future as far as labor from the Isles was concerned. A good plowman in Scotland was receiving from thirty to forty pounds a year "and found," which included his bread, milk and house. This amount would, he felt, stagger North Carolinians.

On the other hand, if factories could be started, that would be another matter! Labor for factories could easily be drawn from abroad. Indeed, not only labor but capital as well. In his enthusiasm for the idea, the Londoner even volunteered to join in such an enterprise by raising "any amount" in England if a good strong company of landholders would join in and form an organization in Buncombe. Why, there were countless things that could be made in that grand county!

The Britisher's idea foreshadowed the great transition that was gradually to take place not only in Western North Carolina but over the whole South. From a purely agrarian economy and way of living they would grow at least partially industrialized, more and more so as decades passed. As for English capital, a later experience in the French Broad country demonstrated how easily (at least for a period) money could be raised in England and Scotland for development enterprises in America, especially in the South which had had little commercial expansion.

Confusion existed in personal relationships and confusion compounded with chicanery held high rule in the local courts. Individual grudges, party politics, money-grabbing schemes and all manner and degree of crimes committed during the war began to be aired by processes of the law. For instance, at Burnsville in North Carolina's mountainous Yancey County, a former private in the Federal infantry was indicted, during the spring of 1867, in six or seven cases for "offences done while he was a Federal soldier": breaking up and destroying Confederate guns, for one thing. Suits were brought against Confederate and Federal ex-soldiers alike for army foraging during the war. Juries for all cases were scrupulously chosen according to the sympathies of the defendant and his judges. One lawyer said during a case a generation later that he knew his client—a Confederate sympathizer— was as good as convicted when he noticed on the jury foreman's coat lapel, during second day of trial, a G.A.R. button. It was just such a detail that a good lawyer could never afford to miss when passing on a potential juror.

During the summer of 1867, other old quarrels were taken out of the mothballs. None was more partisan nor emotional than one in Madison County. During the war, this county had been probably the most divided in allegiances of any in North Carolina. And this trial grew out of a murder which had occurred six years previously, at the very beginning of hostilities. Pieced together from various evidence and petitions, the story—illustrative of all the high feeling and discord of the times—seems to have been this: In May, 1861, on the day North Carolina had set to elect delegates to the convention on secession, there was a crowd in the little riverbank town of Marshall. The county sheriff, a stalwart secessionist, stood on the main street and "husawed," as witnesses described it, "for Jeff Davis and the confederacy." A man in the crowd replied with a husaw for "Washington and the union." The sheriff promptly drew his pistol on the unionist and followed "pistol in hand some ten or fifteen paces" as the man backed away. A stranger intervened, and the sheriff's attention was soon diverted to another man who had presented himself at the voting headquarters.

After asking the voter, "What are you doing here with your gun?" he again "presented his pistol" and began to advance on another retreating victim. In the general swarm, however, the sheriff spied an even likelier enemy, a man with whom he'd already quarreled in the past and whose sentiments he knew to be positively unionist. As he swerved his aim in this third man's direction, the man dodged behind some bystanders, and the sheriff was forced to choose a proxy, the man's son, upon whom he leveled fire; the ball passed through the boy's arm and struck a rib.

Having drawn blood, the sheriff retreated to a nearby house. The owner, fearful of further bloodshed, slammed the door behind him. But the sheriff was unquenchable. Rushing upstairs and throwing open a second-story window, he waved his mighty pistol once more and called to the crowd below, "Come up here all of you damn black Republicans and take a shot about with me." As one witness later phrased it, this "very much Exasperated the crowd, there being on that occasion 144 votes cast at that precinct for union against 28 for secession and a good Deal of Liquor had

been drank that day." The conclusion to the whole matter was that the father whose son had been hurt wounded the sheriff still at the window and finally, when an officer went in the house to arrest the sheriff, the father rushed in behind him and fired a second, fatal shot.

Well, the "husawing" sheriff was dead, and the man who killed him fled the county and finally joined the Federal Army in Kentucky and, soon after his enlistment, he also died. But half-a-dozen years later feeling was still running high over the incident and a suit, asking ten thousand dollars, was begun against seven men accused of being accessories to the death of the sheriff. Of course the conflict was never resolved because by its very nature only time could dim the issues and angers.

As a single but rather complex example of what transplanted Confederate citizens might experience in the decade following the war, the hodgepodge notebooks of one old Thomas Lee reveal his times as well as his character. Sorted and assimilated, copies of letters he wrote, accounts due, notes payable, penmanship exercises, newspaper notices and letters received fall into a revealing pattern.

A zealous Confederate in a predominately Union East Tennessee community, Lee moved sometime during the war to a gap in the Blue Ridge Mountains in Buncombe County, on one of the very headwater streams of the French Broad, and bought a tavern, or "stand," that had been run there for some years by a family named Sherrill. As Lee explained to a business firm, he was living fourteen miles southeast of Asheville, on the Turnpike Road leading south, he owned real estate there which cost four thousand dollars and he had due him in East Tennessee about six thousand dollars. Since he didn't expect to realize at least one third of these debts, he had put only two thirds of the notes in the hands of attorneys for collection.

Those processes of collection must have chastened Mr. Lee in "the law's delay," however, for several years and many letters later he was still urging attorneys and debtors to send him some token payment. Sometimes his temper wore thin, as in 1869, when he wrote one debtor: ". . . in your letter you invite me to come back to Tennessee to live. This Sir under the circumstances I regard as an insult." He called himself an "absquatulated Rebel" and advised his friend to flee when "the lion roareth and the wangdoodle mourneth."

Working to collect from delinquent debtors on one hand so he could pay impatient creditors on the other, Mr. Lee also had other troubles. In a letter of December 18, 1867, he mentioned the various suits in which he had been implicated in East Tennessee concerning confiscation, treason and war damage. One of the lengthiest of these suits was brought by a man named Walker against Lee and several others whom he accused of being instrumental during the war in causing his arrest by Confederate soldiers and a subsequent imprisonment in Richmond. Mr. Lee answered the charge promptly and with his usual vehemence, saying that at the time of Mr. Walker's arrest he (Lee) was and had been for nearly three months in the neighboring state of North Carolina.

There was also the matter of the corn Mr. Lee had purchased on credit during the war year of 1863. By the time he had journeyed across the mountains to Rutherfordton, North Carolina, several times and finally discharged the debt in February, 1870, he found that he had paid $100.52 for just ten bushels of corn.

Mr. Lee was not spending all his time writing letters and listing grievances, however. He had set up a trading post in the Gap. A ledger entry might read: 4½ lb. pickled pork–56¢; Upper leather–75¢; 1 hand tobacco–20¢; 2 lb. pork Ham (no bone)–20¢; 3 pairs of small shoes–75¢. In addition, he kept his house open as an inn for sojourners from the lowland summers. During the fall and winter he ran a flourishing stock stand. He sent a notice over Tennessee and Kentucky to be distributed at other taverns informing stock drivers that he was prepared to keep stock at the old and well-known stand at Hickory Nut Gap on the road from Asheville to Charlotte.

Besides being storekeeper, innkeeper and stock man, Mr. Lee also branched out into salesmanship. In 1869 he asked a Nashville concern about its proposal to furnish agents with the genuine improved Common Sense Sewing Machine. This enterprise did not materialize as successfully, however, as one two years later concerning the Woman's Friend Steam Washer. Having purchased rights for sole salesmanship in Buncombe County, Mr. Lee wrote the Pennsylvania manufacturer within a few months, telling him that although he had commenced selling the steam washer the people of the vicinity seemed to be very cautious. However, he inquired how much the rights to four more counties would be. He pointed out that although these were sparsely settled mountain counties, they might be profitable for him because they were close to his home. Perhaps part of Mr. Lee's difficulties arose because the mountain people were not only very cautious but very "broke" too.

If these complications of debt and lawsuit, friendships and enmities, these undertakings of store, tavern, and salesmanship, were all part of just one man's life after the war, some idea of the times can be glimpsed by multiplying these experiences by even a small proportion of the population. If much of Mr. Lee's bitterness and sarcasm was one of the early unhealthy aftermaths of war, it was healthy to see it gradually being superseded by enterprise and self-reconstruction. By the beginning of the next decade after the tragic war, as soon as 1870, many citizens of the region were looking to the future rather than the past.

One prominent Ashevillian wrote, in a bold jet-black penmanship, from the state capital at Raleigh, to another leader in Asheville, the following foresighted comments:

Raleigh, N.C. 29th, 1870

My dear Sir:

. . . I'm sorry to learn the depressed state of business there.
I think the people ought to be active and buoyant notwith-
standing the scarcity of money. There is a fair [possibility]
that the Railroad will reach them at no very distant day from
some direction. Are they ready for it? I am afraid not. How
much have they got to ship, if the road were there today! How
much could they have next harvest and fall! Our farming
population especially need to bestir themselves. They want
grazing grounds, orchards, etc. etc. these can't be gotten ready
in a day, it takes *time* and the road will be there before they get
ready. . . . Why don't all our farmers have cultivated fruit?
They could do so as easy as not. And I might add, they could
as easy as not have cultivated cows, horses, mules, hogs, wheat,
corn, potatoes, cabbages, turnips, etc. etc. Don't you think so?
They only need *labor* and a little money to do this. We need
intelligent labor to make our mountains blossom as the rose!
God bless the mountains and the people who live among
them! My heart swells with emotion when I think of them!

Such men and women as this, filled with emotion *and* application, loyalty *and* energy, were the ones who took the broken pieces
war had left behind and shaped them into new life. Whether they
had been Confederate or Federal soldier or sympathizer, it took
all of the best of each to recreate what all had helped destroy.

It was inevitable that many of the rootless young men fresh
from soldiering should turn to the great West for a new life. The
return of one of these seekers brought the quality of legend into
the booming twenties of North Carolina. In the autumn of 1929,
a young Asheville businessman answered the telephone one day
and heard the inquiry: "Who's this?"

"George Coggins," he replied.

The stranger's voice was disappointed. "What's your pappy's name?"

"Henry Allen Coggins, the Mayor of Beetree. Why?"

"Now we're getting somewhere. My name is Henry Allen Coggins, I was born on Beetree, and I'm your great-uncle, boy!"

"Couldn't be. The only Henry Allen Coggins I ever heard of was killed at Gettysburg."

"That's me, son. I was there all right, but they just nicked me with their bullets. And when I got away from that Yankee prison I just headed across Illinois to Missouri and Texas and Oregon. Meant to get back home before this but one little thing after another, you know."

The great-nephew was too astounded to reply.

"Well, I'm here at the station, son. I've got Texas dust all over me and I'd like to get on out to Beetree."

George Coggins found his great-uncle with patriarchal beard, snowy sheaf of hair, erect shoulders, keen eyes and contagious laugh surrounded by a spellbound crowd of railway employees and travelers. Then, and in days to come, his tales of fighting Yankees and Indians, chasing cattle rustlers and riding the range, bagging grizzlies and panthers and leading wagon trains across the continent, were to fascinate family and friends and strangers. He could tell of the day he and his six brothers marched away clad in gray, and how some became officers and some became heroes and some just fought and never came back. And how he had finally made it.

"I never took any oath of amnesty. I never will. I'm still just an unwhipped Rebel.

"If I hadn't been a good teamster I don't reckon I could have made my way in the West, but that first trip out I joined up with a wagon train going along the Oregon Trail. After I learned the way I come back and helped move another train out. As I got to know the dangers along the trail and come to know the route better, I was finally trusted to lead trains into the territory. Seventeen hundred miles across.

"The times we were attacked! The day at Pecos River when we finally beat off three hundred Indians but they captured most of the mules we had. Or the time we had between eighty and a hundred wagons in the train and was making slow time. Two of the families got impatient and I couldn't hold them back. They pulled on ahead of the rest of us. It wasn't long till we caught up with them. Wagons burned, cattle slaughtered and quartered, horses stolen, six men and two women massacred."

In the months that followed, before he went to the final West, Allen Coggins visited his old homesite on Beetree, drank out of the family spring and remembered farther back than the new West, when these mountains of home had been the old West. "Well, everything has changed so much. Asheville wasn't much more than a mudhole on the square when I left. Now it's showing off these skyscrapers and big resort hotels. I like it better on the Swannanoa at Beetree. That's where I want to be buried."

Perhaps Allen Coggins thought he had fought the last great war. With zest and confidence, he had reconstructed the broken pieces of his life, and it was in like manner that the people turned their attention from conflict to new livelihoods, new places.

In the French Broad country there was also the boom of an old industry which helped bridge the gap between war and the coming of the railroad. And the river had made that industry feasible. Without it, without those great droves of livestock that poured through East Tennessee and Western North Carolina for the next two decades, it would have been perhaps impossible for many families throughout the region to have kept their precarious economic hold during the years of readjustment and renewal.

# 9

# The Great Drives

A river is not only a highway in itself, but frequently it also provides, like the ancient buffalo trails and Indian traces, the route of least resistance and marks the way for thoroughfares to follow. Thus the French Broad River not only carried its mountainous crops of virgin timber from the hills to the lumber mills and later paper industries, and its rafts of foodstuffs from the bottom lands to the cities, but, more important, it carved a passage for commerce through the steep and unyielding Appalachians of Eastern Tennessee and Western North Carolina to the broad cotton lands beyond.

To the north and west of the French Broad gorge lay the grasslands and cornfields of Kentucky and Tennessee. To the south and east waited the ready markets of South Carolina and Georgia. Between them stretched North Carolina and two hundred or more miles of transportation, depending on the point of departure; but most difficult, most picturesque, and most challenging, waited the seventy-odd miles of the French Broad River canyon.

Narrow, rough, clinging to the cliffs, this was no highway over which the farmers of Kentucky and Tennessee could haul their great crops of corn and grain and hay to the deeper south markets, and so perhaps the ruggedness of this one third of the French Broad land became the major reason for the enormous droves of livestock that dominated, for three quarters of a century, its people, economics, and society. Grass and hay and grain from upcountry fields, transformed into energy and fat on mules and cattle, corn carried as fat on the ribs of hogs and fowls was most easily transported along the muddy, winding roads of the nineteenth century, and was finally most easily sold as fresh meat to the cotton plantation owners and tenants in the lowlands.

Therefore, the road leading up the French Broad grew in use from 1800 when that inveterate traveler, Bishop Asbury, met a drove of thirty-three horses on the tributary Swannanoa, through the 1830's and 1840's when the stream of livestock became almost as constant as the waters which it followed, increased to what the drovers themselves called a flood, until around 1885, when the flood ceased almost as dramatically as it had begun.

This French Broad road of the drovers was a triumph of scenic beauty, the despair of builders and an economic necessity; one of the few roads in the United States that required the ingenuity of side-fords. These were described, in the grave terms of an eyewitness, as, "places where, in the construction of the road down the river bank, the builders encountered large precipices, usually ends of mountain spurs, whose bases the waters of the stream washed. In order to get around such precipices the road was built at their bases into the water, usually for not more than an eighth of a mile around. These were called 'side-fords' and were impassable at times of floods in the river." To help in the upkeep of this road, tolls were charged by the various counties. The usual fee was fifteen cents for each rider and his horse, five cents for each man on foot, two cents a head for hogs, and ten cents for a single horse being led. The ferries charged a cent a head for the livestock.

Of this same road, a traveler wrote, in 1849: ". . . [it] runs directly along the water's edge nearly the entire distance, and, on account of the quantity of travel which passes over it, is kept in admirable repair. It is the principal thoroughfare between Tennessee and South Carolina, and an immense number of cattle, horses, and hogs are annually driven over it to the seaboard markets." A short forty years later, the road was described as being but a wreck of its former self. During these brief decades an economic upheaval had occurred, railroad expansion had mushroomed and a bitter war had been waged. The scene of the big drives was shifting from the near Southwest to the Far West, taking with it the color and drama, the pulse and legend that are part of life where men and animals depend upon each other for livelihood.

Where did they come from, these drovers who rode horseback in front of their surging stream of livestock, these drivers who followed on foot and kept the line orderly, kept it moving along, and, above all, where did this mass of livestock feed and fatten?

The cattle and mules came partly from Kentucky, partly from the grassy balds on some of the high mountains of Tennessee and North Carolina and the lush fields of wild pea vine in their valleys. These grassy balds were whole mountaintops where timber gave way to hundreds of acres of thick virgin grass and cattle grazed on open range. Heavy summer rainfall kept the grass green and abundant from the time the cattle were turned out in early May. When fall came, with frost to nip the pasture and a summer's weight accumulated on the hoof, the herds were brought down from the mountains and started on their journey to market. Cattle and mules were the easiest of all the livestock driven on these trips, and, according to numbers, were of middle importance.

Least important, but still numerous enough and cantankerous enough of temperament to arouse amazement were the fowls. Only a few droves of ducks are recorded, one being mentioned by a traveler of 1857, who said that near Warm Springs, North Carolina, a health resort six miles from the Tennessee border, he saw 373 head of Kentucky cattle in one herd and another drove of four hundred ducks. But flocks of turkeys were an annual event. Down from the hills of Kentucky and Tennessee, where they had roamed the woods in a half-wild state until their final fattening on extra corn or grain from the year's harvest, most of the turkeys were driven to Spartanburg, South Carolina, which was the nearest rail center for produce from the hills. At Spartanburg they were sold to slaughtering houses from which they were shipped to various parts of the country.

Thousands of turkeys were driven up the French Broad every year, and their passage was a sight to behold. Four or five or six hundred turkeys to a flock, led by an old master gobbler who strutted and gobbled his way through the dust and rocks and mud, making way for the other high-stepping noisy birds to follow. The column they made might be four hundred yards long, but it was kept in line by the owner who rode horseback in front, and two or three drivers who followed behind or on each side with long whips decorated at the end with pieces of bright red cloth, usually flannel. The flannel flags and the calls of the men kept the birds in line until night began to fall. Then they roosted. If they had arrived at a stand—the local tavern for men and animals—it was the drivers' good fortune; if not, they would have to make out as best they could, for the turkeys took to the trees and no mere men could dislodge them from their roosts. Since a flock could cover only eight miles a day at best and two hundred miles was the average journey, it is likely that the men slept outdoors frequently. The most pressing reason for arriving at the stands, however, was to obtain feed for the flocks. It took bushels of corn to feed them and stout old trees to roost them. For the rest, they were a slow, noisy, ludicrous old bunch of tourists, these hill-bred turkeys on their way to the holiday platters of the city folks.

But by far the greatest traffic of this era was in hogs, and most of the hogs were from Tennessee. In the census of 1840 Tennessee was the greatest corn-producing state in the Union. Her nickname became the "hog and hominy" state, and production of the two went together just that closely. Corn brought the best price when it became pork. It was estimated by the keepers of the tollgates that between 150,000 and 175,000 Tennessee hogs were driven up the French Broad every year, and the tavernkeepers rivaled each other in their boasts of how many hogs they had fed for a single month. David Vance, whose stand was at Marshall, North Carolina, said he had kept 90,000 one month, while innkeeper Barnard, farther up the river, said he had lodged 110,000!

The owners, called drovers, were, then, the prosperous farmers of the region. Many of their acres had come to them, their fathers or their grandfathers as grants for services rendered during the Revolutionary War, and along the rivers and creeks it was rich well-tended land. Some of these farmers were from the upland, too, the narrow coves where fields were tilted toward the sky and a log house crouched at the head of the hollow. Many of their hogs were fattened almost altogether on mast, the acorns and nuts of the forest where they ranged.

Sometimes, but not often, there were professional drovers who, for their own speculation, bought up the farmers' hogs and drove them to market. It was a hazardous venture, for the price the hogs brought depended directly on the price of cotton, and there could be great fluctuation in that market. But it was usually the farmer himself, up from the tall-stalk, heavy-eared corn of the bottom land, down from the mast-rich, corn-trimmed hillsides, who rode at the head of his own drove, full of hope for the journey and a ready market. River-bottom or hillside farmers, they were men of common ancestry, Scotch-Irish for the most part, with a few English and "low-black Dutch" thrown in for variety; men who, as the old-timers said, followed after good judgment; men with given names like Cass and Ponder and Add and Pleasant, Burrell and Asa and Eb and Dunk, with the ancient Biblical names, Adam, Shadrach, James, John, Joseph, David and Job.

The drivers were friends or relatives or community adventurers, who took this way to see something of the world. These were stout men who undertook to drive fifty or a hundred hogs apiece through dust and mud, across fords and ferries, through mountains and villages, herding, feeding, butchering when necessary, on a journey that would take the better part of a month, and

all for the pay of ten to fifteen dollars, "with found." Found meant
a room to sleep in, sometimes with bed—more often without—and
food.

They were expert hog callers and whipcrackers, these drivers,
and when they uncurled the long leather strip from its stout thick

stock and brought the "cracker" snapping above the backs of their
"poky" animals, the sound was a mixture of dynamite and lightning. Like an army they depended on their feet, needed good
home-tanned leather shoes and socks of hand-carded, hand-knit
wool; also like an army, they marched on their stomachs. The food
at the stands where they stopped had to be good and it had to be
plentiful.

The great hog drives brought into existence a unique culture
along the route they followed. Its center was the tavern, and these
stands were unlike most overnight stopping places because they

were equipped to take care of not only a large number of people but a horde of animals as well.

There was the long, rambling, two-story house sprawled on some wide margin of the river or close beside the turnpike, with perhaps a breezeway attaching it to another low and rambling wing, all built of hand-hewn logs mellowed gray by wind and rain and sun to match the weathered white-oak shingles of the sloping roof. At each end and in the middle rose a chimney, and when the blue smoke began to pour forth from them in the late afternoon, it meant that fires were being built in the narrow bedroom fireplaces for the drovers to sleep by, in the wide-throated fireplace of the main room, where many of the drivers would sleep on the floor, and in the great deep fireplace of the kitchen where kettles of food and pots of coffee were boiling for the hungry men to come. Just beyond the building itself were wide fenced-in lots where the hogs could be turned in for the night, and hard by the pens were the cribs full of corn. The standkeeper had to have on hand immense quantities of feed to care for all the stock that passed his way, and from this fact came another influence of the drives. The farmers on the upper French Broad in North Carolina began to raise corn for the transient livestock. Farmers could find a steady market at the nearest stand, for, as one observer said, "These 'stand' proprietors usually were also merchants. They sold goods to the farmers to be paid for in corn when gathered in the fall." They would send out word to their debtors that on a day named they would receive in corn payment of all debts; and "on that day the farmers would come with the wagon-loads of corn, sometimes a string of such wagons extending for a mile in length, and, commencing at daylight and continuing until midnight, paying their debts with corn stored into the merchant's large cribs at fifty cents a bushel."

The standkeeper, in turn, charged the drovers seventy-five cents per bushel for the corn. Sometimes he got his pay then, sometimes he took it out in crippled hogs which he could butcher and sell or use at his public table, and often he took a due bill, waiting until the return trip when the drover could bring him cash settlement. Between the farmer with his corn and the drover with his hogs, the standkeeper made a neat profit and was the only one of the three who ran no risk from weather or disease.

When the rich yellow on the poplar leaves was beginning to fade and the maples were flaming into their brightest red and gold and the overripe hickory nuts and chestnuts were thumping to the ground with every gust of wind—in mid-October—the drives began. Now the stock was gathered in from the open range, lot-fed a month or two to add fat to the frame already developed, and for the people, all the garden vegetables and fruits were picked and preserved, dried or pickled or cellar-stored, crops were harvested, and only this journey remained, this venture beyond the mountains. Up the French Broad they came, across the Pigeon River, over the North Carolina line, and every five to ten miles, sometimes closer, they found a stand.

Each stand had its own distinctive quality, stamped with the personality of its owner, and over the years the drovers came to look forward to certain places for their special features. There was the Widow Frisbee's where the sauerkraut dipped out of the wide, cloth-covered crocks had the finest flavor of any on the trip; and the Fletcher tavern at the little North Carolina village of that same name, where the proprietor, a man of wide variety, was a doctor serving his area day and night yet running his farm and tavern, too. There was the Widow Patton's, where apple brandy was manufactured at its government-licensed distillery, and a decanter called Black Betsy stood on the sideboard from which anyone might help himself free and welcome, and there was the stand run by Wash Farnsworth at Laurel River. Wash was a Negro, probably the only Negro encountered on the whole journey till South Carolina and Georgia were reached, and his stand was a series of cabins apart from his own, where the drivers stayed and enjoyed the rest and food as they did everywhere. Largest and most typical of all was Alexander's stand. Known from Cincinnati to Charleston as a sum-

mer resort, it came into its own during the fall drives when ten or a
dozen droves might be stopped there for a single night. Since a
drove might have anywhere from three hundred to a thousand
hogs, and at least one driver was needed for every hundred animals, there would be between thirty and a hundred men and between three and ten thousand hogs penned and fed. A lot of corn
and space needed, a lot of food handy in smokehouse and cellar!

In the middle of the afternoon, if the droves were behaving
well and the way ahead was easy, the drover would spur up his
horse and ride on ahead to the stand to tell its keeper how many
lodgers for house and pen would be there for the night. Later in
the day, the sounds of the drove itself would come up the valley, the
long peculiar shouts of the drivers, the cracking of their whips, the
grunts and squeals and lungings of the hogs. And what a welcome
sight Alexander's tavern must have been to them as they came up
the dusty rocky road, or through the churned-up mud if the
weather was rainy.

They drove their hogs into the lot and measured out the corn,
eight bushels for every hundred head, for the hogs were fed only this
one time a day. They had no corn in the morning except such
scraps as they could forage; they did not travel well on full stomachs. When the livestock was cared for, the men went to look after
themselves, for the rule at the long dining table was much the same
as at the trough outside: Those who came first got the feed.

At heavy basins of water, or at an outside spout, they washed
their grimy hands and arms and faces, dipped big drinks of fresh
water into the curved gourd lying by the water bucket on the shelf
just inside the kitchen door and then went in to the plentiful table.
Steaming bowls of sweet-smelling cabbage boiled in an iron kettle
half the day, platters of spareribs and sausage sharp with sage and
seasoning, pots of dried beans rich with grease, sweet potatoes
baked to a yellow crumble, plates of hot biscuits, golden nutty-
smelling corn bread and pungent cracklin' bread, all washed down
with pitchers of fresh-churned buttermilk, sweet milk, pot after pot

of strong black coffee. Heavy, hearty fare that would stick to a man's ribs through heavy hearty work. The cost of such a meal was twenty-five cents.

After supper, there was the veranda, if the evening was in October, or the fireplace stacked with quick-blazing pine or long-burning hickory if it was in November or December. And here came one of the rarest pleasures of the trip, the chance to talk with men from other places, to pick up political news, exchange opinions on the President and the state of the nation, compare crops and seasons and prices, joke and argue and learn. The Kentucky horse drovers teased the North Carolinians: "Why your pore ole French Broad River plumb wears itself out splashing over all these rocks and ledges. Water's so weak we hate for our mules and hosses to drink it!"

A drummer from up North told the drivers: "Reason I came South and did so well is because up North people say, What do you know? Out West they say, What can you do? Down South here they say, Come in." After they were in bed for the night, the drivers teased one another by pulling off the blankets or hiding each other's shoes. Simple straightforward humor of the frontier everywhere, a humor sometimes broken by rowdy violence.

But mostly they talked about their hogs and the market. Had cholera struck during the summer? Sometimes that one disease would wipe out a fourth or half of all a man's hogs in a few short days or weeks. Had the season for corn been good—hot days and plenty of rain? And the season for cotton, had anyone heard about that? For the price of pork and cotton had a set ratio: If cotton was ten cents a pound, the hogs would bring five cents a pound. The price of one was usually half the price of the other per pound, and as the money came from Northern industry for the raw cotton of the big plantations, so some of the money moved on quickly from the planter to the upcountry farmers who provided a staple food for his Negro workers.

Comparing the markets for the year, the drovers often settled among themselves which they would visit first. In agreeing on this, they did not compete with one another, and no matter how many farmers there were at each of the terminals, Anderson or Spartanburg or Savannah, they held to one price. The few times when an irresponsible drover—usually not a grower himself, but a speculator who had gathered together some cheap hogs—cut the prices, disaster followed for all the farmers waiting to sell. Prices fell as rapidly as the November leaves. Their market ruined, the farmers might lose not only their year's labor and investment, but the capital to finance the year to come as well.

In some of the towns, planters had a certain drover from whom they always bought their hogs. Their relationship was built on mutual confidence and integrity and dependence. This gave a certain security to a business full of insecurity. Hogs grew lame and crippled on the journey. At best these could be left at one of the stands, where the keeper might take them as part payment on the bill and use them to feed the next batch of drivers. Or on the ferries, some of the hogs might grow restless and break through their pens to drown in the quick rough current of the river. Every mile or two the hogs began to root along the ground and then they flopped down to rest their short legs. When the old leader stood up and shook himself, the others got up too and moved on.

Occasionally fights broke out. Then the drivers used the direct and harsh approach and, with the nearest rock, knocked out tusks and teeth. And there was always the poundage lost by the hard trip up the French Broad gorge. From the time they left the bottom lands of the river till they came to Asheville, each hog lost between ten and twelve pounds. From Asheville on to South Carolina and Georgia, they would hold their own, perhaps even gain back a few ounces, but the mountains' toll always had to be reckoned with.

So the men compared experiences and exchanged knowledge and made an early bed before the roaring fires. The drivers were bedded down on the floor on pallets, if enough were available, two or three men to a pallet, but most often they rolled up in blankets and, feet to the fire, slept in a semicircle as only men could sleep who had put in a hard day's labor.

Morning was a surge of activity—fires being built, sides of bacon brought from the smokehouse and sliced into thick salty rashers, eggs gathered in a bushel basket, broken into pans of bubbling grease to provide the platters of fried eggs that were the breakfast staple, doughboards spread with biscuits rolled to thick, light consistency, and pitchers of molasses fresh from the cane stalks, pound prints of yellow butter carried from the springhouse. Out in the pens, the stirring of the animals, their squeals and grunts as they nosed along the ground for any grains of corn left over from the night before, and their shrill protests as herds were separated.

Each drover's hogs had their own "marks," which were mutilations of the ears, and sometimes brands as well. These marks were as various as the owners, and they were filed in the records of the county courts as insurance against any disputes of ownership. The language of marking and branding was as specialized as the nicest bureaucrat could ask. For example, some of the marks described in the court records are: "A half crop, in the upper side of left ear and two splits in the right ear." "A crop and two slits in the left ear, a swallow fork and an under bit out of the right ear." During the latter days of the drives, after stock laws had been passed in many of the counties and there was no need for permanent marking, the owners might identify their hogs temporarily by brushing tar along head or shoulder.

Breakfast over, accounts settled, hogs separated and counted, the herd was ready to move out. If several droves had stopped at the same stand for overnight, the favored place in line was, of course, at the front. Then there was no risk of getting behind a slow herd and being hemmed in for the day. The road was in better condition, too, and if there were ferries to be crossed, first chance at using these slow hand-pulled rafts that could carry, as a rule, only fifty or sixty hogs at a trip, gave advantage to first arrivals.

So the new day's drive began, full of fresh vigor. Gradually the slow animals in each herd began to fall behind, until sometimes by afternoon the last driver of the lot would have fallen an hour or two behind his companions who had the faster, probably thinner, hogs. Then the driver might sing to keep himself company along the lonesome road with only the river on one side and deep woods on the other. When the drivers who were together started a tune, and the drovers leading on horseback joined in, the sound of ballads and jigs and hymns, punctuated by shouts and cracking whips, would roll up the canyon, or along the road between the cotton fields, telling the world that the hog drovers were on their way.

Thus they reached the towns, Traveler's Rest, Greenville, Columbia, Augusta, even the magic city, Charleston, found pens and stables and inns, rested for a day, getting the "feel" of the place, and began to sell. From ten days to two weeks, the selling lasted, and during that time the men from the mountains came to know the plantation owners, saw more Negroes in an hour along the streets of town than in a whole year among the hills at home, heard news from up North and from across the ocean, and saw, during and after the Civil War, its effects on the cotton economy of the lowland. The drovers got their money, paid the drivers who had finished their work, and sometimes bought what goods they could carry on horseback to take back home with them.

The journey home was light and fast. Sometimes the drover would have brought a horse or two on lead-strings behind his own, so that some of the drivers might ride home, too. But many preferred to walk; they knew short cuts through the mountains that horses could not take, and they made good time. The riders returned home in four or five days, settling accounts along the way and paying due bills they had signed only a few weeks before. Sometimes the drovers carried several thousand dollars home with them, and so they seldom rode after dark. In all the decades of the drives, however, there are only one or two tales of robbery, and they seem to be apocryphal. The weirdest one tells of a certain stretch of woods near a certain tavern where several different drovers had been robbed and murdered over a period of years. It was rumored that a Negro was the murderer. At last, however, one of the drovers who happened to be traveling alone was prepared for the robber. When he leaped from the bushes (and indeed he was a black man) and seized the bridle, the drover shot him before the bandit could quiet the horse enough to take straight aim. With his body across the saddle, the drover came to the tavern and told his story. Then the stricken wife shrieked that the murdered man was her husband, that his face was shoe-polish black, and that he had carried on this grisly ruse for years.

And so the drovers came home, with money and with something more. Their horizons were broader, their sympathies deeper, their interests more national. The sense of the interlocking economy of their country grew in proportion to their dependence on the great Northern markets for cotton. They followed the rise and fall in prices of crops they did not raise because these remote matters touched directly on their own. They had talked with men of different sections and opinions, they had seen a farm culture altogether different from their own, and when they settled down beside their mud-chinked fireplaces for the long, hill-bound winter, they had much to ponder on.

Between 1880 and 1885 the river of livestock dwindled to a trickle and then dried up altogether. The railroad had thrust its tracks farther and farther into the mountains until, at last, all the farmers could send their animals more quickly, more cheaply, more safely by rail than by hoof. So the drives ended. The dozens of stands they had supported along their route fell into disrepair and many finally disappeared. Of the turnpike itself, we have already described the disintegration. But the main mark the drives left behind was not on the people or the roads—it was on the land itself.

Providing corn for these swarms of hogs and mules and turkeys that came up the river each year had become more and more of an enterprise. So large a demand brought about the clearing of many mountain acres ill-suited to growing corn. With no system of crop rotation, little money to invest in fertilizers and the dwindling of the corn yield after the first couple of harvests, much of this land so quickly and indiscriminately cleared was left to wash away in the quick-melting snows of winter and the sudden beating rains of summer. The French Broad still runs red with its second and third topsoil. Only in recent years have the people begun to understand that this water reddened from the butchered earth is draining away lifeblood as precious as was once the blood of the livestock which tramped along this route on their great half-remembered drives.

# 10

# The Green Path and
## the Iron Track

One morning in January, 1869, the youngest engineer on the Raleigh and Gaston Railroad, an eighteen-year-old boy named W. P. Terrell, was working in the railroad yards with his Negro fireman, making ready to take his work train on its regular daily run. The Raleigh and Gaston was a small railroad in the central part of North Carolina, but it was a link in the chain of communication that was already part of the post-Civil War railroad boom, and when Terrell saw Colonel Albert Johnson, the company's president, approaching him, he left his fireman with the repairs and went to learn the purpose of this unprecedented visit.

The young employee, who had started on the line as a fireman, engine repairman and general handyman before he was promoted to engineer, listened attentively as the company's foremost official told him what he wanted. It was a simple request. The engine and crew were to be brought back into the yards before dark that night; the engineer was to say nothing to anyone, but at eight o'clock he was to bring the engine to the track in front of the state penitentiary.

By eight o'clock the night was soot-black. William Terrell couldn't find a glimmer of moon as he waited outside the gloomy prison. The engine was all fired and ready for its unexplained mission, its warmth felt good against the January chill; the fireman wasn't much company, dozing in one corner; time dribbled by. After an hour of waiting young Terrell wondered if he could have misunderstood the president that morning. Still he waited.

Then he heard the rattle of carriage wheels rounding the curve near the prison. Several men alighted, lanterns were lit, and president Johnson hurried over to the engineer. In a low voice that carried the hush of secrecy and urgency, Johnson gave the boy more instructions. These were as easy to fulfill as the ones of that morning, and as mysterious. First, Terrell would be taking a passenger to Haw River, about fifty miles away. After the stranger was deposited there, the engineer was to go on to the company shops, only a short distance farther, and report to the master machinist with a request that some sort of work be done on his engine. Most important of all, the trip was to be made in complete darkness. There was a blind siding some miles out of Raleigh where Terrell must pull aside and wait till the Charlotte train due at one A.M. was past. Then he would have a clear track to Haw River. Colonel Johnson repeated: No mention of this run to anyone, as little noise as possible, and no light.

The engineer promised to do as he was told but even when his passenger came to the engine and boarded it, the dim glow of the lanterns on the carriages was not enough to let him see the man's features. Wearing a dark traveling cloak with a small trunk and suitcase beside him, the stranger took a seat by the window near the fireman and remained looking out into the darkness. The three men set out on their strange journey. No one spoke. The wheels clicked along their rails. At the place where the blind siding stood, Terrell pulled his engine off the main track and waited in the quiet darkness until the Charlotte passenger roared out of the night, bathed them in a swift glare of headlights and passed on toward Raleigh.

Between that siding and Haw River, all sorts of ideas gamboled through Terrell's mind. Because he was a busy young working fellow who rarely took time to read newspapers or discuss issues of state government, everything but the truth occurred to him. He had not heard that a commission had been appointed to examine the affairs of the Western North Carolina Railroad and particularly two of its officials: a native North Carolinian named George Swepson, and a recent import from Maine named Milton Littlefield. Terrell, along with most of the other inhabitants of the state and especially that hopeful group in the inaccessible western part, certainly did not know that some four million dollars' worth of bonds were missing from the company treasury.

But the young engineer did know that he was going to see this passenger's face before they parted company forever. And so, when the engine pulled in at Haw River and Terrell lit a lantern to help the man climb out, he held it first directly in front of his face. It was a pleasant face with features nevertheless sharp and pronounced beneath a head of white hair. Then the man disappeared down the steps and toward a carriage waiting by the station platform. Someone had been expecting the stranger. That someone drove the finest carriage Terrell had ever seen, and he watched as his passenger entered it, and the carriage disappeared in the darkness. Disappearing with it were the president of the Western North Carolina Railroad, George Swepson, and four million dollars in bonds. When the eighteen-year-old engineer and his fireman returned the engine to company shops and later back to Raleigh, they heard the uproar that had been created by the flight not only of Swepson but Littlefield as well. Law was precarious in those days of reconstruction, however, and Terrell and the fireman kept their story to themselves.

The state searched throughout this country and finally in Europe for the railroad officials and funds. The commission investigating their activities reported, generously enough, "They operated on the basis of personal charity—particularly to themselves." The men eventually returned to North Carolina. Unfortunately many of the bonds did not. And the result of that night flight, complete with black cloak and suitcase loot, in young Terrell's engine, was to threaten the very existence of the Western North Carolina Railroad and to delay for a decade and a half longer the already long-postponed opening of the great French Broad area west of the Blue Ridge barrier. For this episode—known and related only by Terrell himself in later years, but as credible as many more authenticated incidents of this undertaking—was only one of a long series of conflicts and disasters, man-made and natural, that thwarted every attempt to lay the iron track into the upper French Broad valley. Politicians, swindlers, war, poverty, pneumonia, granite and mountain mud were a few of the successive, sometimes simultaneous, enemies that leeched the strength of every attempt.

When, however, droves of livestock poured each year from the rich lands of East Tennessee along the river route through the mountains to markets beyond, and when pampered summer visitors began to select the Western North Carolina mountains for their scenic leisure ground, it was obvious that the moment had matured when pioneer ways must yield to progress, or at least to efficiency. Progress brought its own typical language. In Rogersville, East Tennessee, as early as 1831, a newspaper called *The Railroad Advocate* was begun precisely for the purpose set forth in its title: advocacy of railroads for East Tennessee, and by the following year it could send forth this impassioned plea:

Railroads are the *only hope* of East Tennessee. With them she would be everything the patriot would desire;—without them, she will continue to be what she is, and what she has been, a depressed and languishing region—too unpromising to

invite capital or enterprise from abroad, or to retain that
which may grow up in her bosom. They are the only improvement at all suited to her condition.

Four years later, in 1836, the tone had not changed, and
spurred on by the interest of Western men of prominence such as
General William Henry Harrison, then a senator from Indiana,
and by the hope that a railroad line between coastal South Carolina and the West would "have a powerful tendency to avert this
dire calamity" (civil war), a railroad convention was called for July
fourth in Knoxville.

It was believed to be the largest convention ever held in the
South up to that time. There were 381 delegates from nine states.
The local newspaper praised them especially for their willingness
to sacrifice their local interests in favor of "a long pull, a strong
pull, and a pull altogether." There were reports—one by an engineers' group of which John C. Frémont, the "great pathfinder,"
was a member—which stated unequivocally, "There is no route
within the limits of the existing charter by which a railroad can
be carried across the Blue Ridge that must not pass along the valley of the French Broad river . . . this valley affords by far the best
channel of communication between the Ohio River and the Atlantic Ocean."

There was a "sumptuous and elegant" barbecue. And there
were orations. Chief orator of the occasion was South Carolina's
eminent and eloquent Robert Y. Hayne, also the convention's president and chief dynamo behind the effort to unite Ohio and
Charleston via the French Broad. Quoting briefly from a colleague,
he soared to the edge of exaggeration:

It is greatly to be doubted if the topography of the world affords so singular and so striking a feature as the valley and
river of the French Broad. Drawing its waters from a thousand
tributaries from the topmost elevation of the Blue Ridge . . . it

forces its way through hills, cliffs, and mountains, which otherwise would be inaccessible. [Then he asked] whether the mere
existence of such a passage through the mountains . . . does
not mark out,—as with the unerring hand of Nature—*this* as
the great channel of communication between the South and
the West, by which these two important sections may be
bound together?

Pointing out that goods ordered in Northern cities were frequently not received in Knoxville, at the mouth of the French
Broad, until three months later, he went on to demonstrate the
transformation that would be effected in North Carolina alone by
the proposed 107 miles of railroad within its borders and the two
million dollars that would be spent in its construction. With a truly
Southern flourish he closed by proposing a toast for the French
Broad railroad route: "The South and the West! We have published the bans. If any man know aught why these should not be
joined together, let him speak now, or forever hold his peace."

Well, no one spoke—but the joining was destined not to take
place for nearly another half century. For immediately following
this rosy convention of 1836, an eminent opponent of Mr. Hayne's
swung into action again. John C. Calhoun was resolutely set
against the French Broad route through the Blue Ridge. He favored a passage by the Tuckaseegee or through Georgia to Muscle
Shoals. And the prestige of Calhoun was a factor to reckon with in
that state at that time. Probably Senator Robert Hayne was the
only man of sufficient stature to oppose him effectively on this public issue; it is certainly a fact that with Hayne's sudden death—
following yet another railroad convention in Asheville in 1839—
Hayne's dream of a railroad down the French Broad died too.
Calhoun "scotched" the enterprise from its beginning; the Panic
of 1837 crippled it; Hayne's death left it without a leader. The
Civil War both buried and resurrected it.

During the war years, all railroad building froze to a stand-

still in the Southern states except for purely military purposes, but promptly after the war the importance of railroads to restoration and to industrialization became apparent.

Now immediately before the war, the lower French Broad area had seen a real spurt of rail building. In 1860 the Cincinnati, Cumberland Gap and Charleston had begun energetic construction on that part of their road from Morristown, Tennessee, to Paint Rock at the North Carolina line, a distance of forty-four miles. When war came, the graded stretches, the half-finished bridges, the twelve miles of laid ties were all abandoned. Then, after Appomattox, when the states could look homeward again, the inviting old French Broad route between the Atlantic coast and the growing West asserted itself once more. From the Northwest the Cincinnati, Cumberland Gap and Charleston, with nearly a million and a quarter dollars in aid from the state, completed its line from Morristown to Wolf Creek, Tennessee, four miles short of its Paint Rock destination. And there, in December, 1868, the rails halted. There was a gap in the tracks from Wolf Creek, on the west, to Old Fort, North Carolina, on the east. The French Broad and its waters cut through the very heart of that picturesque and forbidding country that remained to be penetrated.

To accomplish this feat that had faced nothing but failure previously, the Western North Carolina Railroad was revived. Enter Messrs. Swepson and Littlefield and the general upheaval of Reconstruction, and a maze of fraud and counterfraud such as not even the perpetrators could unravel. Exit the bonds which North Carolina had issued to pay for the completion of the railroad and the hopes of many workmen who had already been hired (but not paid) along the route. The Western North Carolina Company gasped and struggled and finally, in 1875, was purchased by the state.

About this time a niece of James Fenimore Cooper, Constance Fenimore Woolson, published a travelogue thinly disguised as fiction in *Harper's New Monthly Magazine*. It was called "The French Broad" and at one point its hero says: " 'I have noticed a phantom pursuing us all the way from the other side of the Blue Ridge. . . . Ruined culverts, half-excavated tunnels, shadowy grading, and lines of levels. I have even fancied that I heard a spirit whistle.' "

Whereupon a native explains, " 'The ghost of the poor mountain railroad, Sir. Swindlers made off with all the money and the robbed mountaineers gloomily make fences of the ties—all that is left to them.' "

Such was the condition when, in March, 1875, an act of the North Carolina Legislature provided that: "The Warden of the

Penitentiary shall, from time to time, as the Governor may direct, send to the President of said company all convicts who have not been farmed out . . . to labor on said railroad, provided the convicts assigned shall be at least five hundred, and the number so assigned shall not exceed five hundred." The penitentiary superintendent was required to furnish all supplies such as guarding, feeding, clothing and doctor's bills and the pay for each convict by the company was set at "not less than fifty dollars each per annum." And we may safely assume it was not more than that either.

With the state of North Carolina furnishing this labor, the company of J. W. Wilson was given a contract to finish the road across the mountains to Asheville. An able honest man had entered the Western North Carolina Railroad picture—the following year, 1877, Wilson was elected simultaneous President, Superintendent and Chief Engineer of the railroad company—and three years later he had completed the road to Asheville. They were long, dramatic, grueling years.

The largest, most obvious obstacle facing any road builder was the grade on the eastern slope of the Blue Ridge. The sharp ascent was 1100 vertical feet in three miles. Wilson solved this by switchback or development grading, so that the track would loop up the mountain by curving back and forth. In this way about two thirds of the climb was overcome in seven and a half sinuous miles.

Another problem was the embankment area that came to be known as the Mud Cut. Excavating a passage through one of the sharp promontories of the mountain, the workmen had drilled through hard rock and removed nearly eighty thousand cubic yards, when the great slide occurred. One hundred and ten thousand cubic yards of soft rock and earth, loosened by the removal of its hard rock foundation, rolled down in a thunder of devastation and wiped out all signs of human labor at that spot. They began again. The loose earth, soaked by rains, became a jellylike mass; in addition mud seemed to boil up from under the tracks. Sometimes in the mornings the level of the tracks was raised as much as twenty feet higher than it had been the night before. It was spiritbreaking, backbreaking work.

And it was work done by hand and sweat and, yes, even blood. There was no machinery—only "pick and shovel, carts and mules, axes and saws and hand drilling of rock." Instead of bulldozers and steam shovels and dump trucks, there were only heavy picks swung in a rhythm of near desperation, shovels loading leaden masses of Appalachian mud, and horses and mules straining under the long haul of the wagons. Even the dynamite was homemade. All the drilling of rock was done by hand, and sometimes the old pioneer method of fire and water (fires built on rock to heat it, then doused with cold water to make it crack) was used.

One of the engineers had invented an explosive mixture that was used as dynamite: corn meal, sawdust and nitroglycerin. A dough of the meal and sawdust was first made up, then a set proportion of the nitroglycerin was added. This was packed in tubes of heavy paper. One old-timer, recalling the building of this iron track when he was a boy, told of being hired to stir a tubful of the concoction for half a day at a time. Observing its power when applied to earth and rocks, the boy decided he would use a sample of it to his own ends. Smuggling some of the dynamite out in a five-pound lard bucket and stuffing a cap in his pocket, he went to his favorite chestnut tree, the largest for miles around, and dug a deep hole near its trunk. This would be a speedy direct method of gathering chestnuts. He poured the bucket of dynamite into the hole and placed a cap to the charge, as he had seen the railroad workmen do. Since he had no fuse, he improvised by running a row of dry leaves from the base of the tree to a nearby vantage point where he could watch the effortless harvest. He fired the leaves and crouched for the explosion. It came. "With a deafening roar the mountain shifted and a cloud of dirt arose." When the smoke and dust had settled, the boy was buried up to his neck in dirt, there was a small cavern where the old chestnut tree had stood, and "a small section of the forest had vanished."

Workmen could dig out the venturesome boy, but there were other miscalculations and accidents less manageable. It is the human story that is the tragic and half-told portion of this railroad's building. During heaviest construction there were 1455 men and 403 boys laboring to clear the path up the steep mountain, and over a thousand mules, horses and oxen. The backlog of workers was the convict force. Nearly all Negro, they had been transported for the most part from the eastern area of the state. Accustomed to a warmer climate, the chill of the mountains, the dampness of mud and tunnels and the discouragement of constant slides soon left them vulnerable to the ravages of flu and pneumonia. The standard food was navy beans and corn bread. For Sunday breakfast there was the luxury of biscuits. Sometimes there was fat pork and a vegetable—cabbage, potatoes, black-eyed peas. Blackstrap molasses was a treat. Since 6¼¢ a day was the average allowance to feed a convict, there was little room for the bare necessities and no inclination for the niceties. In an alien climate, with such a diet, pneumonia was the scourge of the camp. One North Carolina resident remembered where there were four hundred unmarked graves huddled near the last tunnel on the route, filled by victims of pneumonia. How many solitary graves were scattered elsewhere along the railroad track, no one has revealed or estimated.

On Saturday, work stopped at four in the afternoon and the convicts and other laborers took their required weekly bath. Then, if there was a banjo or guitar handy—and there usually was—someone "made music" for the camp. The lonely, bawdy, sentimental, realistic music of all railroad camps, all men in stripes everywhere.

Near the summit of the Blue Ridge the peak of hardship was reached too. This was the drilling of Swannanoa tunnel, 1832 feet long. Delays in its building due to slides cost over half a million dollars and 120 lives and necessitated still another feat which gave rise to the saying that the train came to Asheville before the railroad.

Because the company held some of its rights by virtue of an agreement to have a locomotive reach Asheville, the capital of Buncombe County, before a certain date, and because it was apparent that work on the tunnel could go much faster if attacked from both ends, Major Wilson decided to send his locomotive "Salisbury" across the mountain on improvised track. Timbers were laid on the old stage road and along temporary track the locomotive was hauled by teams of mules and oxen, straining and grinding for a little distance up the mountain with the help of the convict force. Then the engine was halted while the track behind was taken up and laid on in front. Thus the "Salisbury"—by laborious pulley—crested the Blue Ridge and broke the quiet of a Sunday morning in October in the little village of Asheville. The first locomotive had crossed the mountain barrier and entered the upper plateau of the French Broad watershed. Drilled from both sides, the Swannanoa tunnel was finally completed, and Major Wilson sent an exultant telegram to Governor Vance. "Daylight entered western North Carolina this morning through the Swannanoa tunnel."

The Asheville newspaper was no less exultant:

The news that Major Wilson on Monday morning completed the laying of the track through Swannanoa tunnel will be hailed with delight by the people of Western Carolina. For the last two decades these people have been anxiously looking for this result—have been waiting for the snorting of the iron horse through the bowels of the Blue Ridge—and now that this great feat has been accomplished, they feel that the strong barrier between them and the outside world has at last been pulled down, and that they may soon be reckoned in truth as "a part of the State of North Carolina."

Consistent with the whole previous history of the Western North Carolina Railroad, the final cave-in occurred at Swannanoa tunnel just after Major Wilson had dispatched his telegram of victory to the Governor. Twenty-one laborers were crushed to death.

It was another two years, January, 1882, before the railroad completed its course down the French Broad to join with its western link at the Tennessee state line. An editorial in a Knoxville paper greeted the completion:

> In a few months the French Broad road will make us [Knoxville and Asheville] next-door neighbors and the Queen City of the Valley and the Metropolis of the Mountains will stand side by side to witness the driving of the silver spike.

So the dream of three quarters of a century was finally realized. Senator Hayne, the eloquent orator from South Carolina who had bent all his energies to the French Broad route between the South and West, and five hundred and more wretched nameless convicts who had spent their strength against the mountain and rocks and mud: all these were dead. But the rails were laid, leading almost like the tracks of some animate monster, both into and out of isolation.

Now the tallow candles on mountain tables could give way to oil lamps, New England factory cloth—gingham and muslin and percale—could replace rough linsey-woolsey, and the expansive agents for sewing machines and organs, lightning rods and enlarged pictures, would travel over the watershed, penetrating creeks and coves with their own particular symptom of "civilization." Like almost everything else, the railroad had come to the French Broad country the hard way—through a wilderness of conflicts, frauds, ruinous bankruptcies, blasted careers and tragic deaths. But, also like much else in the region, at its completion the Western North Carolina road was considered the marvel of railroad engineering in the United States. And its route was one of the celebrated scenic experiences of the day. Described in magazines, brochures, travel books and stories, the French Broad was the source of many a purple passage and pathetic fallacy. A character in one enthusiastic novel described the scenic mountains of the route: "In comparison with them, the Catskills are a suburb; the White Mountains ornamental rockwork; and the Adirondacks, a wood-lot." The old economy, of words as well as land, had given way to a new influence. The iron wheel had set its track forevermore on the old green path beside the tumbling waters.

# 11

## The Big Boom

Timber was the living gold that covered most of the French Broad country when Indian and white man first entered it. In quality, quantity and variety the region was blessed with rich, seemingly limitless forests. As late as 1896 a Knoxville newspaper quoting from Volume Nine of the *United States Forest Report,* said:

> The timber in the east part of the state [Tennessee] on the high ranges of the South Allegheny or Smoky Mountains is covered with a heavy body of hard woods, mixed at high elevations with hemlock, pine and spruce and constitutes the finest body of timber now standing in the United States.

With millions of acres stretching over the entire French Broad watershed, it was inevitable that lumbering should become and remain the flourishing occupation of the region. The whine of sawmills, the temporary raw ugliness of lumber camps, the husky cries and shouts of loggers to their teams, the week-end gambling and fighting and fiddle playing, all enveloped in the constant sound of well-honed axes and the bright teeth of crosscut saws biting into thick green trunks of virgin timber—these filled coves and mountainsides with the look and sound of progress. The spirit of progress reigned rampant, too, characterized by energetic wastefulness and an optimism that assured everyone the trees could never be exhausted, at least not within the limits of anyone's foresight. An experience which overtook the East Tennessee village of Newport and its surrounding country during the 1880's was both colorful and typical of many of the early experiences of the industry and the times.

Alexander Alan Arthur was a man who was never destined to follow an ordinary occupation in the ordinary ruts of breadwinning. He was a man to lead and influence other men; he was a builder who could not foreswear leaving the imprint of his imagination on the towns where he lived, the crossroads he passed through. Early in the 1880's, A. A. Arthur appeared in Newport, Tennessee. The epitome of elegance in his Prince Albert coat, his fashionable hat, sideburns, and lord mayor air, it was not long until the rustic town of Newport—only a few hundred people scattered along the railroad track that had lured them, in 1867, from the old town on the French Broad to this site on the tributary Pigeon—realized a Presence had arrived. Behind him loomed the dim outlines of a company as imposing and international as its representative. The Scottish Carolina Timber and Land Company, Limited. Its head office was in Glasgow, Scotland; its American head and general manager was Mr. Arthur.

On the remote reaches of the Pigeon River, Arthur had located a fine stand of virgin timber. Although the terrain was steep and inaccessible for hauling logs, he had solved that problem by turning a liability into an asset. He proposed to build booms along the river and float his timber down to Newport and, when necessary, on to Knoxville. With a true entrepreneur's flair for the dramatic, Arthur brought into the quiet village an assortment of people such as it had never known before, and introduced ideas much grander than any the villagers had previously entertained. Englishmen, Scotchmen, immigrants from the Transvaal of South Africa, and English and French Canadians—these were some of the foreign nationalities from which the executives, office workers, yardmen, lumberjacks and river crews of the Scottish Carolina Timber and Land Company were drawn to converge on the wilderness of East Tennessee. At first, while the offices and accommodations were being built in the town, and mess halls and bunkhouses were being thrown up in the mountains, homes of every sort were opened to help take care of the newcomers. People who had never been beyond the confines of their own country line heard strange accents at their supper tables and learned the wideness of the world; other residents, more traveled, brushed off their memories of Philadelphia or Boston or Washington and began to dream about Newport's becoming a metropolis here in the mountains.

Such dreams were part of the natural atmosphere surrounding A. A. Arthur. A tall well-built man, inclined to portliness around the middle, with typical Scotch or English coloring—blue eyes, fair skin with ruddy overtones, reddish-brown hair and stylish mustache—he had about him the well-fed, intelligent suaveness of a man accustomed to importance: important friends and events, large transactions brought to successful conclusion. The fine cloth of his black coat, the fit of his trousers, the very heaviness of the gold watch chain lying across his stomach, even these objects were invested with a life of their own, because *he* had chosen them in the faraway cities of the world, because they had been worn in the company of Leaders on Occasions far above the average experience. Born in Canada, educated in Scotland, Arthur had been engaged in timber operations in Sweden before coming to Boston sometime during the 1870's. Through friends there he met an aristocratic-appearing young lady sixteen years his junior from Lowell, Massachusetts.

Nellie Goodwin had been Mrs. Arthur only a short time when her husband brought her to Newport, Tennessee. She was twenty years old and extremely handsome. With dark hair piled softly above her high forehead, she posed for a portrait before leaving home: in a white satin dress lavishly trimmed with gold thread and embroidery, her waist was slim and supple as a wrist, her profile was fine and chiseled.

A town in the southern Appalachians was at that time quite a contrast to a city in Massachusetts. There were a large number of goodhearted, hardworking farmers, but a limited few residents who were highly educated and culturally sophisticated. Intellectual interests were limited mostly to three, perhaps four, afternoon or evening clubs where papers were read after which "delicious refreshments were enjoyed by all." Music was saved for Sunday morning and the choir, or the entertainment at a political rally. Young ladies went away to school and studied voice or "polite literature" or china painting and upon their return became the arbiters of local "culture." Stimulation of the intellect by well-reasoned difference of opinion was considered slightly ill-mannered. The town was too small to attract traveling companies of actors or singers, and even its most ambitious social affairs had certain limitations. Perhaps it was,

therefore, a combination of disappointment as well as youthful pride that kept Nellie Arthur from mingling with the local people. Newport seemed to her a terrible place, and she gave it little chance to prove differently. Even the servants were beyond her understanding. The Negroes were slovenly and knew none of the recipes she especially cherished; white helpers also cooked in an unfamiliar way and were as independent as judges. Finally she sent back to Boston for two Irish girls who had been with her family for many years. When Katy and Mary arrived and climbed off the cars at the little depot, they burst into tears to see where their young mistress was living—perhaps, rather, existing.

But Arthur himself was on the crest of the wave. Unshakable optimism was the element that bound his character into a memorable whole, and he was not going to let the difficult countryside or the dark predictions of mountain prophets ("Wait till the Pigeon gets on its big britches one of these spring freshets and you'll see how stout them little booms you're building will be. They'll never hold the Pigeon.") swerve him. Capital from Scotland and England was plentiful. It had become the fashion there to invest in American land development and enterprises. Several of the largest stockholders of "The Scottish," as the company came to be called, had arrived in the United States and in Tennessee to aid in the business's growth.

There were the Fergusons from Edinburgh, a bachelor Mr. Campbell also from Edinburgh, who spent most of his time working at the source with the crew in the mountains, and a bachelor from Glasgow with the intriguing name of Frederick Hope P. Moncrieff, who spent all of his time in the town office. One of the girls of Newport remembered years later when she was an elderly lady how Mr. F. H. P. Moncrieff "glistened with Old World sophistication." He was a ladies' man, friendly and adaptable, and he undoubtedly won the allegiance of the townspeople when he became a member of their "Current History Club" and was finally one of the attendants in a wedding involving the village's leading family.

That he "maintained an apartment on Main Street and a Lodge, handsomely furnished in the mountains where he and Mr. Campbell entertained week-end parties," added just the right amount of dash to make Mr. Moncrieff a really fascinating novelty in this locale.

Another family were the McCallums, from London and South Africa, who had arrived with three sisters-in-law, the Misses Draper, also from South Africa. Mrs. McCallum and her sisters owned nearly a million dollars' work of stock in "The Scottish." And others —Lieutenant Cocherane, from Scotland by way of the Sudan, where he had been deafened by the roar of artillery during battle —all were fastening their hopes on this enterprise to make their fortune and farewell.

About 1882 the Canadians arrived, a hundred or more. Arthur had imported them to work in the logging operations on the mountains and in the river during the log drives. Their dialects added that much more flavor to the oddness and interest of the whole undertaking. They found that the preliminary work in the mountains took almost two years before a mill could even go into operation. Then the logs began to roll. Great solid lengths of cherry, ash, pine, oak, tulip (or yellow) poplar—mostly tulip poplar. Old sawmill men in the mountains today shake their heads and say, "Ain't none left like it now. Ten feet across, a-many and many of them yaller poplars. Sawed them out into twelve by twelve and twelve by eighteen boards and they had to be solid clear or they didn't bring much money. The rest? Just left to lay where it fell." The heart of the yellow poplar was all they wanted.

The hum of work in the logging camp, the crash of trees, and the lopping of limbs, the giant splash of river as the logs catapulted down the flume out onto the water: this was activity such as Arthur had imagined when he formed his company. He rode, lord and master, on a shiny black stump-tailed horse over his domain, never settling the bulk of his weight into the saddle, but always standing in the stirrups as if personally overseeing in the wilderness the birth

of empire. Nearly seventy years later a few of the workers could recall the sight of Mister Arthur on horseback, riding over the mountains half-standing in the stirrups, his voice reverberating through
the mountain canyon.

Downriver a great boom, or in fact a series of booms, had been
built by chaining heavy logs together at an angle across the river.
Here the trees were caught as they came down out of the mountains
and held until they could be brought up on the banks and sawed at
the mill, or—in a few cases—floated on down to the French Broad
and Knoxville. On the riverside above the boom were the yards for
stacking lumber, the huge band sawmill, and the company buildings: a commissary, a weighing shed near the railroad, and the
main offices.

Lumber occupied only part of Arthur's fertile mind, however.
He must further the development of the places with which he came
in contact. A map was drawn up showing what the ideal Newport
of the future should be. Above the main part of town, there was to
be a park and a Circle with Villa Sites scattered over it. All streets
running north and south were to be named for native trees in alpha-
betical order: ash, beech, cherry, etc., and all avenues running east
and west were to be named for Indian tribes, Cherokee, Huron,
and so on. Large areas for factory and power developments were
set aside, a steam tannery was indicated on the flatlands up the
river, and parks were plentiful. A town hall, clubhouses for varying strata of society, and a college were shown on the map. On
the heights across and above the river, a Grand Hotel on "The
Palisades" was planned, along with the leading residential area.
Along the river, the site of the future Pigeon River Regatta was
indicated.

To the local people miring up in mud along Main Street during a rainy spell, growing corn in the fields atop those palisades,
boasting of "seventeen business houses, one harness shop, one school
and three churches," the map of The Scottish must have seemed
a breathtaking vision.

But Arthur and his company were already influencing the town in many ways other than the obvious economic ones. For instance, beginning in 1883 and continuing for three or four years, tournaments became one of the favorite pastimes. Local merchants, farmers, what few professional men there were, participated in the tilts, mounted their steeds and lost their mundane identity for a day. They became the Knight of St. George, the Duke of Nola Chucky, or one of another dozen or so titles, and did combat for the Queen of the Tournament. It was an innovation probably dearer to the hearts of the local ladies than the local men; the pioneer was still pretty close to the surface to relish such fancy trappings for just a plain old fight.

One of the main things Arthur planned was his home: Arthur House. A big Victorian dwelling, it was to serve as a showroom for all the native woods, and consequently each room was to be finished in a different wood. Sitting room, drawing room, dining room, bedrooms—each displayed the beauty of the mountains' hardwoods: cherry, black walnut, oak, maple, or the softer timbers—pine, poplar, willow and others. A carpenter from Quebec and a French-Canadian wood carver had charge of the interior work on "The Mansion," as it was locally called, and they found their greatest problem was that of adapting to the various grains and qualities of the woods. In one room the lumber might be so hard it could scarcely be nailed in place without splitting, and in the adjoining room it might be so soft that a nail would go through it as if through soft butter.

While "The Mansion" was being built, Mrs. Arthur went into confinement in Knoxville and had a daughter. When she returned to Newport, it was as mistress of the newly completed Mansion. The Scottish and the Arthurs had reached a peak. A Knoxville newspaper reported that in the "thriving little city" of Newport "the Scottish Carolina Land and Timber Company contemplate erecting a second sawmill, the capacity of it to be the same as the first." Pyramids of sawdust were mounting behind The Scottish mills;

the river was choked with logs riding down to the lumberyards;
the splendid house was finished and plans were afoot to begin development of the whole town; stockholders abroad, officers and
employees on the site, and local neighbors: everyone was happy.

Then the mountain river showed its character. Living up to
the gloomiest mountaineer's prophecy, in a sort of rampaging
prophecy of its own, the Big Pigeon flooded, sweeping boom and
logs and all before it.

It was spring of 1886. Rain had been general through the
area, but during the week end a cloudburst came on the upper
watershed of the Pigeon. Saturday afternoon the already swollen
river began to rise even faster, and all The Scottish people rushed
to help reinforce the booms behind which floated a dammed-up
fortune in logs. Arthur himself spent the night in the still downpour-
ing rain amid the surging water, directing ways to strengthen the
chains against the rapidly increasing mountain torrent. The river
had put on its "big britches" sure enough.

One of the company's engineers came home around midnight
to drink some coffee and gulp a bite of food. Mrs. Arthur had come
to stay with his wife during the long dark hours of waiting and
listening to the rising river and the straining logs. As the engineer
left to go back to the river, he told his wife and Mrs. Arthur, "Listen
for the whistle. If you don't hear the whistle by midmorning tomorrow maybe we'll pull through and beat the river. But if you
hear that whistle, you'll know we're all gone to hell."

Just before daybreak at the depth of the dark and rain, the
waiting women and all the rest of the wakeful town heard the
great crash as the booms burst, and the cry of the whistle signaled
the men's defeat. Logs from thousands of trees boiled over the
broken dams, smashed together in a grinding roar and surged on
down the current like giant toothpicks tossed by some elemental
energy. Homes along the river were suddenly dismayed to hear
this avalanche of sound sweeping down toward them. Ripping out
chunks of riverbank, lodging on boulders and in fields where the

water had overflowed, millions of board feet of tulip-poplar logs were carried down the Pigeon into the French Broad, on down the French Broad and into the Tennessee. For years to come logs could be found down the length of the rivers (Lordy, clean to the Gulf of Mexico, some said), where they had lodged as the waters diminished.

The Scottish Company's stockholders abroad received word of the disaster and promptly sent a representative over to Tennessee to investigate such an enormous loss. Hindsight was much clearer than foresight. The representative felt that a flood should have been foreseen. Definitely foreseen. The company was virtually wiped out. All their investment up to that point had been represented in those logs, and now it was gone. No fresh operating capital was forthcoming from England or Scotland. The Scottish closed down activities.

An experience had come to its end. Mr. F. H. P. Moncrieff left for Northern metropolitan centers; the Misses Draper took their losses and returned, excepting one, to South Africa, where their brother-in-law, Mr. McCallum, soon committed suicide. The French Canadians returned to their Northern woods. The heavy parchment-type stationery with the imposing letterhead (The Scottish Carolina Timber and Land Company, Ltd. Timber and Mineral Properties, Haywood and Madison Counties, North Carolina, and Newport, Tennessee. Head Office, 157 Vincent Street, Glasgow, Scotland) scattered like dead leaves in the wind. The company commissary became a saloon. Its sign greeted anyone entering town as "The First Chance," and on the reverse side warned those leaving that it was "The Last Chance."

But the man who had been the personification of the Scottish Timber and Land Company was not discouraged. He was an inveterate American optimist, a true career promoter. This failure of one company merely launched him on the establishment of other, more impressive ones. Within a year he had moved to a large home in Knoxville where, in January, Mrs. Arthur could entertain with a musicale for the benefit of the Knoxville Relief Association, "duets, solos and a reading" being the features of the occasion, and he had visited the site of Middlesboro, Kentucky, and seen the possibilities of building there the Pittsburgh of the South, near the Cumberland Gap and its surrounding iron and coal fields. He had visited Asheville and seen the possibilities of raising initial capital among some of the wealthy tourists there. Co-ordinating the two ideas, he gathered his groundwork capital from a group of four young Northern men visiting in Asheville and put it to work awakening interest in this city he proposed. The millions of dollars Arthur brought from England to develop his new dream, the overnight boom and sudden burst of that dream, too, are not a part of the French Broad story. But they illustrate the invincible vision and force of this extraordinary man who had brought the first real twinge of twentieth century progress into the lower French Broad country. Elegant and bombastic, a man of great illusions, even his gold-crested English china had a prophetic personal motto beneath the family crest: Fac et spera. Act and hope. He had left behind in Newport a residue of both qualities. Looking at the grandiose map that lay discarded, after the Scottish Company's failure, a group of the town's citizens adopted the dream and formed the Newport Development Company. While the old logging trails of The Scottish washed out to bedrock, and tops and limbs of the giant poplars rotted to mulch, something still remained of the company and its manager. It was the air of confidence that was to characterize the beginning of so many lumbering projects in these mountains, the sharp wasteful defeat when one by one they failed to make that single but fairly important item called profit. Yet they would go on, each taking his turn, slashing and cutting and wasting, till the sawdust pyramids grew thick and gold as broomsedge on the abandoned hills, souvenirs of a newer tribe of Mound Builders. Arthur House, The Mansion, became the home of one of the area's congressmen. The wood in its walls is all that is left of The Scottish, all that remains of the original forest that covered the steep watershed of the Big Pigeon River.

When the band sawmill came into the wild domain of the French Broad, a cycle began that is not yet concluded. When the big boom on the Pigeon broke that Saturday night in 1886, it could have been a prophecy: There was no boom built by man that nature could not break, there was no waste practiced by man that would not be matched by a greater complementary waste to follow. Unfortunately, there was no one equipped to hear the prophecy. The time of the cutting of trees had come. It is still here.

# 12

# Ghost Towns in the Valleys

The French Broad region has more than its share of touring America's commercial hotels, mountain inns, motor courts, tourist homes and trailer encampments. From the river's headwaters to its mouth, this is a resort area, and people who are "enterprising" take the term seriously. They know that climate and scenery have been causes of immigration ever since the years following the Revolution. Their tourotels of today often have an ill-assorted, sheepish, "woods-colt" look, but they spring from a solid, legitimate background. Their ancestors were the sprawling old resort hotels, well-girded by generous porches, set in the midst of ancient trees and well-trod lawn. They were built for the "comers and stayers." Their offspring today are for the "comers and goers." Therein lies a difference and a tale.

Part of the region was a thriving resort area before the Civil War. The first summer visitors to Western North Carolina and Eastern Tennessee came in the stagecoach. It was a long, difficult, dusty (or muddy) trip, made worth while only by a visit of several months' duration. The slowness and hardship of travel by stage severely limited the growth of the mountain towns. Then came "the cars" and the heyday of the watering places. It took a long time for railroads to dig and tunnel and blast their way through the mountains, but blast they did, bringing new life to the settlements on their path. A new mode of summer living prevailed. It was dealt a death blow by Henry Ford and Harvey Firestone. When the auto put America on the highway, it snatched her forever from the leisurely veranda. The era of the promenade and the bathhouse was past.

But to return to the beginning. Three circumstances, among many, were of special influence in the development of these French Broad watering places. The first was a physician's illness, the second a courtship by proxy, and the third was a season of crop failure.

In the year 1821, probably in the low-country heat of late spring or early summer, James F. E. Hardy left his home in the Newberry District of South Carolina. He was nineteen years old and he was in poor health. Toward the mountains he traveled. Some weeks later he arrived at the village of Asheville on the banks of the French Broad. The hill town had already gained some small reputation as a healthful location by the irony—which no later historian nor Chamber of Commerce president seems to have noted—that the distinguished English botanist, John Lyon, had died there in 1814. Perhaps it was sufficient tribute to climate that he had come in 1802, ill with tuberculosis, and lived on for twelve years. Sadly enough, this small, poetic collector of plants was only forty-nine years old when he died—but our Mr. J. F. E. Hardy, who arrived seven years later, justified his surname and proved he was made of different stuff. Three years after leaving South Carolina, or by 1824, he had married an Asheville girl, built the finest residence of the town, and presumably cured his illness, for he began a practice of medicine which lasted for sixty-one years.

He was the most prominent physician of the region and he conducted himself accordingly. With a lordly manner and imposing countenance, he took part in almost every phase of the town's development, became cashier of its first bank and presided over the hospitality of the numerous handsome homes he built. Former acquaintances from the lowlands were his guests, and they carried the fame of the mountains home with them. South Carolina had discovered escape from her malarial, disease-ridden summers. A trickle of hot-weather residents began to stop at a wide spot on the turnpike named Flat Rock.

There was only a small inn at Flat Rock, run by one William Brittain, which was little more than a shelter from the weather. It was obvious that although the Buncombe Turnpike, completed in 1828, had given mountain passage to the seaboard dwellers, and although a few South Carolinians had taken up permanent residence in the hills, another impetus was needed to bring any resort boom. Romance provided that impetus.

Susan Cole Wright Turnour Bottom Edge Heyward was a woman who knew about romance. She lived in the Low Country, on a plantation near Charleston, and was part of the lively international society of that worldly city. The ladies of South Carolina were then, and at the watering places during the rest of the century, considered the most experienced of any in America (Virginia included!) in the ways of the fashionable world. And none was more experienced than Welsh-born Susan Cole who had been married five times, who had arranged a marriage to its successful conclusion between one of her sisters and Lord Berkeley, and who had come to America upon wedding her fifth husband, Mr. Heyward. Heyward owned considerable property in South Carolina and upon his death left Susan a life interest in extensive plantation holdings, a generous annuity—in short, left her weathy and once more single.

Sometime in the 1820's Mr. Charles Baring, whose father and uncle had founded the banking firm of Baring Brothers in London, set out for America on a journey which was a happy combination of business and pleasure. His cousin, Lord Ashburton, also in the banking company and in fact its representative in Canada and the United States for some years previous, had yielded to the numerous charms of the South Carolina widow Heyward. He sent cousin Charles to pay suit for him and plan a marriage between the lady and himself. Well, the New England situation of Miles and Priscilla and John repeated itself under the swinging gray moss and the languid warmth of Charleston. Lord Ashburton, cousin or no cousin, was left to shift for himself, and Charles took possession of Susan's affection and annuity. Happily, neither decreased with the years.

If the records of her birth are accurate, Susan Heyward must have been in her late fifties or early sixties when she married for the sixth and final time. But her life until 1845, when she died at the age of eighty-two (another tribute to climate and loving care) sounds like a gay young girl's romance. To Charles she was "Susan, my lady" and to her he was "Charles, my love." During the first years of their marriage, Susan was not at all well. Charles had a long talk with the eminent Dr. Mitchell King. Now Dr. King had come up to the mountain country in 1817 with three other lowlanders, surveying for a possible railroad route through the mountains, and had been impressed with the landscape and the climate. Within the next dozen years, all of these four men on the surveying scout built summer manor houses in the region around Flat Rock, and when Dr. King was consulted about Mrs. Baring's health, he promptly advised summer in the mountains.

In 1830 and 1831, Charles and Susan Baring bought and built the estate which was to be the hub of the "Little Charleston of the Mountains" for years to come. An English country house set in a landscaped park, its manners and traditions became famous throughout the region. There was a tumble-down stile like the one at Stratford-on-Avon. There was a deer park. There were fox hunts, complete with pink hunting coats and thoroughbred hunters and —the one factor not alien to the hills—hounds. There were parties and dinners, drives along the Little River Road—which must have been a rugged road for primrose pleasure at that early date —and the glittering function which came once a year to climax the summer and celebrate Susan Baring's birthday. Arrayed in the same color for each of these special parties—the purple of roy-alty—with matching headdress of flowing plumes, wearing her favorite jewels, the diamonds she lavished on every possible occa-

sion, the lady who had come to the mountains for her delicate
health set the pace for gay and vigorous festivities to celebrate
birthdays which were to accumulate until she became eighty-
two.

A woman of wit and sophistication, Susan Baring carried her
way of life to the mountains, rather than adapting herself to the
new surroundings. This was true of the ever-increasing caravan
which came from Charleston early each summer, bringing more
than carriages full of handsomely dressed ladies and gentlemen,
well-trained servants, wagonloads of household furnishings, trunks,
pantry provisions and the niceties of Charleston and Europe—
bringing also a way of life, pleasant, well-founded in money from
plantation and shipping and merchant enterprises, and impossible
for the residents in the mountains of Western North Carolina or
Eastern Tennessee to imitate, where farms were limited, money
was scarce and trade was almost nonexistent. The Flat Rock settlement brought probably the highest development of American civilization into the heart of one of the most simple and picturesque
regions of the American continent.

They were, then, these seasonal residents of their mountain
Charleston, a little world set apart from other settlements on the
French Broad and its tributaries. They were international in origin
and interest: Count de Choiseul, French consul at Savannah, after
visiting the Barings, built a French chateau called The Castle; Edmund Molyneaux, British consul at Savannah, came in 1841 and
lived at Brookland Manor; old Dr. King, friend and classmate of
Otto von Bismarck's, carried on a frequent correspondence with the
Iron Chancellor. They were the American diplomatic and social
leaders of their day, who knew much about the intrigues of France
and Germany, the state of affairs in England, and there is little to
indicate that the majority of them knew much about the new region
into which they had practically pioneered. Their lives were as
widely separated from the lives of the local farmers as those farmers were separated from the Court of St. James. Or as far as the

little Baptist church on Mud Creek, near where the Barings first built their Mountain Lodge, was separated from St. John-in-the-Wilderness, the private chapel Susan Baring built for her family and her slaves, which soon became the church for the whole community and was, naturally, Episcopal.

Not that this earliest resort in the French Broad area did not influence all that area's people. Of course it did, particularly by providing a market for farm products which had previously been without a market. To Farmer's Hotel (opened around 1850 by Henry Farmer, a nephew of Susan Baring) the farmers took their produce for the summer visitors' use. June, July and August became the "Lowlander Season," when eggs, gathered from nests hidden in barnyards and haystacks and under laurel bushes, sold for the fabulous price of five and ten cents a dozen. A chicken of frying size might bring eight cents.

The colony at Flat Rock, the village of Asheville, and the picturesque route down the French Broad gorge to a town named Warm Springs which was beginning to acquire the air of a spa—all were attracting more travelers from all parts of the country. The Buncombe Turnpike was finished, but that was not enough. And the state as a whole was made aware, in 1848, of the third factor which was holding the mountain area's development in check: lack of roads.

The season—rain, sun, coolness, warmth, each in the right proportion—the season means everything to a farmer. In 1848 the season in the mountains was bad. Crops failed. Corn, the staple item of table, farm and market, was scarcer than in many a year, and all the lesser crops were cut in proportion. The price of corn soared from fifty cents a bushel to a dollar and fifty cents a bushel. The thing that made the region's plight dramatic, however, was the fact that in the state's eastern coastal plain crops were lavish, corn lay rotting where it had grown and fields were fertilized with fish. One section with an overabundance was unable to help her hungry neighbor because of transportation difficulties. So the North

Carolina legislature of 1850–51 set aside $12,000 to survey "a route for a railroad from Salisbury to the Tennessee line where the French Broad river passed into Tennessee."

It was to be thirty years later, as we have seen, before "the cars" reached Asheville and 1882 before they arrived near the Warm Springs, but another powerful stimulus toward the creation of a resort area had been set in motion. The health-restoring elements had been dramatized by the residence and enthusiasm of certain prominent physicians; the arrival of a wealthy leisure class had brought the prestige always necessary to a vacationland; the improving of stage-coach routes and the opening of railroad connections removed the isolation yet left intact the seclusion which was part of the mountains' charm. The era of "the springs" had arrived, characterized by one skeptic as "a general muster under the banner of folly."

Health and pleasure were the attractions of the watering places: the first providing a worthy excuse for the indulgence of the second. Advertisements of the period mentioned immediate cures, upon use of the mineral waters, for "Diseases of the Liver, Dyspepsia, Vertigo, Neuralgia, Ophthalmia or Sore Eyes, Paralysis, Spinal Affections, Rheumatism, Scrofula, Gravel, Diabetes, Consumption and Chronic Cough, Diseases of the Skin, Tetter, Indolent Ulcers, General Debility, Sleeplessness, and Nervous Prostration." The waters of many places were reputed good for barrenness in wives and impotence in husbands.

The Warm Springs, most famous of all the French Broad watering places, mentioned in one of their brochures that partaking of their minerals would "bring the bloom back to the cheek, the lustre to the eye, tone to the languid pulse, strength to the jaded nerves, and vigor to the wasted frame." From all contemporary accounts of the social life of the place, its patrons arrived with cheeks already in full bloom, eyes overflowing with lustre and pulses in need of no stimulation beyond that of moonlight on the river or the shady turn in a lover's walk. For, as one traveler noted, "every resort has its sunrise views, its sunset views, its lover's retreats, flirtation corners and acceptance glens."

When they were not enjoying the vices of these glens and corners, how did the visitors to these rural havens entertain themselves? A letter to the local paper by a lady visitor from the Deep South gives, in rather breathless style, a "Panoramic View of Asheville, N.C.," as she called her article, during the peak of the summer season:

> Asheville, North Carolina! Behold the Scene! Drink, and drink deeply in the beauty and grandeur of the surrounding country and your very senses will be steeped in intoxication. . . . Go to the summit of Mount Beau Catcher and feast your eyes on the lovely prospect from there. . . . Asheville is full of people from everywhere. . . . They are laughing, talking, dancing, flirting, as they do at summer resorts. Faintly upon the Summer morning floats the slumbrous, intoxicating melody of Strauss' passionate waltzes, and the slow time of the dancers dancing in time.
>
> There is a bouquet of lovely young ladies registered at the Eagle. [After telling us that this bouquet is garnered from Raleigh, the state capital; New York; Athens, Georgia; Baltimore; Virginia; Charleston, our lady continues:] Asheville is at the height of its gayety. There are between two and three thousand guests in the city. . . . There is a handsome young gentleman from Raleigh, Mr. Batchelor, that dances the Racquet very gracefully. The hotel is beautifully shaded in front, and has long delightful verandas.

Ah, Mr. Batchelor, of the intriguing name and the graceful Racquet, how many of the bouquet did you gather to your affections on one of those shaded—but never shady—verandas? How pleasant must have been those morning waltzes with the dancers obligingly "dancing in time," when all society was elegant and

aristocratic, ladies were never less than cultivated, stylish and rav-
ishingly beautiful, and the gentlemen were unfailingly handsome
and charming.

The efficacy of the springs' surroundings in promoting romance
is obvious from such items as this society tidbit tucked away in a
Newport, Tennessee, newspaper of 1883:

> A party from Sevierville went to Henderson Springs to
> spend a day last week. After dinner, Miss Mollie Henderson,
> leaving her escort to await her return, stepped into a buggy
> with Mr. G. M. Maples for a drive. When next seen they were
> in search of a magistrate to consummate their union. It was a
> "run-away" match and a complete surprise. They went on
> their way rejoicing.

For the rest of their lives, we trust.

To balance the picture, however, and keep it from becoming
too lush with wisteria blossoms and wistful sighs, an occasional
visitor wrote from the back-yard point of view, so to speak. In
January, 1839, an Englishman named J. S. Buckingham began a
journey through *The Slave States of America*. Two years later he
published his account of those states, and defenders of the region
still insist that he was a biased embittered reporter. But his view
of the resorts is in bracing contrast to most, and although the book
is filled with constant comparisons and references to other parts of
the world—all distant, exotic and familiar to the widely traveled
author—and although there is a slight, perhaps understandable,
superiority or snobbishness tainting his manner, he was an observant spectator who drew his own conclusions. His opinions on the
pastimes of the "comers and stayers," their reasons for migration
to the mountains, and his pessimism over his surroundings, are typically provocative:

> We reached Flatrock, a single house, without a village,
> kept by Col. Young, and here we alighted for the night.

There were about fifty persons staying at this house, some for health, and some for pleasure. . . . [They] included first families in Carolina. Yet the place appeared to us to possess no one attraction, but that of climate.

I had often been at a loss to account for the eagerness with which such places are visited year after year by the same persons, when all the charms of novelty are gone; but I had heard, lately, from native authority, a solution which seemed more probable than any I could offer to my own mind. It was this: that as marriages in the South are contracted so early in life as to lead to frequent subsequent regret in one or both of the parties, and as they are not so often contracted from love as from considerations of fortune and connections, home becomes wearisome, tedious, and monotonous; and anything which offers the relief of change is acceptable to both, but especially to the ladies. . . . Thus they visit these springs and watering-places, where, as a gentleman truly observed to me, they do not "kill time," for that implies a battle with the enemy, or at least an active struggle, by energetic and lively amusement of some kind or other—but where they rather "lose time" in so complete a manner, by listlessness and trifling, that they are unable to give any account of themselves or others what has become of this, to them the most worthless of all possessions—since their great aim is to devise new modes to get rid of it.

Besides the baths and morning waltzes and flirtations to "lose time," there was also gambling. And the wide green lawns provided generous croquet grounds where the gentlemen could measure wickets and study shots and the ladies could lean prettily on the mallets and pout over misjudged strokes.

A great pretense at botany was also part of the pastime. Some of its devotees were doubtless sincere in their thirst for knowledge, and Colonel Wilder's famous Cloudland Hotel on Roan Mountain

was especially popular for the mineral and botanical study it af-
forded. But the larger number of plant enthusiasts followed "flower
pressing," and whether the winter value of those dried and flattened
summer posies held greater scientific than sentimental attachment
is open to question.

Just before the Civil War, on July 11, 1860, still another tourist to Asheville described the resort's amusements and general appearance:

> . . . a long piazza for smokers, loungers, and flirters, and a
> bowling alley and shuffle board, with coaches and trotting
> wagons at the stable; poor women picking blackberries, poor
> men bringing fowls, school girls studiously climbing romantic
> rocks and otherwise making themselves as pretty as possible,
> children fighting their black nurses, and old gold spectacles
> stopping me to inquire if I was the mail, and if I had got a
> newspaper.

At the same time, the health-giving features of the country
were not being overlooked. Almost from the days of the first doctors who came for reasons of their own health, lung specialists
were present. Glassed-in porches were built on several of the hotels
so that the popular fresh air of the period could be plentiful winter or summer, sleeping or waking.

In 1875, Mr. Edward King wrote that: "Thither [to Warm
Springs] the rheumatic, and those afflicted with kindred diseases,
repair yearly in large numbers, and find speedy relief." Business
flourished and when the old hotel burned, foundations for the new
Mountain Park were laid immediately. It was finished in 1886 and
by this time the land had changed hands, the town had changed
its name to Hot Springs, and the advertised temperature of the
springs had jumped several degrees.

The queen city of the French Broad resorts was still Asheville, situated in the heart of what one pamphleteer described as

"The Land of the Sky, Nature's Trundle Bed of Recuperation." Although there were springs nearby—one situated on the west side of the French Broad, near the Asheville Depot, boasting of waters containing iron, sulphur, and magnesia—the emphasis here was more on climate and scenery than baths or imbibings.

In September, 1888, Dr. Karl von Ruck established the town's first well-known sanitarium. There are conflicting accounts that Dr. von Ruck was born in Constantinople, Turkey, and in Stuttgart, Germany, but he was of German descent and during the Franco-Prussian War had served on that country's medical staff. After coming to the United States, he received his doctor's degree and then here and back at home in his native country, he continued special study of throat and lung diseases. It was a little boom for the mountain town of North Carolina when he chose her as site for his Winyah Sanitarium. Since climate was at that time considered the primary factor of cure for tuberculosis, the mountains around the French Broad territory soon sprouted numerous sanitariums, and afflicted travelers from many parts of the world came there not only as temporary guests but as residents.

Well, they are gone forever now—these old gathering places of the health and pleasure seekers, who came for a season and frequently remained a lifetime along the banks and tributaries of the French Broad. The old Buck, in the center of Asheville, the first hotel west of the Blue Ridge; the imposing Patton, on the left bank of the river at Hot Springs, built during the 1830's, enjoyed for over fifty years until it burned in 1884, destroying the long veranda with its thirteen white columns representing the original thirteen states of the Union. Even the memory of a place named Sulphur Springs, on the outskirts of Asheville, has become dim.

There were so many small and large hotels scattered along the streams and up mountain coves. Near the little town of Newport, there was Carson Springs with a rambling wooden frame hotel. Its verandas were built out over the springs and embraced a great old beech tree where initials of courting couples could be carved in its bark during the break in a summer night's dance or on a long rainy afternoon when the croquet grounds were deserted. A stranger from Massachusetts, a Mr. Peterson and his wife, ran this hotel, and the eccentric behavior of the host, who let his small energetic wife do most of the labor while he cared for an alleged heart condition, was only outweighed by the bounty of the table they provided. As at most of these hotels, service was family style, with platters of meat, bowls steaming with vegetables, cruets tart with seasoning, compotes brimming with honey and fruits, pitchers sweating with cool milk from the springhouse and pots boiling with coffee. And always, trays of hot breads. Those breads the Northern visitors so often criticized but without which no Southerner's meal was complete: biscuits, corn bread, yeast rolls, muffins, battercakes. From Georgia, Alabama, Mississippi, and the Deep South country of West Tennessee around Nashville and Memphis, visitors came to enjoy the Peterson table, drink the mildly medicinal waters and enjoy the mountain coolness.

On the border between Tennessee and North Carolina, at the headwaters of the northernmost tributary of the French Broad, the Toe River, was Roan Mountain, and atop Roan was the Cloudland Hotel. Roan was one of the highest peaks of the Appalachians with unique grassy balds covered by beds of rhododendron and its hotel had a spacious distant view from an altitude of 6,200 feet. One of its attractions for its patrons was that, being astride the state line, it gave them a chance to write home that they slept in one state and dined in another. A rambling frame building, it was described in the mid-1880's as a rude mountain structure in which big wood fires were kept blazing. When the wind rose in the night and darkness, and the loose boards rattled and the timbers creaked, the traveler recorded that the sensation was not unlike that of being at sea.

Leader of the hotels, however, was the Battery Park, built in 1886 on a hill 125 feet above Asheville's public square, surrounded by a twenty-five acre park. It was a massive ramble of frame construction, 475 feet long with broad porches running its length, oriel

and bow windows breaking the front, and numerous gables adorning the whole. Because climate had become a product, the Battery Park porches were featured in summer by great boxes of flowers and in winter by being enclosed with glass. A description published seven years after its opening said that within the Battery Park all was comfort and elegance, that its spacious entrance hall displayed every evening a brilliant gathering of guests, who in little groups—the ladies with their fancy work and gentlemen with their cigars—passed the hours in informal sociability. Special entertainments were given in the ballroom, with a stage of its own. The Battery Park was lending reality to an attitude that was growing throughout the region: The Chamber-of-Commerce, come-hither tone that was to make the mountains of Western North Carolina and Eastern Tennessee a paradox of tourists and isolated mountain folks.

In 1885, Mr. Charles Dudley Warner gave a picture somewhat different from the local one recorded in dazzled diaries and overblown newspaper accounts. His voice was tinged with humor, however, and since humor is probably the quality most needed to make a successful traveler, it seems as if Mr. Warner must have been happier than many tourists during his travels in this region. He thought Warm Springs ill-kept, but added that he no doubt liked the place better than if it had been smart, and he enjoyed the négligé condition and the easy terms on which life was taken there. There was a sense of abundance, he felt, in the sight of fowls tiptoeing about the verandas, and to meet a chicken in the parlor was a sort of guarantee that he and other guests should meet him later in the dining room. The guests, he noted, were very pleasantly Southern. He told of colonels and politicians standing in groups and telling stories which were followed by explosions of laughter, retiring occasionally into the saloon, and coming forth reminded of more stories, and all lifting their hats elaborately and suspending narratives when a lady went past.

Warner also visited Asheville. He was one of the first to observe the contrasts that were even then being established in this "fourteenth cousin of Saratoga." The one contrast he particularly mentioned was to grow more obvious during each succeeding decade and was to keep Asheville from ever being completely Yankee or Deep South: "The enterprise of taste and money-making struggling with the *laissez-faire* of the South." The mingling of Northern wealth and Southern abandon. He felt that the willful gaiety of the town gave it a melancholy tone, but he appreciated "the blooming girls from the lesser Southern cities, with the slight provincial note and yet with the frank and engaging cordiality which is as charming as it is characteristic."

It was the peak of the boom for the watering places in the French Broad country. To these springs and hotels came people who at a later date would be gasping over the canyon of the Yellowstone rather than the canyon of the French Broad. The "Lowlanders," who set out from their malarial flatlands with a caravan of carriages and trekked up through the foothills and into the mountains on a journey that cost at least two weeks every year, were looking for the same things many of the tourists who hurry through so rapidly today are seeking: A combination of comfort and ruggedness, the uneasy balance between a luxurious personal surrounding and an untamed natural background. They simultaneously sought new experiences yet managed to establish many of their old ways of life in the country they visited.

The gulf between their intention and their reality seems somehow illustrated in a poem one of the lady elocutionists of the day recited to an audience at Warm Springs, North Carolina. She was "making a tour in North Carolina and Virginia, giving recitations at the principal watering places" and the poem she delivered herself of at the Springs was written for her by Mrs. Mary Bayard Clarke. To imagine the parlor where Miss Bowen rendered her act, dark with dust-heavy carpets and draperies, plush with heavy furniture covered in horsehair or velveteen perhaps, complete with library table holding the stereoscope and a current romantic novel, and to imagine the people, politely attentive, dressed in their light summer's best, is as much a part of the incongruity as the limpid nicety of the verses is incongruous to the wild unmannered portion of the river they attempt to portray. A sample of the afternoon's long recitation, titled *Racing Water,* conveys its general flavor:

> "Racing Water" who can paint thee,
>     With thy scenery wild and grand?
> It would take a magic pencil
>     Guided by a master hand.
> Down the canon's rocky gorges,
>     Now they wildly, madly sweep,
> As with laughing shout exultant,
>     O'er the rocks they joyous leap.
> Tah-kee-os-tee—Racing Water—
>     Was thy sonorous Indian name,
> But as "French Broad" thou are written
>     On the white man's roll of fame.
> Perish that! but live the other!
>     For on every dancing wave
> Evermore is shown the beauty
>     Of the name the red man gave.
>     Of the name the red man gave.

Those were the days when summer was long and languid. There was time to cover a small area thoroughly, to press its flowers and walk its winding half-hidden paths. They were days of the sound of rustling skirts and petticoats along the splintered magic piazzas, the sound of sudden male laughter booming out on the evening air just after dinner when the men stood apart under pungent wreaths of cigar smoke. It was the time of the smell of lavender water, and summer greens and corn boiling in the big old kitchens, and honeysuckle out along the turnpike.

And just around the corner waited the motor car.

Susan Baring of the six husbands and the purple plumes rests at her St. John-in-the-Wilderness. Carl Sandburg, poet of the proletariat and biographer of Lincoln, dwells at the Flat Rock plantation built by Christopher Gustavus Memminger, Secretary of the Confederate States of America. The Battery Park Hill has been bulldozed to a level with the rest of its surroundings and the hotel is now a brick skyscraper, compact and efficient as a biscuit cutter. In 1937, Warm-Hot Springs was reported to have a population of 637, about the number of people its hotel once accommodated.

Only Tah-kee-os-tee remains much the same, leaping down its "rocky gorges," gathering to itself all the warm and hot and sulphur and magnesia waters of the miraculous, now-unfashionable, nostalgic springs.

# 13

## The Only Thing Free
## Was Their Enterprise

In the 1880's, there was a crossroads forty miles east of Knoxville called French Broad, Tennessee. It boasted a general store, a boat landing, a few scattered houses and the plantation home that commanded the fertile river-bottom acres of the famous French Broad farm. John Stokely, whose great-grandfather had come into the wilderness of East Tennessee the year after the Revolution with a patriot-soldier's grant of land, whose grandfather and father had accumulated a half dozen of the finest farms along the Tennessee part of the river, John—a hard-working thrifty-trading farmer—lived, with his wife Anna Rorex, in that spacious antebellum house above the tended rolling fields.

It was like several other houses along the lower French Broad, where the river emerges from the mountains and widens into a silt-rich channel and bottom lands that gave rise to a way of life unique in the South. Here was a combination of plantation and mountain life that embodied many of the best features of each and thereby achieved its own distinction. The broad level acres, the square brick home, the languid heat and ancient fertility—these the

French Broad farms had in common with deeper South plantations. But there was also the regional isolation, the self-reliant independence, the hard work without a tradition of slavery or even any considerable tenant labor—and that was the inheritance from the mountain farms.

Bordering the lower third of its length, these holdings that were less than plantations and more than farms grew and flourished along the river. There was, perhaps, none more illustrative of this curious yet sturdy combination of qualities than that of the Stokely family whose small enterprise grew from these riverbanks to other rivers across the nation, from one ocean to the other, and from the Gulf across the boundary line into Canada. The foundation of their story is typical of many in the area; here began the largest home-founded business still in existence on the French Broad.

When Anna Stokely and two of her sons and a neighbor invested, in 1898, $3,900 in crude canning equipment and an even cruder building on the banks of a little stream which flowed into the nearby river, they hardly foresaw a corporation that would be doing $100,000,000 in business in 1950 with more than sixty plants scattered throughout the United States. Because of the loamy richness of their river-bottom land, the Stokelys could grow more than their limited market of 1898 could absorb. Because they came from a family where resourcefulness and work were necessities, they put their minds and shoulders to the problem of this surplus.

In 1890, at the age of forty-four, John Stokely had died suddenly. Anna was left with nine children, vast acres of farmland and little cash. But the pattern had already been set. The corn and wheat and hay grew and tasseled and ripened gold in the fields. Teachers came for four months' school at the one-room building nearby, boarded at the big house and sometimes stayed on for years. The seamstress, doctor, dentist, came once a year and stayed a week or a month catching up with work for the neighborhood and bringing news and stories of other families and farms in the section.

Altogether it was a remarkably self-sufficient world. Everyone had his part to do; it was unthinkable that he might not do it. Now the time had come to test the strength of the pattern.

Because she wanted to give her sons responsibilities and experience and because she was also determined that they should have college educations, Anna Stokely devised an unusual and valuable system of farm-college rotation among her five sons. The boys were acquainted with work. When they were still small their father had put them in the field with the hired hands. A neighbor passing the farm one day saw the little fellows hard at clearing a patch of upland, and he spoke to their father. "What's the matter with you, John? Don't you know you can't grow any kind of crop on that rocky ground?" And John Stokely said, "It'll grow boys."

The first year after her husband's death, Anna turned the management of the farm over to her oldest boy, Will, then seventeen. With the younger ones working under Will's direction, he was in charge for one year and then his mother sent him to Wake Forest, a Baptist college in piedmont North Carolina. The second son, James, stepped in as manager at home and after a year running the farm he followed his brother to college and the third boy took over the farming operations. In turn he went to college and the fourth began his duty at home. When this one left for school, the fifth took over and the cycle was complete—Will, the oldest, was graduating and ready to return home. This combination of education and experience was undoubtedly a decisive factor in these Stokely boys' later success.

Their letters from college were full of insight and advice for their mother and the farm at home. For instance, in October 1892, James wrote his mother from Wake Forest:

> I am glad you got the hogs off as well as you did. There was no money lost in feeding them. I guess I did the right thing when I took the large hogs in preference to the small ones; for if we had got the small ones, you couldn't have sold them so

soon. . . . Where are you plowing and sowing wheat now? As it has not rained, I guess the ground is getting very hard; and I guess it pulls the horses hard; but it won't do to stop and wait for rain.

In December James was saying,

Dear Mama . . . I am glad you have a carload of cattle. Tell the boys they must put the big fat on them and make money out of them. I think they ought to get the clover piece turned against Christmas if they can for it would give it more time to freeze out; but that little hill-side next to the river ought not to be plowed until spring, for in the case of a freshet it would wash away.

As the boys finished college and came home, the limitations of the farm became apparent. Run the way it had always been, and the only way that anyone in the area had ever thought of farming, the land—choice though it was—could only support one or two families and their helpers well; some of the boys would have to look farther afield. As James said later, "Our college experience had broadened our visions somewhat and when we came back to the farm we began to look for some way to broaden our opportunity of making a success of the business that our ancestors had followed for a number of generations."

James himself thought of taking up law, but after a few months of graduate study at the University of Tennessee, in Knoxville, abandoned the idea and went to work as manager of a large farm owned by a cousin and neighbor, Colonel Swann. He stayed there one year, until the autumn of 1897, the year during which the idea grew of canning some of his family's surplus crops. An old man who lived from boyhood on the place, half hired hand, half companion to the boys, tells of the first time he ever heard mention of a cannery.

"Hit was a hot summer day, we'd just come up to dinner from bustin' middles down in the bottoms alongside the river, and after we's all through eatin', out there in that big dining room, just leaning back in our chairs resting a little, Mrs. Stokely she looked around the table—they was all there, Will, James, John, Hugh, George—the girls were too, I reckon, but I forget now just which ones, and their mother said, 'Well, boys, I've seen you almost through college now. I wonder what you're planning to do.' They looked at one another a little and Mister Will he spoke right up, said he wanted to go on farming. Some of the others said they'd farm too, and Mister Hugh said, 'The farming's not for me. I want to make something out of myself and live in style. I'm going to Harvard and be a lawyer.' He did, too. Then, after a little bit, Mister James spoke. They all listened when he said anything, kind of quiet, you know. 'I've been thinking,' he said, 'about trying to can some of the tomatoes we grow here on the place. Set up a little cannery.'"

Years and generations of self-reliance lay behind that tentative solution to a problem that might have seemed insurmountable. It embodied an idea that would gather increasing importance throughout the South: diversification.

During the rest of 1897 plans were laid to run a cannery and a store combined. The family approached Colonel Swann and asked him if he would like to become part of the business by contributing some capital. He agreed and on January 1, 1898, a partnership was formed by Mrs. Anna Stokely and Colonel Swann, who invested $1,300 each in the business, and two of the sons, James and John, who invested $650 each. Their initial capitalization could hardly have been more modest, the store they built that winter and the canning shed they set up the following spring were as simple—yes, crude—as could have been expected; their knowledge of the canning industry was nonexistent. But Stokely Brothers had two important assets, and judging by the quick death of hundreds of small canneries that burst into being and collapsed in failure during the years of Stokelys' growth, they must have been decisive factors.

First, they had their own raw material and the most ideal conditions for its constant production. During countless seasons the old French Broad had been depositing sediment washed from the mountains down to these level lowlands. Every five or six years the river bottom lands overflowed and the richness of organic matter renewed the soil. In view of this fact and the unusual climatic conditions—hot midday sun because of latitude, with plenty of rain and relatively cool nights because of the nearby Great Smoky Mountains—they soon found they could double crop their lands when vegetables were grown instead of grain.

Second of the two advantages Stokelys had was their human resource. They had themselves—five brothers interested and able in five different facets of the business: William, the farmer and judge of livestock and crops; John, the extrovert who enjoyed people and commerce and the processes of selling as well as the pleasures of farming; the youngest, George, the engineering wizard who had gone to Massachusetts Institute of Technology and come home with not only knowledge but ideas as well; Hugh, who was following his own successful law career in Birmingham, Alabama, could and did give counsel on the ever-increasing legal problems that confronted the business; and James, the combination of all these others with something in addition: the genius to develop them into an effective whole. In a family that was never particularly imaginative, he had the imagination Americans most admire, that for business creation and development. In Emerson's phrase, if any company was really the lengthened shadow of one man, that company—in its first quarter century—was Stokely Brothers. Without any other single one of the brothers, the company would certainly have had a difficult time, but without James it simply never would have existed.

And so they had themselves, brothers working in harmony and respect for one another without disruptive discord or struggle for power. They also had the people who lived around them, the human reservoir from which they could draw labor and some of their materials. During the early years of Stokely Brothers there were no industries in the area. Cash income for mountain farmers was almost unknown. As the first canning shed expanded and multiplied into other little plants scattered up the river and streams, the men and women who came for a few weeks or months of work were pleased at the possibility of supplementing their produce barter with cash pay. The abundance and intelligence of its laborers was a blessing to the company; its own diversification and distribution of money was a blessing to the laborers. During those early years, there was an unusual balance of benefits for everyone who came in contact with the company.

In 1898 Stokelys was entering an industry which was between booms. During and just after the Civil War, small factories had sprung up in many parts of the Midwest, but by 1880 the men were being separated from the boys, as it were, and the growth that was to come after 1900 was to be more solid and permanent. Van Camp and Heinz and Campbell and Libby were already in the field; Del Monte emerged the year after Stokelys, when eleven California companies combined to form the California Packing Company, and American Can Company consolidated three years later.

When their store at French Broad was completed, Stokelys laid in a supply of merchandise from Knoxville wholesale houses and the surrounding countryside. Almost everything was sold on credit, and the bill was usually paid in produce either for the cannery or the store itself. As for the factory, it was about a half mile across the highway from the store on a creek whose water could be used in the canning operations. It was only a "shake roof," open at the sides, about sixty feet long and thirty feet wide. The equipment included some metal tubs, several peeling knives, a few thousand cans, solder and soldering irons with which to seal the cans, and enough wooden boxes to hold the pack. That first summer they canned only tomatoes. From sixty acres of their own and a few neighboring farms, the family harvested enough tomatoes to

put up four thousand cases of #3-sized cans in three weeks. They had chosen tomatoes because it was a crop which grew well on all their upland, it was a vegetable they had canned for years at home and knew how to handle, it could be packed after cooking at the boiling temperature of water, and it was a popular product with a wide variety of kitchen uses.

With the crop grown and canned, it now remained to be sold. James and John took some samples and went down the river to Knoxville and a hundred miles farther South to Chattanooga where, after an initial setback or two, they met with success in their wholesale and retail contacts. They made arrangements to ship that first year's pack by river boat down the French Broad to Knoxville and from there on down the Tennessee to Chattanooga. There was a river landing on the family farm and a little warehouse was built there. The cans, in wooden cases, were hauled by wagon from the factory to the warehouse and, when the boat arrived, the cases were put on a slide down to the landing. For several of those first years the French Broad was the primary means of shipping their goods, and once again the Stokelys had cause to feel grateful to the river that had made their land what it was and now provided an outlet for the products of its fertility. The boat took about a day coming up the river from Knoxville and about a day to wind back down. In the autumn, when most of the shipping was under way, four or five hundred cases of cans to a load, the river was often low; frequently the boat was hung up for half a day or more. But the pack went through.

It was a good feeling, to have concluded successfully a year at a completely new venture. When plans for the following year were made, only Colonel Swann was unhappy. Disagreement as to future salaries caused him to sell his interest in the business for what he had invested plus five hundred dollars profit. Upon reorganization, brother Will took Colonel Swann's place as an equal partner.

The first five years of Stokely Brothers were the peak years at French Broad. John looked after the store, James ran the canning business, Will was farming for himself, but part of the time helped look after the factory they had built on the nearby Dutch Bottom farm, and George was still in school although he worked on the farms and in the factories during the season.

This was a time of small but important expansion. Each year a new canning plant was built. There were several reasons why it was better to have several small scattered buildings rather than one large factory. First, transportation was difficult. Hauling ripe tomatoes or berries for a distance over rutty, rocky roads, especially in the jolty farm wagons, soon ruined them. But with factories near the fields, haulage was at a minimum and delay in canning fresh products was also at a minimum. In addition, gradual building required less immediate capital outlay, and the family was for firm steady growth rather than a large gamble. Rather than take sizable salaries for themselves, the boys reinvested their profits in the business and consequently, for the first quarter century of Stokely Brothers' existence, their management was underpaid according to any comparable industrial standards. But James as President and Treasurer, John as Vice President and Secretary, Will as Vice President and George as Factory Superintendent had always submerged their own interests to those of the family enterprise they were building. Money, time, energy—and finally it would be no exaggeration to say life itself—they were willing to give for the success of their creation. George, when he became a co-partner of the business in 1905, had even made the proposition that his salary be paid only out of profits in excess of those made in any previous year, for he didn't consider that he "would be worth anything to the business unless more profits were made when he was working for the firm than before he began working for them." An unusual proposition, but this was an unusual partnership.

As new plants were added, new products were grown and canned. String beans, blackberries, huckleberries, quartered apples, peaches, sweet potatoes. These were familiar local foods and at first the company had to use what it could find at hand, for jogging the farmers out of their old corn-wheat-livestock pattern proved to be a large job of education and persuasion. In order to put up quantities for even a sizable Southern distribution, Stokelys needed the produce of many growers in the region, but East Tennesseans were independent, set in their ways, and suspicious of newfangled crops that seemed, perhaps, less "manly" or substantial than corn, tobacco or hay. James Stokely sent a statement to the local newspaper at Newport and made this characteristic challenge:

> It is our conviction that a farmer should plant a variety of crops. If one is hard hit by the season, perhaps another will be alright and save the day. . . . If there is one keynote of success for the farmer, it is, we believe, to arrange his crops so that he will have something to do every work day in the year, and do it. It is our ambition to be instrumental in doubling, within the

next ten years, the value of the farm products of this section. It is going to be our purpose from year to year to give the farmers of this section a good market for some farm product that is not grown extensively now because we have no market for it.

A few years later, with the aid of advisers from Wisconsin, and to the surprise of the industry as a whole, Stokely Brothers became the first successful canners of sugar peas in a location so far South. Here, more dramatically than ever before, the advantage of the rich river land, hot maturing sun and cool mountain nights, was demonstrated. Now, instead of having only one season of perhaps six weeks on tomatoes, about six distinct canning periods had developed, during which at least two different items were usually processed simultaneously. Peas and turnip greens were first in May, then string beans and blackberries, followed by beets, sauerkraut and peaches. In August came sugar corn and tomatoes, followed by sweet potatoes and lima beans and, last of all, apples, pumpkin and lye hominy. In later years pork and beans, and other products, would be added. From the planting of the peas in February to the last hominy kernel sealed in December, the industry had become a year-round project.

The company grew but the family did not become more complacent. They cut every corner, used every by-product. They set up sawmills and built their own crates. Where they cut off trees they immediately planted tomatoes, famous for growth in "new ground." Vines from their peas, stalks and fodder from their sugar or hominy corn were ground into ensilage and used to fatten a large herd of beef cattle every year. This turned a waste product into a profit but it did more: cattle helped maintain the invaluable fertility of their land. All the phases of their canning and farming dovetailed with a beautiful precision. As production increased, need for selling increased, and here again the French Broad location played a decisive part in early success. Because of their Southern situation and earlier harvesting of crops, Stokelys could place their canned goods on the nation's table weeks ahead of their Northern and Midwestern competitors.

This growth had been achieved step by step, from the sale of the store in 1902 when it was realized that the cannery would require all the family's time, to 1905 when the company built a large warehouse and established central offices in Newport, a town of fifteen hundred people on the Big Pigeon River, three miles above its confluence with the French Broad. By then George had also entered the business, and he and James moved from the farm to headquarters in town. The next year their mother, Anna Rorex Stokely, moved too and the family life at "French Broad" was dispersed. There were many people through the area who would remember life as it had been in the big house there: The five brothers and four sisters and their mother, sharing work and pleasure, entertaining house guests with picnics on the river in summer and hunts at Christmastime, enduring sieges of typhoid fever, bringing home brides. Ten years after they had left the place the head of a large Southern wholesale company was to tell James in the course of a letter:

> I remember most pleasantly my visit to your mother's most hospitable home on the French Broad river a few years since in company with several of my friends, and I believe I can truly say that I never in my life enjoyed a visit quite so much as I did that one, and the memory of it has frequently given me repeated pleasure. I can never forget your mother's kind and unassuming hospitality, and the recollection of George's hearty laughs and good fellowship will ever be fresh in my memory.

One of the company's primary reasons for moving to Newport had been the railroad. They realized that shipping by water would limit their future markets. The railroad at that time was their only solution to this problem, but its use created new problems which were to plague the company for decades to come. First and last among these were the discriminatory freight rates that prevailed in the South. At first James tried to fight the rails with threats of the river. In August, 1906, he wrote the Southern Railway agent at Knoxville concerning a freight rate increase: ". . . Now if you put into effect a fifteen-cent rate to Knoxville we, of course, will see to it that a steamboat is run regularly from Knoxville to our section." A compromise was reached on this occasion but the essential problem remained, and although their fertile farmlands were to remain in the family, and the headquarters were situated on an important tributary, Stokely Brothers in a sense had left the French Broad. They were reaching for the entire South, eventually the whole U.S.A.

This was prophesied by the trip George made in 1908 to Indianapolis, Indiana. The company had decided to expand and consolidate its large central factory in Newport and, with the habitual caution and common sense that tempered their enterprise, the brothers wanted to know all they could about the most efficient factory construction. The Van Camp plant in Indianapolis was supposed to be the finest in the country. So George, always full of zest and eagerness and quick intelligence, went to reconnoiter. He did not go as a visiting executive conducted on tour by fellow officials. He took an overall-wearing job as day laborer and stayed almost a month, studying every detail of equipment and process. He wrote James: "I am trying to get the way everything is canned and bottled down to a nicety. As far as machinery and arrangement is concerned, we can make many improvements over Van Camp. I am very ambitious over the corn, catsup, and pork and bean business." He had never worked harder in his life, he said, than for Van Camp's, and when he returned to the little company in East Tennessee, he came full of enthusiasm and ideas. Stokelys enlarged and consolidated their new plant on the Big Pigeon. But the climax of the story did not come until twenty-five years later, in 1933, when the Stokely mountain farmboys returned to Indianapolis and purchased the Van Camp Company. Where one of their founders had helped unload tomatoes and tend machinery, they now set up headquarters for their multimillion-dollar enterprise with Will's son, William, Jr., as President, John's son, John B., as Vice President, and James's son, Alfred, as Assistant to the President.

By then the three originally most active brothers in the company were dead: George and his mother Anna, killed together in a train accident in 1916 when he was Mayor of Newport and only thirty-two years old; John of a heart ailment in 1919 and James with a heart attack in 1922. Will and Hugh had helped guide the company in the twenties until the second generation could take over. The span of their lives had been short, but they had been representative of the highest character of the region, the epitome of determination and optimism. When a large crop disaster had struck, James had written, "I don't think we will put up a single can of peas this season. This is a pretty serious set-back but we are not worrying over it as we are satisfied that the good that will eventually come out of it will overbalance the loss that we have sustained. It will put us on our mettle to so successfully manage the affairs of the concern as to completely overcome, in a short time, the temporary set-back." During the recession of 1921, James added grimly: "A fellow that never goes up against any hard situations is not going to develop very much."

This James Stokely, the company's leader for its first quarter century, is still something of a legend among those who knew him. To the stranger he seems more fiction than fact, a man who shared the company's profits equally with his brothers although he bore a greater burden of work and responsibility, a man whose honesty was noteworthy even among the most honest, whose fairness and sense of justice often seemed extreme. He had written: "You know you have always heard that 'if a fellow takes care of the pennies, the dollars will take care of themselves.' I believe it is equally true that if we concern ourselves about the little acts of service, the big things will take care of themselves." James had taken care of little acts and little people—with some large results. Twenty-five years after his death one plant manager said, "Jim Stokely was the finest man I ever knew. I believe if I had something to divide, I'd get a fairer cut with Jim Stokely dividing it for me than if I'd divide it with myself."

The company, like life and the river and all else, went on. It grew from the French Broad across forty-eight states. It grew from tomatoes to over half-a-hundred items. It grew from sole family ownership to include ten thousand stockholders. It grew from a $3,900 investment to an annual $100,000,000 business. It became a larger enterprise and in many ways a different one. Today it is a corporation among other corporations. Its officers protect the stockholders, its unions protect the workers, the government protects the rights of the public. Once upon a time officers and stockholders and workers and public were one.

The journey from the French Broad has been a far one. Yet its roots still lie in the rich river loam and in that summer day there in the big house above the river when the voices of the past and the claims of the future met, and James told his brothers he had thought of trying something new—a little cannery.

# 14

# The Chateau and the Boardinghouse

On green upland rising gently from the broad sweep of the river before it reaches Asheville reposes the most elegant private residence in America. Originally surrounded by 100,000 acres of forest and farmland, studded with treasures of man's art from many parts of the world, this marble confection was the flowering of one man's taste and is the repository of many men's talents. Biltmore House.

On a side street in Asheville's downtown business area, hemmed in by concrete and dinged by city smoke, rests the most famous boardinghouse in America. Once the home of a lusty family whose appetite for life was too large to be satisfied by a single town or region, this gabled frame Americana was the root of one man's art and the revealing of many men's lives. The Old Kentucky Home, famous as the fictional "Dixieland."

Separated by only six miles of real estate, the two houses are as different as the periods they represent—one the French Renaissance in the style of the great chateaus of Blois and Chenonceaux and Chambord in the lovely tended countryside of the French provinces; the other, on the style of prosperous middle-class Midwest, common at some time through most of the United States in the raw little towns of its vigorous unkempt countryside. They are as different as the men of whose lives they were an essence: a quiet slender intellectual with little of the common touch, but strong in imagination, wielding the power of one of America's greatest family fortunes; and a turbulent giant of a man with frequent impatience for the niceties of fashion, but stout in imagination, stoking the power of individual creative genius.

The fruits of his imagination each man left behind him: one an estate and the other a literature, and each lures thousands of visitors every year to visit the country of the upper French Broad. Some of the visitors become enraptured with only the wealth and beauty of the Biltmore House (opened to the public in 1930), some experience only the sense of reincarnation hovering above the Old Kentucky Home (opened to the public in 1949), where another vicarious fictional life seems suddenly made real. A few visitors expose themselves to both weathers of life, trying to understand the flower and the root, appreciating each man for his own distinctive role in artistic history.

In George Vanderbilt and Thomas Wolfe and their common meeting ground on the banks of the French Broad, there is more than a legend of Midas and the Poet. There is the personification of a split in our national creative life that has been too often represented as difference breeding conflict and contempt and too seldom understood as difference signifying growth, increasing mutual respect. Those who have looked toward Europe and its traditions for inspiration have been witlessly admired because the very distance of their sources often lent them an air of enchantment, and just as witlessly condemned because they have gone beyond national boundaries for experiences that recognize no artificial limits. And those who have looked homeward, whose inspiration has come from deep knowledge of their native soil, have been thoughtlessly praised because the very proximity of their sources often lent an air of authority to what they said, and snobbishly condemned because the background or lives seemed commonplace—in a calling that could admit no class or caste. Too frequently both the Vanderbilts and the Wolfes of the world have been rejected or embraced for the wrong reasons, just as were these two here in their home countryside. When travelers of many nationalities, from varied occupations and modes of life, trek to visit Biltmore House and the Old Kentucky Home, they must be paying their respects to something universal, something made articulate through these structures.

George Vanderbilt was an adopted lover of the North Carolina mountains. Thomas Wolfe was the mountains' born son. This is the story of how one sought and how one fled the countryside they both cherished.

Sometime in the late 1880's, George Vanderbilt visited Asheville, stopping at the rambling old Battery Park Hotel atop a hill at the edge of town. From its verandas the view southwest was magnificent, the towering sentinel of Pisgah and lesser ranges of mountains scalloping the horizon with blue uneven peaks, and as he sat there one day with a doctor friend he decided this was the place to fulfill a dream he had long nourished. Here he would build the most distinctive home in the United States to house the art treasures he had and would collect from over the world. Forthwith a series of small transactions took place which the Asheville *Citizen* of January 3, 1889, noted, with editorial curiosity:

> Some months ago Mr. Charles McNamee, a lawyer from Richmond county, New York, came here and at once entered upon the purchase of tracts of land just South of Asheville and across the Swannanoa river. It has leaked out that the millionaire George Vanderbilt is his client, but Mr. McNamee is reticent. . . . A few thousand of us would really like to know just what kind of cat is in this particular bag.

Of course the cat jumped its bag soon afterward and prices jumped too. But his agents succeeded in gathering the approximately 100,000 acres which finally comprised the estate, and in 1890 construction of Mr. Vanderbilt's dream house began. When it was opened on Christmas Day five years later, Biltmore House was the culmination of work by architect Richard Hunt; Frederick Law Olmsted, the landscape gardener who had designed New York City's Central Park; sculptor Karl Bitter; stonecutters and carpenters from many countries; a thousand laborers employed for years; and an expenditure of five million dollars. Its one hundred rooms stood on a five-acre foundation. Most of its Gobelin tapestries, antique English and French furnishings, rare paintings and porcelains and books had been chosen by their owner just for this house.

Vanderbilt's presence in the mountains made folks suddenly aware of private money in amounts of which they had not previously conceived. He was their first contact with America's royalty. Reactions to the arrival of fortune in the region were as varied as the people living there. In the *Chatauquan* for June, 1895, a Northern reporter told of an old Negro man who was the independent though ragged owner of a small property and was a "veritable thorn in the flesh to the millionaire" because he owned "nine acres of land in the heart of the vast estate, and though $10,000 have been offered him for this property, which is worth about $5 an acre in its present condition, he absolutely refuses to sell. He calmly declares that 'he has no objection to George Vanderbilt as a neighbor'." It was years later, after the Negro's death, that members of his family sold his small acres to be added to Vanderbilt's, and at a greatly deflated price.

A more widely known resident of the neighborhood wrote some columns for the New York papers on the construction of the house. His name was Edgar Wilson but he was famous under the pen name, Bill Nye. Nye had only recently bought a place on the river at Buck Shoals, and he said:

> George Vanderbilt's extensive new grounds command a
> fine view of my place. I was over there yesterday to see how

the work was progressing. It is a beautiful site. One can see from the foundations of his prospective mansion for miles up the beautiful French Broad River.

One reason I have not yet finished up my place is that I want first to see what George does, and thus get the advantage of his experience. He does not mind that, he says. . . .

The servants will occupy rooms entirely apart from the family. Mr. Vanderbilt will keep help the year round. He has set out his pie-plant already, and yesterday ordered a span of horseradish plants.

A railroad running from Biltmore, on the main line, to Mr. Vanderbilt's place is owned by him, and is used solely for conveying building material and salaries to the men. . . .

Mr. Vanderbilt is very popular here, especially on Saturday evenings; but he is not loved alone for his vast wealth . . he is known as a quiet, studious, thorough gentleman and scholar. . . . The climate of North Carolina, especially of Buncombe County, is really its chief charm. It is, in fact, why both me and Vanderbilt came here.

Enterprising real estate brokers were quick to seize the commercial angles of the estate and advertisements for land and houses began to include such appeals as: "Close by George Vanderbilt's chateau," or "Adjoining the Vanderbilt estate." Thus Biltmore House ("Bilt" for the Dutch "Bildt," ancestral town in Holland from which the family had come, and "more," an old English word designating rolling upland) began wielding both the subtle and obvious influences which for years to come neither owner nor town could altogether alter.

The conscious influences imposed on the French Broad country by the Vanderbilts were for the most part constructive and permanent. There were three main fields in which they pioneered new and better methods: agriculture, including horticulture and animal husbandry, mountain handicraft industries and forestry. Frequently more important than the project itself were the personalities imported to foster or run it. From all over America and parts of Europe, Vanderbilt siphoned the ablest specialists his money and vision could attract. Beyond the great iron gates of his estate entrance, he gradually built a model village patterned after the English squire's village, financed its church and school and hospital.

There were no local markets where vegetables could be bought in winter and its seven greenhouses alone could provide lettuce, cucumbers, parsley, cauliflower, tomatoes, green vegetables, small fruits, even pineapple, for the tables of Biltmore House. As the thoroughness and ability of the Scottish-born gardener and his helpers produced an ever larger abundance of vegetables, a market wagon was outfitted and Biltmore Estate peddled its quality produce through half a dozen of the town's residential streets and to the hotels. At first some of the local farmers resented the fact that so wealthy a competitor should enter the field, but as time passed and the estate did not lower prices for produce but raised the standard of freshness and attractiveness (for example, they used raffia to tie bundles of vegetables, rather than the old strips of rags that had been the local custom), resentment turned to imitation.

The sight of the neat tiered wagon loaded with carefully washed bundles of select vegetables was a symbolic addition to the streets of Biltmore village and Asheville. It introduced two elements that were to be inherent in the Vanderbilt enterprises: quality and diversification. The latter caused Vanderbilt to establish, at first, a pig, chicken, sheep and dairy farm on the vast acreage of the estate. But because only the dairy reached the quality and financial success necessary, it is the only one of the projects flourishing today. One of the first thoroughbred herds in the South, fifteen hundred strong, it is now, and has been since its institution, one of the finest Jersey herds in the world. Its offspring are in every state from coast to coast. Such a standard, set in a region where cattle were sometimes turned out to find mast like wild pigs and squirrels and where the purity of breeding was low, certainly had its influence on the local farmers.

The second important constructive addition made by the Vanderbilts to the over-all community began as a gentle knocking by opportunity which Vanderbilt and his wife were quick to answer. Two Northern ladies named Miss Vance and Miss Yale rented, in the summer of 1900, one of the new houses in Biltmore village. Miss Vance's hobby was woodworking and, as the peck-peck-peck of her hammer resounded through the house and even carried outside, three of the little village boys heard and became curious. They peeked in windows and the back door to see what the stranger-ladies were doing. Miss Yale invited them in, so wide-eyed and so young with minds like sponges, and one of them was the blue-eyed son of the Scottish gardener. Evening after evening they came back, watching Miss Vance work while Miss Yale explained what she was doing. For many years these two ladies had been wanting to work through their church on some specific program of benefaction either here or abroad. Now they suddenly wondered if Providence had not answered their wishes in a rather roundabout way. They asked little George Arthur and his companions to be their first class in woodworking. When Mr. and Mrs. Vanderbilt heard about this class in the village, they came to call. And Mrs. Vanderbilt said to the ladies, "Of course we can't let you go home again now, you know." And the Biltmore Industries were born. The boys, in ever-increasing classes, carved under Miss Vance's direction, and Mrs. Vanderbilt brought Biltmore House visitors around to see them. As the boys' abilities grew, these visitors often wanted to buy some of the beautiful little objects made from the native walnut and cherry. Soon, of course, regular sales developed.

This was fine for the boys of the region, but Mrs. Vanderbilt had seen a glimpse of the mountain women and girls, with the limited  opportunities in their lives. Since many of the homes already had looms, she wondered about weaving. Why didn't they learn to make good material and do fine needlework like so many of the women of Europe?

Miss Yale and Miss Vance traveled through the back country of North Carolina's mountains, stirring up interest in this new hobby and livelihood, delivering the wool to little cabins or substantial houses, anywhere the women were lonely and eager, suggesting methods of washing and dyeing and patterns of weaving, and returning to pick up the finished product. There were times of discouragement when some of the women would say they had no mind for such follies, but would rather hoe in the fields beside their men; moments of humor, like the day New England's Miss Yale rode her horse up before a mountain cabin and the woman said to her, "I'm proud to see you. Light and strip." Miss Yale lit, but was pleased that to strip she needed only to remove her outer riding habit.

The woolen homespun became a success both as craft and business venture. The weaving and woodworking expanded to larger and larger workrooms and shops. The Industries themselves, as the Vanderbilts had established them, were later sold and re-sold. But in many a household through the village and countryside where Miss Yale and Miss Vance had come to live, their names would be remembered even above the Vanderbilts. These two had gone into people's homes and given them the dignity of work, the pleasure of creation; given them respect that nourished self-respect and opened doors of self-expression and new livelihood.

Besides the diversified agriculture and the renewed handicraft industries by which Vanderbilt influenced the region, the third and by far the most important innovation was in the realm of forestry. Here, too, there was an interesting personality involved: the German with the crisp mustache and Prussian manner, Dr. Carl Schenck.

From 1892 till 1895, Gifford Pinchot, just returned from his forestry studies in France and Germany, had been successfully conducting experiments on a 3,500-acre tract of the Biltmore Estate, and when he moved on toward national prominence in 1895, Dr. Schenck came to take his place. George Vanderbilt had seen and loved the Black Forest of Germany. He was eager to have his forests tended as carefully. But there were many problems confronting such an ambition in those days. Many of the woodlands in the estate had been recklessly cut and burned over for years before Vanderbilt bought them, there were thousands of acres of abandoned clearing, and erosion had already begun to scar many a field and hill. Largest problem of all, however, was ignorance. There was no such thing as a forestry school in America. And so Dr. Schenck began one. In 1898 he established his first classes in forest practice—the first in the United States—on the Biltmore Estate, and from day to day worked on notes and lectures, revising texts he had known in Europe to suit the American scene, for there were, of course, at that time no books on forestry by American authors. With his ruddy intelligent German face and little Tyrolean hat with the feather (handy in anger because he could tear it from his head and stamp on it), locally known as "the Kaiser," Schenck wrestled with his problems stoutly. Because Vanderbilt wanted his forests to be profitable as well as sightly, a large part of the job in the woods was to cut mature trees suitable for lumber and still leave the remaining trees in good condition. This selective cutting was in itself a major innovation and required considerable training of skeptical logging crews. Then Dr. Schenck was required to operate a band sawmill such as he had never seen used before and handle hardwoods he had not known in Europe. Many of the logs were floated from the forest downriver to the boom at the sawmill, but the river was erratic, logs jammed on the rocks or drifted onto the banks of farms along the way. Some of the huge chestnut trees cut for tanbark and lumber were abandoned after the bark was stripped because they were too inaccessible to the mill.

With the plantings, his problems again were many and varied. Dr. Schenck had to learn about native soils and climates, as well as about native species of trees, but in both his failures and successes there were lessons for his boys of the forestry school. Because they were pioneers they made mistakes, but because they were scientists they profited by them. And one of the chief difficulties was always the local people. Accustomed to Europe and a traditional peasant class, Dr. Schenck found it difficult to deal with native mountain people on a basis of equality. And there was no place in the United States he could have worked where the humblest, poorest, most unlearned man felt more keenly his right of being "as good as the next fellow." It would have been a rare experience in contrasts to have been present the day Schenck on horseback along a mountain trail met one of the hillmen he had fired from service on the estate. The man, lean and deliberate, looked up at the brisk booted German and said deliberately, "Come down offen that horse. I aim to whup you." And the equally serious Schenck replied, "I'd be glad to accommodate you, sir, but I can't fight you." "And why can't you?" he insisted. "Because, sir," Schenck explained, "you're not my equal."

Despite difficulties and misunderstandings, his forestry work at Pisgah progressed. His roads were so carefully laid out that later highways followed his lead, and fire-protection paths came where he had pioneered. When he returned to Germany at the beginning of World War I, he left behind him foundations on which many a U.S. school of forestry stood. In the midst of a heavy stand of yellow poplar, he waved good-bye to "his boys." "That isn't a stand of poplar; that's a dream of my life."

These were some of the personalities George Vanderbilt gathered together for the beauty and benefit of his estate. They were fine minds, unique artisans, and they made a unique contribution to the area.

There was one other less healthy influence the Vanderbilts had on the town of Asheville. The arrival in a small mountain village of a man bearing a name as legendary in the circles of wealth and society as that of Vanderbilt, such an arrival would naturally serve as green light for the superficial social-climbing set. A summer vis-

itor to the mountain capital early noted this rather ridiculous aspect of things and dispatched some acid comments to the local
paper. After describing the many attractions of the place, he says:

> The false note in the gamut is the Vanderbilt establish-
> ment. I do not mean the thing itself, for it is intrinsically a
> beautiful and gracious contribution to the landscape. I mean
> the artificial atmosphere of snobbery and servility and petty
> ostentation which has been injected into the once bracing and
> pure ozone of the neighborhood. It is like some tawdry little
> court—say the Court of Pretzel. . . . I haven't the least idea
> that this arrangement is Mr. Vanderbilt's preference. It seems
> incredible that a grandson of the tough, hard-headed, simple
> and homely old ferryman should deliberately invest himself
> with the pomp and circumstance of royalty.

There were humorous stories, less disturbed, about Vanderbilt and some of the ambitious townsfolk. When W.O. Wolfe came
home for dinner at noon one day he brought one of these chronicles with him. Standing at the head of the massive dining room
table, slicing his razor-edged carving knife through the tender suc-
culence of a prime ten-ribbed roast of beef, he related the tale of
the colonel, patriarch of one of Asheville's first families, as he had
heard it that morning down at his monument shop on the town
Square. "Old Colonel went to call on George Vanderbilt a few
weeks back, and when he came home he told that old Negro retainer
he keeps around the place there that Mr. Vanderbilt would be returning his call one of these days and he must know how to act in
the great man's presence. 'Now Johnson,' Colonel tells him, 'after
you open the door and take his hat, you must usher him down here
into my library and when you get about a third of the way in the
room, bow low from the waist and announce, 'My lord, Mr. Vanderbilt.' Old Colonel, you see, can't forget or let anybody else forget he was born in England. He coached Johnson some more and

then one day G.W.V. did come, a little slight man, you know, but
when he stepped out of that Biltmore carriage and old Johnson
saw him, he got more and more excited. 'Dis way, suh. Yes-suh,
yes-suh, dis way.' And he led him down the hall and when he
reached the library door he threw it open and hollered at the top
of his lungs, 'My God! It's Mr. Vanderbilt!'"

They laughed with great gusty humor, the Wolfes, at such
deflation of pompousness, for they were people to whom life was
no pretense. Experience was no pantomime to be fitted to a pattern; for them it was the daily drama of self and family and town
felt with sharp awareness. Unlike Biltmore House, it was not the
furnishings, the things, that quickened the Old Kentucky Home
to life: it was the people who lived there. The tall, white-faced
stonecutter with the chiseled features and the flair for oratory, his
small, bright-eyed wife with the prodigious memory and the
strength of mountains in her fiber—and their varied searching
children. Particularly the youngest child, named Tom. For if
George Vanderbilt collected around him big people, memorable
ones, Thomas Wolfe created big people and memorable ones. For
this very creation, his home town could neither forgive nor forget
him.

The autumns of 1929 and 1930 brought two major events to
the town of Asheville. Both were catastrophic in the sense that they
left the place forever changed—changed for the better as years
would reveal. One event was that the two leading banks of the
town closed their doors and depositors were suddenly face to face
with the unbelievable specter of financial failure. The city was even
more bankrupt than many of its citizens, for political chicanery
had poured millions of the city's monies into the banks' unplugged
leaks, and now all was lost. Prominent citizens committed suicide,
retired schoolteachers and aging farmers faced panic with no savings left to lean on, the money structure that had seemed so solid
yesterday had crumbled overnight. People looked at one another
and the wonder of what had happened gazed bleakly back at them.

And Tom Wolfe, the boy with the great brown eyes and enveloping hands and towering frame, published a novel called *Look Homeward, Angel*. Its author had done just that. Now people who had always thought that books were pasted together from bits of dust and ink bound by beads of perspiration and rare drops of inspiration discovered that life—daily ordinary and extraordinary life such as they knew—sometimes spilled over into literature. Some of them might have sometime read that Prince Andrew's sister, Mary, in Tolstoy's *War and Peace* was partially modeled after one of Tolstoy's relatives, they might have learned in some English class that the conditions pictured in Charles Dickens's novels were representations of some of the conditions of English society as he found it (and loathed it and wanted it changed). Doubtless some of the immortal reality of Tolstoy's people or Dickens's scenes came from the fact that they were drawn from the fabric of their authors' lives. But all that had been far away and long ago. Here, now, was a novel dealing with the places and people Tom Wolfe had known. "Why it is Asheville," they cried. "It is we. It is me!" And they searched one another's faces. This was a sense of bankruptcy deeper than even the failure of the banks they were soon to experience. Distilled through the consciousness of a boy who soaked up, spongelike, every detail of the life in which he was growing up, laid open on the pages of a book, were their lives and not only the wonder of life and beauties of seasons and landscapes, but the snickering secrets too, the shadowy corners and evil appetites. He had said this was "a story of the buried life," but what many wanted buried was life itself. Although their daily lives might be surrounded by deceit and some of them openly lived by fraud, still they could not understand why it would not be better to leave "unpleasantness" buried. They were of those people of the world who do not yet realize it is the submerged consciousness that can wreck a whole personality, and the buried bulk of an iceberg is the part that destroys a ship.

With the usual perverseness of humanity, the people of Asheville did not seem shocked at much of the deceit and folly and wickedness and waste that Wolfe found—they were shocked only that he exposed it. They did not look into their civic and social life and wonder how they could cure it of cancerous growths so other adolescents growing up would not be exposed to the same cynicisms and falsehoods. They said, instead, "The book's unspeakable. People don't write about such things. It isn't nice." And others said, "Look at what he wrote about his own family. Why, they're ruined."

The Wolfes were not so easily ruined. On the contrary, they were made immortal. They were, on their mother's side, of the same mountain blood that fed many of these very urbanites who had lived in the city of Asheville for a generation and become in the process too civilized to appreciate any but what they believed to be the most delicate of artistic nuances. They were the people who smiled vaguely when "mountaineers" were mentioned and

failed to remember that their own grandfather had driven a bull-
tongue plow through the earth of old Madison or Buncombe or
Yancey County.

But the Wolfes had never denied their background. They knew
of the vast tribe of their mother's family who had lived in the mountains of North Carolina since the Revolution and married into
other large pioneer families, and they sensed that part of the
strength and uniqueness of their own heritage came from those
source roots. Their mother was a character fitted to saga, to great
folk tales.

Julia Westall Wolfe grew up in Buncombe County out along
the Swannanoa headwaters, during the years when it was emerging
from wilderness toward civilization, and she remembered the rich
look of new ground just cleared of timber, the lean hardship of
panic years when money became tight as winter ice on the rain
barrel. She heard accounts of the Revolutionary War and the Civil
War as they were repeated in front of open fires during long evenings. She worked in the house and out on the farm. When she
finished her education, she taught. Then she met the tall stonecutter from Pennsylvania and began another life. But all her girl-
hood and heritage had equipped her with a natural self-possession
and dignity that was characteristic of the best type of French Broad
mountain person. Talking with a butter-and-egg man who happened by her house and whose mother she might have remembered from long-past years, appearing before a radio audience in
Hollywood, speaking to a class of university students in New York,
visiting with a clerk in a store or a waitress in a restaurant or a
stranger on the train, Miss Julia remained for eighty-three years
her same calm interested self. There was little of the chameleon
about her. She did not change to suit her surroundings. Everyone
decent was her equal and none was her better. She said once, "People sometimes say to me, 'You're not a social climber.' 'Humph.'
I answer, 'Why should I be? I'm at the top now. Always have

been.'" And her lips would press together in a little smile while her chestnut brown eyes twinkled.

The same basic sense of worth, of roots, was in her youngest son. When Tom Wolfe revisited Asheville in 1937, F. Scott Fitzgerald was in town at the same time, stopping at the Grove Park Inn, handsome resort hotel built by Bromo-quinine king, E.W. Grove. They got together, of course, and talked. At last Fitzgerald said, "This is a sterile town, Tom. Why do you come here for characters?" And Wolfe replied, "What are you talking about, Scott? I've just come from Burnsville over in Yancey County. I've been talking with my mother's uncle, John Westall, over there. He's ninety-five, he was at Chickamauga and he told me about it. My God, it was wonderful. I'm going to write it all down verbatim. There's your character, Scott, back in Yancey County. What did you expect to find up here at the Grove Park Inn? They're the same people you see at expensive hotels everywhere. But you go out in these mountains here—sterile, Scott? Don't you believe it!"

Whether or not the people of his home town appreciated or understood, they came alive, the family that lived in that rambling boardinghouse, the family that Tom Wolfe knew and distilled into another fictional family. It is this fiction family that draws readers from all parts of the country to visit the side street in Asheville where, for a moment, they can imagine they know more intimately the characters they have met in the pages of one of Wolfe's books. Do such visitors stand in front of one of the numerous fireplaces of Dixieland, as Wolfe called it, and imagine they see the great roaring flames leap up the chimney-throat as Gant builds one of his fabulous winter-morning fires? Do they see the upright piano and think they hear Helen singing one of the summery sentimental ballads, one of the operatic arias that was supposed to bring her fame and fortune, or beside one of the old rocking chairs can they pause and believe they hear Eliza spinning one of her cocoonlike tales of family relations and mystic warnings, of births and mar-

riages and deaths? Upstairs before an old iron bedstead do they
imagine they see Ben, full of bitter pride and an unquenchable
brightness, go out to meet his dark angel? And where in the house,
on porch steps in the moonlight, in the cavernous kitchen, in hall or
bedroom, do they not see the eager yet withdrawn face of the lonely
lost Eugene?

For even as Eugene was lost in the maze of this house and
family and town, Tom Wolfe was lost in these ancient hills. Although he could write about them magnificently—where else has
October flamed so beautifully to life or the magic Northern snow
descended in more exciting reality?—he was still not a chronicler
of nature as he was of humanity. It was people, the man-swarm of
Manhattan's enfabled rock, that fascinated and compelled his talent. He would hunt through the byways, search a thousand faces,
hope in a hundred friendships, for understanding and an end to
loneliness. For if there was one condition of man's life, one quality
of his experience on this earth, to which Wolfe gave supreme voice,
it was the deep, personal, universal ache of human loneliness. And
the mountains were walls enclosing loneliness, demanding it. They
were monstrous barriers. But the river—ah, the river. The river
moved and changed, yet remained timeless too, and it led out to a
world beyond the mountains. Tom Wolfe chose the river instead
of the mountains and foresaw that he could never come home
again. Even in death lying on a hill above the French Broad, the
essence of him is not there. It lies between the covers of half-a-dozen
books scattered on shelves around the world, books in which one
person's experience is made so vivid that it enlarges the experiences
of his readers, too. That is why people come each year to see where
that life had its beginning and largest impetus.

The chateau and the boardinghouse. George Vanderbilt and
Thomas Wolfe. The rich collector who came to the mountains of
the French Broad because they seemed to match the home he
wanted to build, but who was buried at the age of fifty-one by
distant waters; and the hungering creator who fled the mountains

of home because he was possessed of a craving for experience with all peoples in all places, but who returned at the age of thirty-eight to be buried by the river he had known as a boy. In Vanderbilt's world, the chateau had been the heart of the model village as an English castle was the focal point of many a feudal town, but in Wolfe's world, each individual in that teeming boardinghouse was his own, the only, focal point. As the chateau was a marble culmination and repository for some of the finest flowers of man's talents, so the boardinghouse was a rich maelstrom of humanity feeding one of the rarest talents of American literature. The Loire and the Swannanoa rivers are half a world apart, but the best and stoutest spirit of each met on the banks of the French Broad, when slight elegant George Vanderbilt and great passionate Thomas Wolfe each found means to represent man's groping toward beauty made concrete in art.

# 15

## The Big Law
## and the Little Law

The courthouse sits near the center of town. It is the nerve center of every county seat along the French Broad. Its floors are worn by the shuffling feet, its walls are stained with the lounging backs, its corridors are dingy with the smoke of all the swarming human life centered in its books of record and departments of health and road and welfare—and its courts of law. Belonging to no one, it belongs to everyone. Impersonal as a tool or weapon, it is also as personal as hate and murder. Above all, it is a smell. The smell of many people through many years of heat and cold, the smoke-soaked clothes speaking of airless grease-spattered rooms. Sweat and tobacco and wholesale disinfectant, stale air saturated into every crevice, a human composite as impossible to communicate to an outsider as to escape if you are an insider.

In this building, at the beginning of every quarter year, the dramas that have dragged to weary dénouement or blazed to tragic climax in country coves and town's back streets repeat themselves, to be weighed in the scales of impartial justice. And the French Broad country, being still a region of individuals where a person is more interested in two neighbors' argument over a dog than some journalized account of distant conflicts, still boasts a generous turnout for court days.

The men gather on benches along the courthouse lawn and swap reports on the season for crops, the price of hogs and cattle and feed, political views, their latest harvest of man-stories. The women shop through nearby stores for cotton batting to fill quilt-tops pieced on long lonely evenings, a new pair of slippers (low-heeled shoes, not bedroom wear), and a bottle of "pop" for the baby they're carrying. During the time of trial they ebb and flow through the doors and along the seats—until the climax of a case is reached. Then drawn by some invisible magnetism they are there, all in from benches and stores and cafés, crowding the room with a spongelike attentiveness, soaking up every detail of sound or sight or the general "feel" of the case.

The attorney general has read the indictment: "The sovereign state against Buck Blackburn—that he did assault and murder Creed Fine, insulting the peace and dignity of the sovereign state . . ."

The preliminary witnesses have set the date and time: "It was a Saturday, just getting down toward dark."

"Now what, if anything, did you find under Creed Fine's body when you took him out of the car?"

The witness's face is puzzled and the smooth-voiced lawyer for the defense restates his question for the prosecution's witness. "You helped take Fine out of the car after he was shot?"

"Yes."

'At that time, while you were lifting him out, did you find anything?"

"I don't know."

"You don't know whether or not you found something lying there on the front seat of that car?"

"Well . . ." The small, pinch-faced man shifts in his chair.

"So you did find something?"

"I reckon so."

"Now I ask you, was it a pistol you found on the seat where Creed Fine had been——"

"Object! That's a leading question and the lawyer for the defense knows——"

"All right, all right. I'll state it another way. What did you find there on that seat where Creed Fine had been sitting?"

"A—pistol."

The good-looking young man glances triumphantly at the jury and retires to his corner behind a sheaf of yellow papers and legal volumes bristling with bookmarks.

The prosecutor, the attorney general himself, is standing now. He smiles toward the jury and addresses his nervous witness.

"Was the pistol still in its holster?"

"Yes."

"Still in its holster like Creed Fine never had any intention of using it——"

"We object!" The quick young lawyer.

"Objection sustained." The weary judge.

The prosecutor playing it to the gallery all the way: nodding, smiling through two gold-filled teeth, leaning across the rail between court and onlookers.

Finally, the defendant himself on the stand. Tall, swarthy-faced, with open white collar and khaki trousers, harried and innocent-looking now as an animal in the woods, something underneath in leash capable of large sudden violence. His young lawyer handling him slowly, carefully.

"You and your wife are separated, Buck?"

"That's right."

"And you'd gone to her house to see your babies?"

"Yes."

"How many babies do you and Darlene have, Buck?"

"Three."

"And so you just went by to see your three babies? And who'd you find there?"

"Creed Fine was settin' out in his car in front of the house."

"Now what sort of relationship existed between you and Creed Fine?"

"Come again?"

"Was there bad blood between you and Fine?"

"Oh! Yeah. He'd been deviling me ever chance he got."

"And you'd been avoiding him?"

"Yeah. Whenever I could."

"What did you do when you drove up in the yard there to see your babies and saw this man sitting there?"

"I got out of the car and come around."

"Did he do anything?"

"He opened his car door part way."

"Did you say anything?"

"I said, 'What you doing here?' "

"Then what happened?"

"He started grabblin' around on the seat beside him. He'd said he was gonna shoot me if I come around Darlene any more. I thought he's gettin' his gun."

"What did you do?"

"I shot him."

"Did you mean to kill him?"

"No. I was just tryin' to keep him from killin' me."

"Your witness, General." The young lawyer smiles confidently as he resumes his seat.

The attorney general takes the witness. A solid red-faced man wearing a black tie and striped shirt, with a voice like the crack of doom. Beginning easily, with the mountain accent thick as barley broth on his tongue.

"Now Buck, these here babies you say you come to see that Saturday—how often you been to see them lately?"

"I wouldn't know, exactly."

"Hadn't you been to see these babies once in ten months before this?"

There is no answer. Buck's head is hung as he peers at the floor just in front of him. A ruddy-faced farmer on the front row nudges his companion. "They got him that time." It is like a serious game, every man expected to put up the best fight for his side. Justice plays second lead to wit.

"And hadn't you been arrested once for nonsupport of these babies you say you was so anxious to see?"

"Not exactly arrested."

The questions and fumbles plod on. After a while: "Now Buck, when did you look to see if this gun of yours was loaded?"

"Sometime that evening, I reckon."

"You mean sometime that afternoon before you killed Creed Fine you made sure your gun was loaded?"

He sees the wide trap and says nothing.

The prosecution walks down the aisle before the jury. "Aye, you checked to see it was loaded before you drew it on Creed Fine. Now you tell us *why* you looked to see if it was loaded. I want you to tell this jury *why* you left it loaded, if you can."

Silence for half a minute while people shift in their seats and the court clerk takes a drink of water from the glass and pitcher on the judge's stand. (Some of the courts still have dippers.)

The attorney general leans against the banister dividing the courtroom and cracks out with, "Then let me ask you this: When you pulled the trigger on that gun that blew the top of that man's head off from the ears up, or practically, did you mean to kill him?"

"I meant to shoot him."

"Did you mean to kill him?"

Silence. A baby cries near the back of the room. Its mother jogs it up and down violently in an effort to quiet the crying. Buck Blackburn smooths one hand across his hair in a nervous gesture and says nothing.

The prosecutor appeals to the judge. "The defendant won't answer my questions. I can't ask a simpler question."

"Answer the question," the judge directs.

With heavy patience, pacing toward the courtroom and then whirling to confront the witness, the prosecutor repeats, "Did you mean to kill Creed Fine?"

"No." Barely audible.

"Then what did you think blowing the top of a man's head off would do to him?" Triumphantly. "What effect did you think that would have on his general health?"

Eyes on the floor again. No answer.

"Well now, you couldn't have been in all this great bodily danger after all, could you, if you didn't even mean to kill the man?"

"I was scared he'd shoot me." Doggedly.

"And he was fumbling there on the seat all the time it took you to get out of the car, walk around it and come up there in front of him with your gun. Is that what you're saying?"

"He started fumblin' after I got out——"

"Then you had the gun drawn on him first?"

"No. I went back and got it after I seen him reachin' for his gun."

"Did you even know Creed Fine had a gun?"

"I hadn't seen it."

"You're not answering my question again. Did you *know* he had a gun?"

"Well, I couldn't see it."

"Then you admit to this jury that you killed Creed Fine without knowing he had a gun or ever seeing one on that occasion?"

"Object!"

Back and forth. The hot dingy Saturday afternoon relived. Two V-8's layered with dust, decorated with squirrel tails on radiator cap and aerial, drawn up in the bare dirt yard before Darlene Blackburn's three-room house. Soft-spoken men with eyes wild

as balky mules', full of liquor and anger, sick with a hard unrea-
soned pride that could be satisfied only by killing. And after the
blood, the enormous realization, and fear.

"Why did you go in the house and stick your shotgun under
the floor there? Why didn't you take it home?"

"I thought I'd done enough."

"You'd done a-plenty too much. You knew that, didn't you?"

"I just knew I didn't want no more to do with that shotgun."

The townspeople drop in to hear a bit of the story and look
over the crowd: the clothing merchant immaculate in his light
knife-creased suit, the café owner, the juke-joint operator, in loud
checked shirt and hand-painted tie and movie mustache, the old
revival preacher, pale-eyed and stooped, who remembers only the
names of those who dole him out a few coins from week to week.
Girls in blue jeans and profile sweaters. And the overalled, blue-
shirted country men. The women in limp gingham dresses or more
likely bright cheap rayon uneven around the hem, stained and
wrinkled. Children clambering up, around, over them and the
seats. Inside the rails, the lawyers coming and going, whispering,
laughing, motioning, delaying, deciding; the court clerk, the sheriff; a few select spectators leaning in chairs over by the windows.
The jury on one side: twelve citizens culled because each side believed they would be tractable.

It is time for the summations. The attorney general stands
slowly and grins at the people now packed in the courtroom. He
has taken off his coat and his suspenders match his tie. He pushes
up his sleeves and makes a great vertical motion with one fist.
"Rotten! This case is rotten to the core! Buck Blackburn was a hard
witness. Like my wife's old cow he gave down his milk slow-ly.
But what little he did give smelled to high heaven!"

His voice sinks to righteous resonance. "Ever' man or human
being has the right to live. Now the defense says Creed Fine was
a vile and dangerous man because he'd been indicted for murder.
Then they say, Please, please don't find this boy vile, dangerous

and vicious for confessedly killing a man! That's a narrow, contracted, prejudicial, unethical point of view and argument. They're treating this whole thing like it was just some little difficulty their boy was in, but I'm asking you: What if a hen jumps on a June bug and swallers it—is that a difficulty or a consumption?"

The people along the benches nudge each other. They grin and crane their necks a little farther forward. The attorney general is always good for an old-fashioned open-field fight with no holds barred. He paints a lurid mural of the death of Creed Fine.

Finally he concludes: "Gentlemen, I was born in the mountains. [They have all known the attorney general for more than two decades, but he always repeats this fact of his birth to them.] And I'm proud of it. What sense I have is common, mountain, bay-horse sense, and I'm proud of that too. And ever' bit of sense I've got tells me Buck Blackburn murdered Creed Fine in cold blood with malice of forethought. Remember-ye-this, gentlemen of the jury, once you write your verdict there on that record, it can never be erased. And there is only one verdict you *can* bring in. Guilty of murder in the first degree!"

The people shift positions and watch the defense lawyer as he walks before the jury. They listen to every intonation of his refutation and plea. "—and so he came to see his babies. This man Buck Blackburn tries to make his living by the sweat of his own brow, and like some of the rest of us doesn't get to see as much of his children as he'd like to. And when he came there that Saturday afternoon, what'd he find? A bold vile dangerous man who'd once been indicted for murder, sitting there in a car. A man who, from all accounts, had spent the day seeing just how much liquor he could get on the outside of. And Blackburn walks over to him and says, 'What are you doing here?' That's when Creed Fine started reaching for that pistol there on the seat beside him. Now the prosecutor here is trying to tell this jury that Blackburn provoked an assault. Why that isn't common sense. It isn't law! Asking a man what he's doing doesn't give him a right to start for his gun. And when Blackburn saw that action and remembered past threats, he went back around his car and got his own gun. Not until he was in *mortal fear of his life!*—"

A few more flourishes and Buck's lawyer finishes, wipes his brow with a large white handkerchief. He sits down beside his client.

There is a rustle of relaxation over the room in the following silence. Some of the people ease through the swinging doors. The babies that aren't asleep are slipped a surreptitious cracker.

The judge reads from several long sheets. There is absorbed attention when he comes to the part "—and you will report such verdict as proof dictates and justice demands. If you find this murder in the first degree sentence may be anything from death by electrocution to twenty years imprisonment. Murder in the second degree may receive anything between ten and twenty years. Voluntary manslaughter you may set at imprisonment from two to ten years, and for ordinary manslaughter you may give one to five years or not less than one year in the county workhouse. If you decide the killing took place in self-defense, the injury must have been real or imminent."

It is turning toward the last half of afternoon and clouds have begun to gather over the sky. The people are as restless as animals before a storm and the judge's voice is drowned out in the shuffling confusion. Many farmers are leaving so they can get back up in their coves before a churned mass of red mud seals them out. There are two or three Negroes near the back, and they wait to see one set of white men "give it" to another.

After the verdict—voluntary manslaughter in self-defense, five years recommended—the room and halls empty quickly. The drama itself, the story unfolding, the interplay of wit and skill, this was what most of them had come for anyway. The plea of self-defense has won more reprieves from a killer's electric chair than anyone ever counted and this was just one more.

It's a full-time job, practicing law in these small towns. And

during a lifetime grows the largest necessary ability that only age
and much experience and a rag-bag tenacious memory can com-
bine to make: knowledge of how to choose a jury. The voice in
which old-timers will tell you, "He's the best hand in the county
to pick a jury," reveals the stature of such an achievement. It
means hearing a man's name or glancing at his face and knowing
immediately what part of the county he lives in, which political
faction he follows, what are his family chronicles and characteris-
tics. Such tributary details are frequently more important than
half the direct evidence in the case. One white-maned lawyer, the
patriarch of a French Broad county, recalls one among many such
occasions.

"It was nearly fifty years, half a century ago. Rufus Williamson killed this gambler who came in here and was cleaning out all
the boys in town. They claimed he was cheating, nobody'll ever
know, but anyway they got him in a card game up there back of
the bluffs, and Rufus was hid behind a tree just in line with him.
Shot him straight through the heart. Then the boys took his body
and dumped it in one of those caves near the bluffs. After awhile
somebody found the body, of course. They traced the killing to
Rufus. Never could get him to tell who had helped him. But he
came to our offices—I had two older partners then—for us to de-
fend him. I can sit here now and say in cold blood that I saved
that man's neck. It came about, not by any evidence we uncov-
ered or by any of the arguments those two older lawyers made and
they had silver tongues too, let me tell you, but by reason of one
juror.

"We'd used up the better part of two days and nearly all our
challenges picking that jury. We just lacked one. Then they called
a man named Lish Foster. My partners started shaking their heads.
We all knew the Fosters. A tough-burled bunch from back in the
old nineteenth who'd convict a man just to see him sweat. But I
happened to know this Lish and he was a chickenhearted sort of
man. He'd never had much liking for my man Williamson, but

they'd traded cattle and mules and never had any hard feeling. And then something came in my mind. 'Didn't you and Lish go to school together?' I asked my man. 'I reckon we did. Back when my pap was cutting timber up in old nineteenth.' Right then I knew Lish Foster was our juror. But my partners couldn't see it. They were thinking about old man Foster and his oldest boy. They'd send their own blood grandmother to the gallows, I said, but Lish could never hang anyone he'd been to school with. I finally convinced them.

"Well, the trial lasted nearly a week. But sure enough, when that jury went out to debate, there were eleven of those men for conviction and death and one for imprisonment. That one was Lish Foster. He hung out against those others for a day and a night. Finally boiled down to a disagreement over some word in the

judge's charge and they sent out for a dictionary, which they weren't supposed to do of course, but the definition gave Foster the little toenail hold he needed and he carried them to part of his side. They finally decided against death. That's all we'd hoped for anyway. That one fellow had saved Rufus Williamson's neck."

Sometimes jurors are chosen for filler material. The lawyers know they'll follow the lead the other jurors offer. They're seldom, however, quite as dense as old Matt who sat at the trial of Red-Eye Daley for the double offense of shooting a man and then stealing his still. Matt sat and spat in the spittoon when it was handy and on the floor when it wasn't, the trial boiled around him and finally the jury filed out to deliberate under a spreading beech tree on the courthouse lawn. They debated and discussed, old Matt squatted on his heels and chewed his tobacco cud. At last the foreman said, "Matt hasn't put in any word about all this. What do you think about the case, Matt?"

"Case?" Snorting like a startled horse. "What case?"

"Why this trying of Red-Eye for shooting his partner," the foreman said.

"Shooting? Red-Eye shoot somebody?"

"He killed his partner——"

"Killed him? Lord, they'll hang him for that, won't they?"

Court day has always been part holiday in the French Broad country. One traveler in the mid-1800's described a little North Carolina town as having a "gaunt, shaky courthouse and jail, a store or two, and two taverns." The taverns, he said, were necessary "to accommodate the judges and lawyers and their clients during the session of the court. The court is the only excitement and the only amusement. It is the event from which other events date. Everybody in the county knows exactly when court sits and when court breaks. During the session the whole county is practically in town, men, women, and children. They camp there, they attend the trials, they take sides; half of them, perhaps, are witnesses, for the region is litigious, and the neighborhood quarrels are entered into with spirit. To be fond of lawsuits seems a characteristic of an isolated people in new conditions."

Mounted on their blooded horses or riding in handsome gigs and buggies that were a passionate rivalry between the owners, a veritable cavalcade of lawyers, headed by the judge, made their circuit every quarter from one county seat to another.

The lawyers may have been friendly and jolly with each other on their journeys, but once arrived in the courtroom they "drew the sword and threw away the scabbard." They earned their clients' money.

And if the legal battle wasn't hot enough, there were usually members of the audience who would provide a real fight. As a matter of fact, the crowds sometimes came primarily to see a fight. One of the most famous that ever occurred in East Tennessee was at the old-town location of Newport on the banks of the French Broad. The antagonists were Stephen Huff and Phil Sutton. Sutton weighed 175 pounds. He was round and well proportioned and didn't appear that heavy. Active as a cat, he had strength, endurance and courage. Huff was a larger man of tremendous strength. Friends had primed the men for a match which was set for a certain court day. It was reported that thousands came from all the neighboring counties to see this well-matched contest.

A ring was made on the bank of the river. A man named Allen was Huff's second and O'Dell was Sutton's. The principals stripped to the waist. Their heads had been shaved and their bodies well greased to make any hold of the opponent's more difficult. When the fight commenced, Sutton made the first offensive. He jumped up and kicked Huff in the abdomen with both feet. This was supposed to have hurt Huff badly but he made no sign. The two clinched and went to the ground. It was presently discovered that Sutton had a rock in his hand and was "tearing up Huff's head with it," as an eyewitness later said. At least Huff's friends said so, and one of his neighbors, who was no slight man himself, intervened in the fight. This was considered the most unethical thing possible at such a contest and O'Dell, who was second for Sutton and all for letting the rocks fall where they would, knocked down the interfering bystander. With this, a general skirmish was under way. The two combatants were parted and the rest of the day was doubtless devoted to parting their friends. The backers of neither man would ever admit defeat. They never fought again. Perhaps it was believed that the strain on the onlookers was too great.

During the decades of settlement and growth, the punishment was made to fit the crime. "A rope for rape and a shotgun for seduction" was the accepted law. Roads were few and money scarce, property was guarded with your life. Larceny was punishable by thirty-nine lashes well laid on a bare back by the sheriff. Around 1840 a fellow convicted of stealing a dozen bundles of oats was whipped with eight keen chinquapin switches cut from a thicket growing at the edge of town. Each switch was used for five lashes except the last, which had only four, and at the end, the prisoner who had stripped "start naked" from neck to hips had a truly "blooming back."

A thief who stole a man's horse stole his automobile, his cultivator and tractor, and his friend—and he could be hanged. The third and fourth hangings that occurred in Buncombe County, took place in 1835 for two young men convicted on very circumstantial evidence of stealing a horse. The event of their hanging was typical of the times. If anything outranked court day for excitement, it was an execution. Crowds swarmed over the town, thronged the taverns and grogshops, brought their children for moral education to see the terrible result of a life of crime, and proclaimed a general holiday. By early morning the day in May when Sneed and Henry were hanged, Asheville's public square was packed with people. The few stores were doing a land-office business, a company of the "milish" was on hand to be sure the prisoners remained on hand and did not deprive the crowd of its double-feature spectacle.

The procession to the gallows was rowdy and dramatic. The shackled prisoners sat on their own coffins and were drawn on a wagon through the streets from jail to gallows. There they found two half-completed graves waiting for them. There were sermons, one by the Reverend Thomas Stradley, and then the prisoners again vowed their innocence. But the black hoods were drawn, the nooses were lowered around their necks, and the trap doors sprung.

Manslaughter was punished for many years by branding. A capital M was emblazoned on the prisoner's right hand. There was a tale told in Buncombe County in the 1840's of a man who was particularly hard and bold. He gave no sign of noticing as his right hand and arm were strapped with leather thongs to the railing of the bar enclosing the courtroom. He watched without a flinch as the sheriff, Dave Tate, brought in a small hand stove full of glowing live coals, set it down before him and laid the branding iron to heat. After the iron was held to a prisoner's hand, the branding lasted until he could repeat aloud three times, "God save the state." Sheriff Tate put the iron to his man's hand and the cool nerve didn't break until he'd said the triple oath, "God save the state," then yelled at the top of his strength, "And damn Dave Tate!"

Of course, the greatest single legal problem of the area has always been the making of moonshine whiskey. The character of part of the country and the character of some of the people has conspired to make this so. The steep land that grew poorer with every clearing and each successive crop of corn made it impossible for a man to earn more than barely the cost of his seed unless he measured his crop in gallons rather than bushels. Laurel thickets were beautiful to see, but the only crop use they had was providing good cover for hidden stills. On the other hand, many of these people always followed the line of least resistance. Work was their natural enemy and they avoided an encounter whenever possible. They liked the excitement of outwitting the law.

During World War II the sudden mushrooming of a city called Oak Ridge, near Knoxville, boomed the moonshine business along the French Broad. Located in a technically dry county, with a population drawn from all regions, it provided a prosperous market for the mountain bootleggers. If workers at the atomic city did not know at that time what they were producing, most of them who drank likewise did not know what they were consuming.

Just then, during the war, there was a sugar shortage to over-

come, sugar, of course, being a prime ingredient of "white lightning." Bootleg sugar was peddled to big operators who could dole
it out in turn to their individual producers. Then there were the
bees. For every bee-stand he fed during the winter, a farmer was
allowed five pounds of sugar each quarter year. Beehives sprouted
around mountain cabins like weeds in a seedbed. Honey had always been a favorite sweet but now it became a passion. Today
you can still drive through some of the back country and see occasionally, in some small back yard, row after row of abandoned
beehives.

In Buncombe County, liquor stores are legal, but with the
federal tax of $10.50 on every gallon, and local taxes added to this,
moonshine—peddled at about half the price—still has a flourishing
market. And the capital of the region's production is nearby, in an
East Tennessee valley called Cosby. With some of the finest sky-
line of the Great Smoky Mountains for backdrop, and smooth fields
following the winding creek through the valley, Cosby has at first
glance all the pastoral beauty and tranquillity of an early American print. But its history of lawlessness is long and colorful. Its
name has been well-known for years, not only in the state but
through the South, in Chicago, Cleveland, and Detroit, and
wherever else Tennesseans have migrated and taken their folklore.

Revenue agents combing Cosby have adopted any usable
modern device to help locate stills, and moonshiners have countered
with any device to keep them in the dark. There was a day when
wisps of wood smoke rising from some remote thicket, or corn
sprouting tender green shoots in some out-of-the-way creek bed,
were tattletales of nearby operations. But now small portable oil
burners let a still operate within a few yards of a main highway
and never give a sign. To spot these oil burners, officers have taken
to the air. Search by plane has been used a good deal, but it has
one drawback. It puts the operators on guard and makes their capture less likely, even if the still is taken. As for actual capturing,
there is still nothing to replace the old-time raid. A successful raid

takes careful planning, quiet waiting, quick action and plenty of stamina. Many an officer has been left holding the sleeve of an empty coat when he failed to hang on to some wily moonshiner who skinned out of such encumbrances and "took off" up the mountains.

On Cosby the people can spot an officer's car as soon as it enters the valley. A blast of dynamite is the time-honored signal of welcome. And in recent years the boys have inaugurated a little game of follow the leader. At every store and filling station and crossroads, the officer's car picks up another one or two cars in its train until finally there is a small caravan following wherever he goes. Usually the entourage is quiet and peaceable, sometimes there is a little blowing of horns, but it is slightly disconcerting to have eight or ten cars as unsolicited escort on a secret patrol.

Wood smoke has left the stills and so, for the most part, has copper. Big operators use the less expensive galvanized iron pots. They are subject to rust, but quality long ago yielded to quantity and a fast dollar. These galvanized drums are called "silver clouds."

Methods of putting a "bead" on moonshine have stepped up too. To bring their Cosby best from 90 proof up to 96.25 proof, the latest discovery has been to add one pint of rubbing alcohol to every gallon of liquor. One man tells about going to a house on the creek and finding the family all sitting around a great tin wash tub "proofing the whiskey." This meant they were mixing the first jar or two of the run, which would be exceedingly high proof, with the rest of the run which was progressively lesser proof, and then they were spiking the whole thing with their alcohol "beading oil."

"Them folks down in Knoxville want a big bead," the mountaineers say. "They'll shake up that fruit jar first thing to see how many bubbles they can get fizzing around. Well, this'll give 'em something to fizz, and pull their hair out too." And so the piles of empty isopropyl alcohol bottles pyramid along the Cosby roads and in abandoned fields. No self-respecting moonshiner would drink this stuff: it is strictly for the trade.

One of the largest public menaces growing out of the whole business comes from the boys who do the hauling. Most of the short runs, anything under a hundred miles, are assigned to teen-age boys who long ago abandoned the dull book-world of school for the two-fisted reality of man-talk and a souped-up motor. Some of them never passed the third or fourth grade. But they can dismember a car and put it back together with loving precision. They usually drive a black coupé with a built-up back that will hold a trunk full of loaded Mason jars without any telltale sag of the springs. All the pent-up energy and frustrated creativeness of their barren lives goes into their driving. Qualities which would be admirable in other undertakings—fearlessness, boldness, determination—make their driving a mortal hazard to every other motorist. They burn the highways, thread the back roads and alleys, bank the curves and shoot the straightaways, and link the moonshiners up coves and hollows with big-city bootleggers.

There are two agencies that try to deal with this lawlessness. They are known through the mountains as the big law and the little law. The little law is the local county sheriff and his deputies. Sometimes the little law is tough as tanbark and its honesty is unimpeachable; usually it is sieved with leaks and blinded with bribes. Its raids are desultory and uniformly unproductive. Occasionally a hundred gallons of mash go down the drain, or a dozen cases of already filled fruit jars are brought in as evidence.

The big law is the government officer, the A T U agent, the man in the two-door black car with the out-of-county license. It is the big law raid that sends a man to the penitentiary to "build time."

A few years ago the mountains rang with the reverberations of a triangle story that had a new twist. The feature characters were the big law and the little law and the moonshiners—but no one could decide just who were the villains or who the heroes of the piece.

On a steep ridge where the East Tennessee counties of Cocke and Sevier and Jefferson meet at a common boundary point, there was a still in operation and its presence was apparently known to both local and Federal officers. The only trouble was that the local officers said they were not just sure which county the still was in; some of these ridge boundary lines are rough and difficult to determine. At any rate, on this certain night, the Federal officers went up the mountain to stage a raid on the still, and they did not follow the customary procedure of informing a local sheriff and his deputies as to their plans.

They hid themselves behind strategic trees, bushes and rocks surrounding the stillsite and waited for morning to come, the usual time when distillers came in to begin their run. With the first faint gray light they saw a movement in the woods. There was a furtive reconnaissance by the handful of men approaching. The Federals shouted to their prisoners to drop their guns and raise their hands. When they dropped to the ground instead and started firing, the Federals let them have it. The mountain was filled with volleys and shouts.

Somewhere in the nearby woods a third group of men were listening in frozen amazement to the exchange. The moonshiners doubtless wondered who could have been ambushed at their still. For the A T U agents had only succeeded in killing one and capturing four officers of Jefferson County who had also come on a secret raid that same morning. Although the moonshiners felt the millennium had arrived with the two agencies of justice shooting it out between themselves, feeling ran high in the general area. Government interference in local affairs came in for some colorful drubbing and the moonshiners began to have company in their feud against revenuers. The Federal officers were tried in local court. Acquitted of criminal charges, they were still not acquitted by local opinion, and agents are now a little less zealous with their guns. In fact, there are few killings during raids any more. The days of isolation are gone in moonshining as in all else, and the law breakers know that a clever lawyer is better than a gun, or at worst a few months at the state pen are better than a lifetime in Atlanta.

Big law or little law, it's all a part of life to the French Broad people. A paradox of violence and gentleness, their crimes are not as a rule the impersonal cold-blooded robberies and murders of our big cities and gangs. They are crimes of emotion, sudden as spring freshets, sweeping all before them, over as soon as they begin, and with no gain, or thought of it, to anyone. And almost always they are personal. The people may have adopted all the machine gadgets they can afford, the men may have taken to automobiles with a furious devotion, the moonshiners may have seized every device available to make quick cheap liquor—but their feelings are not yet standardized. They remain—is it ever fair or reasonable to make a generalization about any group of humans?—they are, by and large, a naive, shrewd, kindly-when-they-want-to-be, wicked-when-the-spirit-moves-them people. To see them on a court day, to sit through one of their terms of criminal session, is to experience even today something that smacks of the best and worst that was part of our pioneer past, which follows a law of buried hungers and outer defiance that was larger and older than the man-made code of either the big or little law.

# 16

# Bread and Butter

If the way a man earns his living is the measure by which he spends his life, the people of the French Broad have often been at the same time poor and wealthy, wise and unwise. Poor in money, rich and wise in the self-satisfaction of their work, unwise in the pursuit of that work. Their past has been peculiarly independent, not only politically but economically as well. Not the necessities they had, but the luxuries they could do without were the measure of their freedom, and in the early days of settlement a very real freedom it was. One whose buried memory still stirs grandchildren and great-grandchildren who live along creekbanks or ridgetops to seek some intensely personal, less remunerative but perhaps more rewarding lifework than is usual in our mid-twentieth century. These, for the most part, are the basic labors, springing from the old relationship of man and earth, and man's simplest necessities.

It would be difficult to find a dozen people who have a family history in the French Broad country who don't count at least one farmer, and more likely several, among their ancestors. Even professional men by vocation were also farmers by necessity until recently, and savings were often deposited in lands rather than in banks. Bread and butter was plentiful, pungent bread from home-threshed wheat or unbolted corn meal, sweet butter fresh from the churn dash, but those early breadwinners developed many curious crafts and talents to earn money for the sugar and salt, coffee and spices that they could not grow. In the rugged Tennessee county of Sevier, bordered by the Smoky Mountains and sliced by the Little Pigeon River, there were 1,071 heads of families listed in a census of 1850. Of these, all but eighty-nine were designated farmers, with the exception of one or two candid souls who admittedly "did nothing." Of this 8 per cent of nonfarmers, blacksmiths (14), millers (11) and Baptist ministers (9) led the list. Half-a-dozen carpenters and wagonmakers, five merchants, three each of physicians, tanners, shoemakers and horse traders, a brace of lawyers, coopers, Methodist ministers, hammermen and saddlers, and a single hatter, miner, wheelwright, navigator and cabinetmaker just about complete a fairly clear picture of the pre-Civil War life of that and many a neighboring county.

In more important Knox County, at the mouth of the river, the chief industry of 1860, according to value of the product, was so overwhelmingly the manufacture of flour and meal that all other products, including iron castings, marble, lumber, blacksmithing, leather and a dozen others, in their combined value scarcely exceeded that one item of staple breadstuff production. This shows that the region produced mainly for its own needs and they were the basic ones.

Such outside money as came to the individual farms was usually for some allied work or product, and none of these means of mountain livelihood still followed today is older or more interesting than that of the herb gatherers. To stand in the dusky twilight of a sprawling herb warehouse and smell the bittersweet dust from the pungent piles of sassafras roots and dry tangy catnip leaves and unpleasant Jimson weed and aromatic white pine bark is to sense the primitive medicinal needs that surround us even in a machine age.

In 1849 reporter Charles Lanman, traveling down the river from Asheville to Paint Rock, met a man whom he considered a typical unlearned mountaineer until the fellow suddenly overwhelmed him by asking about the latest news from China. Further conversation revealed that the old man was a "sang digger," and since the "sang" he sold was shipped exclusively to China and Korea he had a very real link with that country. The actual name of the plant was ginseng, and its role in local history is one of the strangest on record. There is no known disease it cures, there is no human condition it has reportedly improved. In fact, of all the two hundred and more botanical species of medicinal herbs growing in this region, ginseng is the most useless. Useless but far from worthless, and consequently close to extinction here in its native habitat. For when a product may bring as high as fifteen dollars a pound, grows wild for the taking and requires only the investment of a hoe, a tow sack and some time to secure it, there can be little doubt its doom is sealed. From the year 1794 when André Michaux journeyed through these mountains and found the plant and told the local people about its ready market abroad, even showing them how to dig and prepare it for shipment, the hunt for "sang" was on.

Deep in the heart of North Carolina's Haywood County, along Jonathan Creek, Nimrod Jarrett and Bacchus Smith were hired by a Philadelphia doctor in the early part of the 1800's to develop the business of gathering ginseng, and they soon established a branch depot in Yancey County on the Cane River. Through 1893 the trade flourished, for in that year the North Carolina Department of Agriculture reported that this mountain section was "one of the chief sources of supply of medicinal herbs" and that "in travelling through the mountains bales of these herbs may be seen collected about the country stores as bales of cotton are seen in the Middle and Eastern Sections. Ginseng in great quantities is shipped to China." The Chinese "doctrine of signatures" makes ginseng a supposed cure-all in that country. The name itself comes from the Chinese "jin-tsang," meaning "manlike," and by the doctrine of signatures any medicine brewed from a plant having the same shape as the afflicted limb or organ will be effective. Since many ginseng roots resemble the complete human figure, it, then, would be a general remedy for all ills.

Catering to this Oriental market, many a mountaineer in the heart of Western North Carolina and East Tennessee learned to look for the inconspicuous green plant with the three large and two small leaves on the same slender stem, growing in deep shade and frequently fifty to seventy-five years old. Young plants, under five to seven years, and cultivated ones were never as commercially successful as the old wild half-hidden ginseng, and as the diggers pushed farther and farther back into the forests, never leaving part of a root to make new growth, uncertain and indifferent as to how to preserve young as yet unprofitable plants because it was impossible to judge their age except by the unearthed root, ginseng became ever rarer and its gatherers worked themselves out of a job. From the seven cents a pound considered "very profitable" when Bacchus and Nimrod were in the business, the price has spiraled to a present ten to fifteen dollars a pound. It is still the most valuable of all herbs, the "growing gold" of the mountains.

But there are hundreds of others infinitely more useful, and plentiful. Of some 250 botanical drugs produced in the United States at least 75 per cent are gathered in the mountains of Western North Carolina. One of the unique features of the industry is that it is supposedly practiced by the most ignorant people of the region, yet it requires technical knowledge as precise as that of most industries. The main difference is that the herb gatherer's knowledge is ancient and traditional. It is an inheritance passed down by word of mouth and daily demonstration, and is often more valuable than the four-poster bed or the west field named in a will. The skill consists of knowing which plants and bushes, vines and trees contain medicinal qualities, and whether the virtue lies in their leaves or roots, berries or bark. In the days when every home was also its own hospital and drugstore, the knowledge also included recipes for use. A rhyme sometimes held the dull fact more firmly in memory.

If she has flu, your daughter Pansy,
Quickly give her
A dose of tansy.

If her fever runs quite high,
There's Joe Pye weed
For you to try.

If she has a cough that's deep,
Give white pine syrup,
It's very cheap.

And now, although they may buy their medicines from the counter of the drugstore at the county seat, many of these families still range the mountains in spring and summer for the bark, flowers, leaves, and in winter for roots, that will eventually find their way into almost every medicine chest in the country. The world's largest dealer in botanical drugs, S. B. Penick and Company, maintains one of its major collection warehouses at Asheville (there is no drugstore anywhere in the world that does not have at least one of this company's products), and here, through the year, come the great tangled bundles of plants and barks and roots that will be baled in burlap to be shipped to manufacturers and wholesalers, or pulverized and packed in the clean round bellies of white oak barrels.

With spring the seasonal procession begins. Comes the last digging of roots before new season's growth sets in, and first stripping of bark just as sap begins to flow. Then leaves and plants and flowers push into growth. In March featherlike leaves of turkey corn are followed by its white queer-shaped blossoms from which a "blood purifier" is made; then white blossoms of bloodroots, *sanguinaria,* used in treatment of bronchitis. Mandrake or May apple, then yellow ragwort, snakeroot and wild ginger that are mountain tonics, with the cohoshes used to control nervous disorders such as St. Vitus's dance. In May the delicate lady's-slippers glow pink and yellow in soft-mulched woods, and Indian hemp, used in treatment of Bright's disease and dropsy, follows the fringe bush; in midsummer come Indian tobacco and common Jimson and pokeweeds used to combat asthma; and in late summer the heather-colored boneset, for colds and fevers, fringes gullies and swamps. The balm of Gilead (or "gilly b'am"), ingredient of healing ointments, especially for earache, is left for winter. Then also the fronds of ferns are gathered, boiled and used as remedy for colds and whooping cough.

These and a couple of hundred other plants offer each year new crops for the uncounted families who will pick, sort, dry and sell them. The drying is most important. Where color in the final product is of no consequence, the family spread their herbs in sunlight and open air, but where color counts, a barn loft or shed is used and in this process of curing a large per cent of the diggers' labors are lost, for it takes from three to six pounds of fresh root to make one pound of the dried. But the one factor dealers most insist on is dryness: roots are dried until they break with a snap, and leaves, herbs and flowers until they crumble in the hand.

It is common regional knowledge that the bark of the buckeye, hickory, holly, Judas tree, sumac and sourwood have valuable curative qualities. Less known is that the despised poison oak is used in treatment of rheumatism, paralysis and some eye diseases. From life-everlasting blossoms, a healing salve is made. Dandelion, pest of city lawns, and dock leaves are rich in medicinal properties. Butterfly weed is a remedy for pleurisy, and the common mullein is unequaled as an ingredient of cough syrup.

Most people, if they think at all along these lines, take it for granted that herbs, roots and barks are used, if for anything, only for medicinal purposes. It is amazing, therefore, to learn the many other uses of hundreds of these natural products. They supply the textile, canning, cosmetic, insecticide, dairy, soap and beverage industries with essential ingredients for their products and operations. The oil of sweet birch, wintergreen, sassafras and peppermint is used to flavor candy, chewing gum, tooth paste and tooth powder.

Probably no product in America so instantly reflects supply and demand ratio as these crude drugs. Amounts paid for the gathered herbs are so changeable that price lists must be issued sometimes as often as once a month. For this is one of those rare businesses in which prices are controlled largely, not by the consumer, but by the gatherer. As certain herbs accumulate, prices on the current list are lowered and that stems the tide of supply momentarily while some more profitable plant is sought and dug. This is not as simple as it sounds, for one uncontrollable factor influences the picture: nature and her vagaries. Wild plants vary widely and unaccountably from one season to another, and only prices can influence the herb gatherers to counteract shortages by prolonged searching of remote corners. It is a unique business from woods beginning to factory ending, this gathering of nature's medicines.

The gathering of her beauties has also been, and is, a business of the French Broad people. They range from the waxy hidden galax leaves of the lowland woods to the tall balsams of Roan Mountain, on the dividing line between Tennessee and North Carolina. Especially before the coming of factories to the area, shipping galax and other evergreens to Northern markets was an important item of trade for numerous families.

There are some who say that the galax grows nowhere else in the world except in the Southern Appalachians. The story goes that a doctor's wife in North Carolina first shipped it out of the state and received two dollars for every hundred leaves. Its beautiful shape, glossy texture and excellent keeping qualities made it popular in the cities. Foresters were among the first to encourage galax picking. Since galax and forest fire cannot inhabit the same area, foresters saw this industry as one sure way to combat fires with galax pickers as volunteer rangers quick to spot flames and present to help stamp them out before they spread. Since the leaves were, and are, pulled just above the roots, there is no threat to new leaves, just as

large and healthy, that will come forth next year. Prices for galax
have ranged, over thirty years, from forty to ninety cents per thousand leaves. Picked in the winter, between November and March,
in large gunny sacks, sorted by the fire at night and tied in neat
bouquets of twenty-five leaves, galax is perhaps the most unusual
greenery by which the French Broad country is represented in distant winter decorations, but there are others too: ground pine,
holly, balsam boughs, mistletoe, Christmas trees.

And the old refrain of waste in the French Broad country re-
sounds here again. One of those minute incidents almost too inconsequential to record and yet too common to overlook, characteristic of too many of the people and events of the river—all in a
story of mistletoe. Along the banks of Big Creek in upper Cocke
County, and down the banks of the French Broad below their
junction, grew, in the 1800's, hundreds of tall white sycamore trees.
Until 1883 there hung from these trees a magnificent growth of
mistletoe, and in the winter when the white-skinned limbs were
bare of all foliage but these dark green leaves with their clusters
of pearly white berries, it was a sight of rare beauty. But in that
year the sight was destroyed forever. A boy who lived on Big Creek
remembered long after: "One day in mid-December some men
came up from Knoxville and, without so much as by your leave,
proceeded to strip the trees of their armfuls of mistletoe, packed it
in half-a-dozen big hogsheads and marked them for shipment to
Knoxville. Then, just as the hogsheads were about to be loaded
aboard the car, came a message to the head man of the crew. He
turned to me (for I was station agent) and said, in a voice as if
choked by a mouthful of green persimmons, 'Don't ship it. They
say they don't want no more mistletoe.' "

The haphazard waste of so small a thing as mistletoe could
be tragic when expanded to include the forests. For years lumbering has been one of the leading occupations of the region and yet
it is still surprising to hear the tales of failure and bankruptcy, to
realize how little money, even, was salvaged from the slaughter of

the trees. From days of the first ax-wielding settlers through the coming of the slash sawmills, the entrepreneurs like A. A. Arthur with his Scottish Carolina Company and the half-dozen hasty companies that followed him (and failed) on the same boundary, the arrival of the band sawmill and the really big operators, the policy has been almost completely one of cut out and get out. Two factors have influenced the really disastrous cutting of mountains too steep for any successful use except timber growth: one, obviously, the quick cash from lumber or pulp or acid woods, and the other, the constant need of marginal farmers for a little more cleared corn or pasture land. That the lumber might scarcely pay for itself under difficult conditions, or that the cleared fields could maintain their fertility and soil only a few seasons at best, required a foresight that was forestalled by the immediacy of family needs for cash. Furthermore, a man needed to be doing man's work and what more manly than following his pioneer grandfather's ways? The groping, thoughtless little farmers were as much the unconscious villains of forest waste as the giant timber companies; today many of the farmers and companies alike who once treated the woods as a mine look upon them as a crop. Industries dependent on wood have, in the enlightenment of self-preservation, developed a program of planting and education that may gradually repopulate many of the blasted hills with the hardwoods and pines and poplars they were designed by nature to support in this great forest belt of the Appalachians. Tree farmers are becoming as respectable as corn growers, and as prosperous.

It is perhaps symbol and prophecy and challenge that the North and West forks of the French Broad headwaters, lying in wide forested cups of Transylvania County, are now owned by a lumber company. Fifty-two years ago, before there was even a satisfactory rail connection ("two strips of rust running into Brevard, the county seat, that was all"), the company's founder, J. S. Silversteen, came down from Stroudsburg, Pennsylvania, and staked his claim on the lumber of the basin where the French Broad is born. Over 140,000 acres he cut, 30,000 of which he had bought from George Vanderbilt. From the virgin tulip poplars—six feet, eight feet in diameter—and the pine and hardwoods, he shipped lumber; from the heavy stand of chestnuts he extracted tannic acid, even after blight struck and left the chestnuts like bleached gray bones on the hills. "There was fine water. An untouched place to develop. Mighty rough. It's nice to talk about pioneering, but it's hell when you're doing it. But I'm still here. It's still fine. I ship lumber from right here to all parts of the country—including the West where they don't have poplar or oak." Flooring for a house in Montana, bread and butter for the French Broad dwellers along the uppermost reaches of the river, from one of the region's oldest occupations.

It was farther down the river that "clearings" really scalped the mountains, making room to raise that man-and-animal staple, corn, to fatten and feed the droves of hogs, cattle, mules that came from and through the countryside till just before the turn of the century. After the Civil War another crop flared into prominence, another of the heavy feeders that required rich new ground for growing and, for a while at least, repaid with high prices. Tobacco seemed momentarily the region's savior, but evidence of its final destructiveness still marks almost every mile along the middle length of the river.

The results of this cultivation were already apparent in 1888 when a traveler in East Tennessee reported that one farmer, who had cultivated a ridge back of his house that was as steep as a roof, nevertheless assured him that it had been ploughed with mules, to which the traveler replied that the harvesting must have been done by squirrels. He reported that the soil was good enough if it would only stay in place, but the hillsides he saw were seamed with gullies, and the discolored state of the streams he passed was understandable when he had seen this cultivated land which was no sooner cleared than it began to wash.

But Asheville in North Carolina and Greeneville in Tennes-

see were flourishing tobacco markets, Greeneville in 1887 selling
some 2,000,000 pounds and Asheville in 1890 selling 5,000,000,
all the bright yellow variety. No wonder the state Board of Agriculture could report in 1893 a great increase in land values, especially in Madison County with its superior bright leaf, and that
"mountain sides and tops that seemed destined forever to wear
their vesture and crown of forests have been brought into cultivation. Men that ten years ago scarcely knew the sight or name of
money have become prosperous and relatively rich."

Almost as suddenly as it had soared, however, the market
now plummeted. As one Cocke County man remembered: "For
two or three years we waited hopefully for prices to come back;
but they didn't come back, and, that we might better forget, we
tore down our tobacco barns and made stovewood of the logs. It
was a good many years before our folks recovered sufficiently from
the debacle of the 'fire-cyored yaller' to try their hand at tobacco
again, and then it was burley, which required an entirely different type of barn." So there was a lull between tobacco booms, but
today, with growing-quotas to control production and ever-im-
proving fertilizer programs to increase yield, burley tobacco is the
main cash crop of the French Broad country. At Greeneville, county
seat of Greene County, Tennessee, during the tobacco season ending in early 1953, a higher average price was paid per pound for
burley than in any other of the fifty-eight markets of the tobacco
belt. Into the 23,000,000 pounds they sold, Knoxville's 18,000,000
pounds, Morristown's 9,500,000, Asheville's 8,500,000, into these
bulk figures were gathered the labors and hopes from thousands of
little individual farms.

Raising tobacco, they say, is a job for thirteen months of the
year. From the first blue wisp of brush smoke that precedes even
spring in the woods and proclaims the burning of a seedbed to be
followed by the white cocoonlike stretches of canvas protecting the
precious plants, from those first signs on the mountains to the final
brown-golden harvest stacked along mile after mile of warehouse

floor, tobacco tending is a combination of labor and luck. No matter how constant the labor, it is all for nothing if summer hail slashes the broad soft leaves to ribbons. No matter how good the luck of seed and weather and market, it will not count if informed labor has not made use of it. You study the faces of old tobacco growers as they stand on a warehouse floor and wait for their year's crop to be sold, their whole year's labor to be evaluated in a matter of minutes, and you know it would take one of the old Dutch or Flemish masters to record the earthiness of those countenances—fine lines around the eyes that come from studying the weather, working against summer sun or winter snow; lines across the forehead that come from studying the problems of disease and insects; deep lines beside the mouth, set by the determination born of bad seasons and fickle nature. They wait for the auctioneers to reach their baskets and their features mask hope and pride as carefully as they will presently hide disappointment or surprise.

Of all major farm crops in the United States, tobacco is the only one still sold by open auction to the highest bidder. On the floor of long warehouses, representatives from all the major tobacco companies in the country move along the aisles looking at the shallow baskets of tobacco already graded and labeled by a Federal inspector. Gathered with them around the baskets are the warehousemen, the auctioneer and the ticket marker. A warehouseman opens each bid and the odd chant of the auctioneer begins. By half-cent increases and practically invisible signals, the bid goes up. A faint nod, a flicker of the eyelash, a movement of the finger: these are the signs an auctioneer must catch from the wary buyers. His curious chant increases in intensity until at last it reaches its climax: "Sold, American!" "Sold, Reynolds!" He names the price, a ticket is fastened on the basket, the men in gabardine overcoats move on, and the man in faded overalls is left to consider his fortune or failure. Some of the cash he collects at the warehouse window will be set aside for the expensive little seeds and fertilizer to begin next season's crop.

In the past decade, two newcomers have appeared to share King Tobacco's throne as a cash-reaper in the French Broad. Poultry and cattle. In 1953 in Western North Carolina, dairying and beef cattle together brought in $10,000,000; poultry, which "came from nowhere four years ago," brought $12,500,000. An acre of Ladino clover and orchard grass has been found to produce more pounds of beef or milk than an acre of corn, with less labor, better soil fertility and no erosion. The French Broad country a few years ago imported milk daily from Northern states, particularly Wisconsin, and today it stands not only self-sufficient but in some sections on brink of overproduction. And yet, beef and dairy cattle are not the land cure-all they have sometimes been represented. There are those who fear this may be the beginning of another era similar to the first tobacco debacle. In a country as mountainous as East Tennessee and Western North Carolina, the TVA forest and soil services, state and government farm bureaus and local demonstrators should take a long look at the advisability of many of the steep pastures trying to catch seed. In a section of the United States known as part of the great forest belt, where grass does not voluntarily follow in the wake of clearing or even cultivation but must, even after continued planting and on as carefully tended fields as those of the Biltmore Farms, be reseeded every seven to ten years, under these conditions many of the hillsides and hilltops now being artificially coaxed by fertilizer subsidies and pasture enthusiasts would seem more wisely returned to their original forests and tree-cropped, with gentler lands receiving the concentration of improved fertilization and farming methods. But the fact that livestock has reached the French Broad again as a big-time industry (during the days of the great stock drives it was here but on a different basis) means almost surely a more prosperous countryside. As one Tennessee lawyer said, telling of a nearby settlement and its recent transformation from unofficial Moonshine Capital of the South: "Few years ago all they did there was hide out in the laurel thickets and make liquor. Now they're getting onto the tourist and chicken bandwagon, they're forming companies for motels and signing agreements among themselves stipulating that no 'intoxicating beverages' shall be made or sold on the premises. And they're raising chickens, big brooder houses and broiler-growing houses you'll see as you drive up the creek. That's what they're tending now. Two biggest feuders on the creek, carried a gun for each other for years because of a fight over a still, now they're in this restaurant company together and a chicken business and they've got a working friendship."

It is groups and individuals working together that make these farms successful. Groups like the Farmer's Federation, a co-operative with a family background (the McClures and Clarkes of Chicago, originally, now of Asheville for a generation), and a business with economic, social and religious purposes. The Federation has led the way in many new fields of endeavor. Once they were helping people back in the mountains sell wreaths made from native evergreens. Now they are at the forefront in the chicken-growing business, improving methods of production and expanding markets at the same time. James G. K. McClure, founder and head of the Federation, is perhaps the only man in the French Broad country who could and does manage, with equal success, an annual picnic at the Waldorf and picnic at Waynesville. At the Waldorf Astoria in New York he acquaints other regions with the work and necessities of the mountain region, and his guest list of over a thousand includes many captains of industry and finance. At Waynesville in Haywood and other county seats through the mountains, he acquaints the local people with their own agricultural problems and achievements, and the guest list includes all who want to come, from town mayor to ridgetop farmer.

Then there are individuals like "Alfalfa Bob" Phillips in rugged little Mitchell County. "Mr. Bob" worked for some fifteen years with the TVA Extension program, learning the meaning and method of good soil practice, and it was one segment, he says, "of a planned but free economy that has enslaved nobody, but through democratic means has inspired our people to live fuller and richer lives." "Mr. Bob" himself did some inspiring, too, by the example of his own rolling pastures and fields of alfalfa, by buttonholing everyone he knew and many he didn't, three hundred or more other farmers, he figures, and telling them of the virtues of alfalfa. That's when he was christened "Alfalfa Bob." Someone has said that more praise is due him who makes two blades of grass grow where only one grew before than to him who conquers kingdoms. And as the idea of conquering nature gives place more constantly to a feeling of alliance with her, more blades of grass, more trees, will green the French Broad hills and valleys.

Because many of the farms are still small and marginal, however, and, too, because some of the people are just naturally artistic and creative, it has been estimated that more than six thousand people within a hundred-mile radius of Asheville, probably twice that if the whole river basin were included, earn all or part of their living by fashioning things with their hands. From hooked rugs to silverware, from amethyst earrings to woolen coverlets, from hand-turned chairs to pottery pitchers, these handicraft industries are something old and something new, something borrowed, something true. Their creators' names are legion: Marshall Mills and Lucy Morgan, Stuart Nye and Douglas Ferguson, Roby Buchanan and Arval Woody; all the men and women, young and old, highly educated and unschooled, who make with their hands something beautiful, durable, unique.

At Boone Forge, in the mountains of Western North Carolina, Marshall Mills has kept alive the art wrought at the forge. At the Williamsburg, Virginia, restoration, the hardware and fireplace accessories, cooking utensils and lanterns and other handwrought iron are products not of Virginia's past, but of the North Carolina mountains of the present.

The weaving revived by Miss Lucy Morgan was lost until she rescued it in the northeasternmost corner of the French Broad area just in time to save it from oblivion. From simple beginnings, her Penland School of Handicrafts grew to be what is today the largest strictly craft school in the United States. Besides weaving and pottery, still her major specialties, there are sixty related crafts taught to students who come from all countries of the world. Here, on the remote Toe River, where casual travelers would seldom penetrate and if they did would expect to find the most isolated and lonely people, is a school community which included in the typical season of 1952 people from thirty-four states, Alaska, Haiti, the Philippines, Finland, North Rhodesia, Korea, China, Japan, Bolivia, India, Germany, Canada and Puerto Rico. Workers in their teens and in their eighties shared knowledge and enthusiasm. It was the artistry and satisfaction of handicrafts that drew from such different people a common joy of experience.

As for Stuart Nye, whose name is known in sterling jewelry throughout the forty-eight states, he never set foot inside a craft school, read a book on silverwork or even planned to work in metals, but he has wound up today a famous craftsman. A friend, who was hard up and moving away from North Carolina, urged Nye to buy the small supply of hammers, equipment and silver he couldn't take with him. "I scraped together the ninety dollars and I was in business. I'd worked in wood before, but never silver. I just loved the silver. It was so soft and lustrous." He made some pieces of costume jewelry for which there was a slow sale. Then one day he created a dogwood blossom in silver, the four petals classic and graceful in their simplicity, and his future was sealed. People liked that lovely little design—they bought it in pins and earrings and bracelets. Stuart Nye hired a helper, then another and another. At last he had a little factory. Salesmen called and pointed out how much more rapidly the girls could make the pins if they used a form die and stamped out the pieces, but they made scant headway with a man who believes hands are to use and feel with. "I think it's remarkable the way the business just grew," he says and shrugs in self-deprecation. "I think it's due to the fact it was a new type of jewelry—very simple. No one before had taken a simple leaf and made a pin out of it. They took a leaf and added a flower, and a stem, and a bud and then set a stone in the whole thing. By that time it was so complicated it had to be interpreted."

Simplicity was the keynote of the Douglas Fergusons' beginnings too. At the village of Pigeon Forge on the Little Pigeon River in Tennessee's Sevier County, Ferguson and his wife discovered some unusual and excellent clay by watching a tribe of dirt daubers build their nests. They fired several of the nests and found the quality of "bisque," or fired clay, very good. When they traced the insects to the clay beds, they found a natural supply of superior clays for the pottery they had been designing. Another old craft was turned into a new business.

Roby Buchanan at the post office of Hawk, North Carolina, had both a craft and an occupation for many years and it was hard to keep them separate. With the water power that ground corn into meal between the heavy turning stones of his mill, Roby also polished the gem stones he collected in the surrounding hills. He ground corn for a living and found gems for a pleasure, although once in a while he did sell some particularly fine specimen. But he never made a neighbor who'd brought his sack of corn to mill wait till he'd finished work on an aquamarine or garnet or moonstone or ruby or amethyst. Gems were "for pretty" and folks wanting them could wait, but meal was the first food in a mountain home and if the barrel was empty it had to be replenished. When the old millrace and wheel washed away in a flood and Roby never restored them but bought an electric motor for his cutting and polishing, it marked the end of a miller and the beginning of a lapidary. Up this hidden little cove and into the unpainted weathered old mill house come tourists and letters and orders. The letters reach him even when they've such scant address as: "Roby, Hawk, N.C." or "Mr. Roby Buchanan, Mitchell Mountains, North Carolina" or just "Stoneman, Hawk, N.C." because he has gone out into his native earth and found beauty buried deep in the heart of rocks and brought it to life and form.

Arval Woody can remember hearing his grandfather tell of hauling chairs he'd made for twenty-five or thirty miles across the Blue Ridge by sled and oxen to sell three for a dollar. And some of those Artur Woody chairs made three quarters of a century ago are still being used today. They're worn at the top and sides by generations of children pushing them over the floor for trains, but otherwise they're stout as new. Woodys have been making chairs, in the country of the upper Toe River where Grassy and Rockhouse creeks come together, for five generations. Not tables or chests or cabinets: just chairs, because they know how to make them handsome—the old Colonial designs with a good linseed oil finish on solid black walnut and cherry—and how to make them strong. No screw or nail or glue is used in a Woody chair, and it cannot become wobbly, because of a family formula worked out generations ago. Thoroughly dried rounds are set into the four chair posts while the posts are still green. As these dry and tighten around the rounds, a stable joint to last a lifetime is formed.

Grandfather Artur made somewhere between 4,500 and 5,000 chairs in his lifetime. His son Martin and grandsons Arval and Walter have made how many? They're in every state in the union, as close by as a neighbor's sitting room and as far away as Finland. From Artur's simple square little kitchen chair with white-oak splits for the seat to the tall ladderbacks and woven fiber seats today, methods and styles have changed, but the basic quality has remained a family pride. Only the dollars the chairs earn have more demands today. "A dollar was good money in those days," Artur used to say of his sales by sled and oxen. "Taxes were mighty low then. We raised most of our food on the farm and a dollar would go a long way at the general store." On fourteen acres of mountain land, Grandfather Woody earned his independent bread and butter and passed a tradition down to the coming generations.

Such are the basic livelihoods of the French Broad country that grew out of the natural surroundings and human needs: herbs and shrubs, lumber and pulpwood, farming—corn, tobacco, cattle, poultry, a half-dozen lesser items of apples and truck vegetables, gladiolus and tulip bulbs—and the old handicrafts preserved among contemporary pioneers. There are other jobs too, new, well-paying jobs down the length of the river. For the part-time farmers and for those who wanted "to go to town," the big factories were the salvation they sought. Beside the aged luster of these old ways, the new ones glittered like chromium beneath fluorescent lights.

# 17

# $\mathcal{TV}$'s and $\mathcal{V}8$'s

The face of the country changes. Railroads and highways thread the mountains, booming smokestacks pierce the sky, log cabins are veneered with imitation brick, and the ways of some of the people change too. Dust-splattered, mud-crusted cars make Rebel's Creek and Bat Harbor suburbs of nearby towns, the geometric palms of television antennae roof-blossoming even on village back streets and up obscure hill coves bring the cities to the country. The V8's and the TV's are taking over, and the French Broad country is not only adapting to them, it is profiting from them and helping make them, as well.

When *familia Americana* in Maine or Montana, South Carolina or South Dakota, Iowa or Texas, spends a "typical" Sunday afternoon and evening—washing the Sunday dinner dishes, reading a newspaper and thumbing through one of the big magazines, going for a ride in the family car, relaxing with a cigarette and finally having a supper snack in front of the television screen—some vital ingredient in every object they use is supplied from the French Broad country.

The French Broad does not seem like an industrial area, but the gleam of the enamel at that sink where the family work, the paper of that *Life* magazine they may read, the tire cord and dozens of essential insulators in the car they drive for their afternoon out-

ing, the paper their cigarettes are rolled in, the basic materials of
the plates from which they eat their suppers and the glasses from
which they drink, and perhaps the very television machine they
watch, certainly some of its parts—all come from this river basin.
Material for the rayons or nylons some of the family wear may
easily be from the area, too, along with a dozen other items, but
these mentioned are indicative of the total picture.

Yet, producing all these machine goods, the people on the
French Broad and Pigeon, Davidson and Nolichucky and Toe still
do not seem like an industrial population. They are not. And
therein lies another of the paradoxes of this region: factories came
to the French Broad and its tributaries because the people were
not of a manufacturing background—but they were highly intelligent. Talk with the chief men of these companies, local officials or
executives from another region, and certain common details will
add up to an interesting total. In varying vernacular they may tell
you: We needed good water, we thought these surroundings would
attract young executives for homesites, we found the raw material
we needed. And they will certainly tell you: We liked the laborers
here. They live on their own land, 90 per cent of them, they have
a pig fattening in the pen, a milch cow in the barn, a few chickens
and a garden; they're not rootless and frustrated, looking for more
security, because they already have it. When factory workers live
at home on family farms they're stable workers. The turnover of
employees is remarkably small in all these plants. And because of
the regional stereotype which exists in most people's minds, pic-
turing Southeastern mountaineers as careless and indolent while
Northeastern workers are brisk and efficient, it is a refreshing surprise to have one of these transplanted executives reveal that in
his opinion and experience just the opposite is many times true.

The erroneous viewpoint that confused literacy with intelligence has in part already been corrected. Because some of the
mountain people had until recently little schooling and often still
clung to old ways and ideas, it was frequently assumed they were

uneducatable and somehow backward. A few initial experiences of typical industries entering the region soon dispelled this idea, however. From the mines of Mitchell County on the upper Toe River, northernmost fastness of the French Broad watershed, to the concrete bulk of Douglas Dam and the tremendous power concept of the Tennessee Valley Authority on the main lower body of the river, companies found that the people were as valuable a resource as water or minerals or timber. Five of the largest and most interesting of these are also five of the most different types of industry in the region, and their story is a revelation of change, perhaps progress.

The oldest of these locally is also the only one native to the region. The Tar Heel Mica Company, founded by David Vance in 1891, deals in one of the minerals that has made the village of Spruce Pine in the Western North Carolina hills seem in many ways more like a Far Western mining town than like a Southern community. Spruce Pine is the center of a 250-square-mile area including Mitchell, Yancey and parts of Avery counties, from which comes 90 per cent of the nation's mica, 75 per cent of its feldspar and the only significant amounts of primary kaolin in the Western Hemisphere. A large part of this mining is done in small operations—"ground-hog holes," the local people call them, penetrate the sides of hill after hill in these counties, and the raw wound of many an abandoned digging gapes on the mountainsides, giving the country an appearance different from the rest of the French Broad watershed.

Ever since the Civil War, when a northern traveler happened to see a large sheet of "isinglass" in one of the cabins where he stopped overnight and from there developed the sheet-mica business, at one time supplying practically all isinglass used in the old-fashioned stove windows in this country or Canada, the uncertainty and excitement attendant on a mineral economy has existed in varying degrees through these mountains. A horseback tourist of 1874 told of being greeted everywhere he went in this vicinity by

the question, "Good mornin', gentlemen. After rocks?" It surprised
him that so many "rock hunters" had been ahead of him in these
mountains and that they had already infected the farmers with
fever over mica and other mineral riches. Some of the results of
this "rock fever" were alarmingly apparent a dozen years later
when both business and tempers were booming, small fortunes were
being made and lost in reckless living, and lawsuits over land titles
and claims were keeping the lawyers busy with a small bonanza
of their own. There was the claim fight over the Cebe Miller mine
that seemed to bring the whole epoch to a climax. Down a steep,
tree-covered mountain you can look today toward the abandoned
mine over whose possession three men were murdered not a hundred yards from where you stand. Two other men were fugitives
from law the rest of their lives, and sharpest irony of all, the rich
vein of mica was already drained of its value.

There were other eruptions of violence too, against "Tallies"
and "Niggers"—Italians and Negroes—brought in to help build
roads or mine. But as gem prospecting faded into the background,
as the only emerald mine operated anywhere in the United States
was abandoned and the less glamorous, more constant, minerals
settled into fairly steady production, as Spruce Pine matured and
people prospered, life also became steadier. Today mica and its
products are used in most of the electrical and electronic devices
being manufactured, as insulators in toasters and irons, in automobiles and Diesel engines, in roofing, oil drilling equipment and
high-quality paints; primary kaolin goes into the making of fine
china, rubber goods, refractories, Fiberglass; and feldspar finds its
way to the factories of glassmakers, into the shining enamel of
bathtubs and sinks and refrigerators, even into some of the dental
plates sparkling before Hollywood cameras and youthfulizing old
age: millions of tons of these minerals each year, in steady flow
and improving quality, with no more event than the daily work
of making a living.

When Peter Thomson of Hamilton, Ohio, selected the cross-

roads of Canton, on the Big Pigeon River, as the site for his projected new pulp and paper mill in 1906, he did so because of three
major resources found here in especially happy combination: first,
an abundance of clean water; second, a satisfactory timber supply;
and third, intelligent labor. That he needed these resources in
quantity is evidenced by the amounts of each now used by this
largest single industry in the French Broad region. Each day the
Champion Paper and Fiber Company at Canton turns some
50,000,000 gallons of water from the Pigeon River through its plant.
It consumes 1,500 cords of pulpwood a day and employs 2,700
people.

When these approximately seventy carloads of pine logs and
thirty carloads of hardwoods are dumped daily into the great ro-
tating drums which bark and chip them, the digesters which cook
them and separate the cellulose fibers in the wood from the lignin,
resins and fats, then into the bleachers, beaters and final finishing
machines, they are transformed into paper of various grades for
many various uses. *Life* magazine takes fifty thousand tons a year.
The American Can Company uses Champion paper for its milk
containers. Government postal cards and many types of stationery,
mimeograph and offset papers are all from Champion. These are
some of the products that the wood and water and workers of the
French Broad produce.

At one point in its process from wood to paper, pulp is nearly
99 per cent water, the pure water of Big Pigeon River. And to
supply those chippers and digesters and rollers, many a hilltop or
tree farm has been stripped of every twig or carefully reduced of
its crop. Which of the two has occurred—stripping or cropping—
depends largely on the individual owner. That Champion was in
the forefront in encouraging people throughout its area to consider
trees a resource which could and must be replenished, is a tribute
to its foresightedness as a business and a member of the community. More specifically, it is probably a tribute to the man who
was the company's leader for some four decades.

Reuben B. Robertson, Peter Thomson's son-in-law and a man of rugged ability both on the business and social levels, was also a far-seer. One of the very reasons his company had come to these Appalachians was because of the seemingly inexhaustible supply of raw material, but he was one of the earliest industrialists not to be lulled by this economy of abundance and to begin a campaign of conservation. In 1920 his company employed its first professional forester, and longer and longer strides were made toward leading other industries, as well as individuals, into a program of forest management. He realized the value of two of his greatest resources at a time when many leaders were either exploiting these resources or underestimating their final importance in an industry's success. They were the resources of woods and workers. Through a prolonged advocacy of good forest usage—selective cutting, replanting, fire control—he was able to help point the way toward what should be a planned feast rather than a possible famine in wood products. Through years of successful industrial relations with his employees —good wages, personal contacts, numerous and constant extra incentives—Robertson laid a firm foundation of workers' good will. These two of the three great natural assets Champion found in the French Broad country, it has handled with more than usual enlightened self-interest. Considered in the reverse light, of Champion's asset to the community, its belching smokestacks have meant cash in a countryside short on cash, it has meant comparative certainty in an economy based almost solely on the uncertainties of farming.

When Enka Corporation of America, owned by a parent Dutch company, located its rayon factories on Hominy Creek in Buncombe County, in 1928, and on the Nolichucky River in Hamblen County, Tennessee, in 1948, it, too, came because of water and workers. With a pipe line to the French Broad river five miles away supplementing their North Carolina stream's supply, and with the volume of the Nolichucky to draw on in Tennessee, water was assured—even in the fifty-million-gallon daily quantities used by the two plants last year. As for the workers, they had never been factory laborers before, and the Dutchmen who came to run this industry saw that learning the rayon processes would be easier if other processes did not first have to be unlearned. Here again, they owned their own homes and farms too; they were a settled people.

The combination of Scotch-Irish employees and Dutch employers was, especially in the early days, interesting. The latter were precise, honest, inclined to be dictatorial; and they didn't like credit. They had put sixteen million dollars in the bank before they bought an acre of land in 1928 and they had no commitments, either in North Carolina or Tennessee, when their plants were built. They had had no land given them and no tax exemptions. The Dutch believed that debts of that sort are never paid, and they wanted to know precisely where they stood at all times. The less rigid, more emotional, thoroughly democratic Scotch-Irish natives watched these Hollanders and waited, laughing a little at the military hierarchy in the executive branch, liking the solid integrity that grew on the community.

There are three main processes which produce the rayon filament yarn that makes cloth for almost every type of wearing apparel, rugs and upholsteries, cable covering, and a cord that goes into making all the standard brands of tires for automobiles, buses, trucks and airplanes. Of these processes, the one used at Enka is called the viscose, and by it cellulose from spruce, pine and hemlock pulp and from cotton linters is transformed into the yellow syrup of viscose. Through the gold and platinum thimble of a spinnerette perforated with 18 to 720 almost invisible holes, the factory simulates a giant silkworm, forcing the viscose through a bath of chemicals where it solidifies into a rayon thread made up of these 18 to 720 filaments.

These are the continuous processes, twenty-four hours a day, three hundred and sixty-five days a year, which the four thousand workers of Enka supervise. Grandchildren of women who never

heard of a material called rayon, who wove linsey-woolsey by chinked stone chimneys along the Nolichucky and Hominy Creek and French Broad, these grandchildren now ride in to work from many of the same family farms their grandparents had and help in the spinning of fifty million pounds of rayon a year.

Pure water was *the* prime consideration that brought another major industry to one of the headwaters of the French Broad and when the new company, manufacturing a product new to American industry, came to name its plant begun in June, 1938, and completed a year later, the name chosen was altogether appropriate: Ecusta, the Cherokee Indian word for rippling water.

Ecusta, the industry, was a culmination of one man's dream and determination. On the day that the German armies under Hitler's direction rolled into Poland, the machines of Ecusta, under the direction of German-born Harry Straus, rolled forth their first sheets of native cigarette paper. Almost a decade of experiment, disappointment and planning had preceded this moment of production when America was freed from dependence on foreign sources for her supply of cigarette wrappings.

Before Harry Straus's experiments, cigarette paper was manufactured in France from linen rags. After he had come to America in 1902 at the age of eighteen, and risen from a salesman of cigarette paper to the controlling ownership of a French mill, Harry Straus began to feel uneasy over dependence on Europe's wandering ragpickers. Why shouldn't cigarette paper be made in the United States, largest consumer of cigarettes? Since linen was made from flax, why not go directly to the raw material and manufacture from it?

The problem was to separate, by some machine or chemical, the fibers of flax from their woody core. Solution to this problem had baffled all government and university and industrial laboratories. The hand method of separation employed in Europe could not be bettered, apparently, and yet it could not be adopted either because American wages made it uneconomical. The dilemma seemed insoluble. Thousands of hours and tens of thousands of dollars went down the drain. Then a secret washing process was developed by which wood and fiber were separated and flotation carried away the flax while the heavier wood sank in the water. With the problem of flax usage overcome, there remained only the matter of finding flax. Growing experiments in half-a-dozen states, from the Eastern Shore of Maryland to Oregon, failed. Doggedly, Straus decided to try the straw from linseed flax, grown before this only for its oil which is used in paints. When his chemists adapted their processes to this seed flax and he produced a sample of paper made from it in his French factory, he was able to interest the major cigarette manufacturers in America in loaning him two million dollars to build the first mill in the United States for the manufacture of cigarette paper from seed flax.

The fact that North Carolina manufactures more than half of this country's cigarettes was only a happy coincidence in the location of Ecusta's site. What mattered most was water, because water is a large ingredient in the manufacture of this paper. For instance, just before the final sheet is pressed and rolled off the machine, it is two hundred parts water to one part pulp. And since cigarettes go in people's mouths, the paper around them must be tasteless. In addition, it must be the approximate thickness of a human hair yet strong and resilient enough to withstand the pull of the cigarette machines. A strip the width of a cigarette must support a weight of eight pounds. It must fold without tearing, it must not stick to the lips, it must burn at the same rate as tobacco, and be pure white.

The millsite was chosen with care. Sixty locations were considered before the rich acres along the Davidson River were chosen. Because it came out of Pisgah National Forest, it was a government-protected watershed, and the purity of the water was analyzed even in France.

Once the site was purchased, construction began in June, 1938.

The next year, French experts came to Transylvania County to teach local people, most of whom had never even visited a large factory, methods of making cigarette paper that were new even to the experts. The company's management had estimated it might take two to three years to teach these mountain people techniques of the industry as they were known to the French. Four months later, the Frenchmen were able to go home. Once again the local population had been not so much underestimated as, perhaps, just an unknown quantity.

One of the lawyers in Brevard, county seat of Transylvania, will tell you: "We were on the cooling board when Ecusta came here and I don't mind saying so. Yes sir, we were laid out: the undertaker had been called, the flowers had been ordered and all we lacked was the embalming. Now it's different. You can see it is. Let some folks holler about industry and pollution of streams; for us, it's dollars on Saturday." With the purchase of Ecusta by Olin Industries and their subsequent construction, in 1952, of a giant cellophane plant on adjoining acres, even more dollars should flow on Saturdays.

And farther down the French Broad others would agree with the lawyer from Brevard. He would be seconded in Greeneville, Tennessee, where Magnavox has the only television factory in the South (in 1953) and the only one in the United States engaged in the complete manufacture of television sets from raw material to final tests. Magnavox found that after three weeks of education for their jobs, most of the people they hired—from Greene, Hamblen, Cocke, Hawkins and Washington counties—could pick up the work and go ahead like veterans. Observant Bert Vincent of Knoxville reported visiting the plant: "I walked along an assembly line where a hundred and two girls sat with small tweezers, screwdrivers, welders and other tools of the trade. Each girl was doing her own little, but very important, job. 'What are you doing?' I asked of one, Miss Martha Shelton, who lives on the Newport Road.

"'I'm fastening down the ends of nine little wires,' she smiled. 'That's all I know.'

"The girl to her right was doing some little something, too. And all the others of the hundred and two girls in that line. And when they were all through they had put fourteen hundred small parts in each set."

At the mouth of the river, where Knoxville was located at the junction of the French Broad and Holston to become an important distribution center of the nineteenth century, there is perhaps the largest concentration of industry. From marble quarries to textiles, from meat packing to iron works, Knoxville has had its own companies, but the greatest effect on both that city and much of the surrounding country has come from three indirect agencies: Alcoa, site of the huge Aluminum Company of America plant, ten miles to the southeast; TVA with power dams and recreation lakes on all sides; and Oak Ridge, with its atomic energy works twenty miles to the west. Here at Oak Ridge during the years of World War II, many a French Broad dweller contributed some small share of labor toward ultimate splitting of the atom. There were a few who stood puzzled on this threshold of the future, glancing back toward the small self-sufficiency they still remembered. The secrecy, the vastness, the total lack of humanization pervading the whole process sent some of the older folks seeking for home again.

One staunch old fellow shook his head in perplexed sorrow: "They said there was work for all down at that Oak Ridge, and ag'in spring come I went down to do my part. But I couldn't stand it. Day after day freight trains rolling in there full of material, first one kind then another, trucks coming and unloading, folks by the thousands—a whole cityful—scrambling and working and me along with them. But never nothing coming out. Them tons upon tons of goods being swallered up and nary a thing being made that I could see. All a-going in, nothing coming out, and it that way all the time, day in, day out. I just had to quit."

Such a long step and such a short time from the day when

each man had grown and threshed his own wheat, ground his own flour and baked his own bread, to this final specialization of work and talents. The manufactures of many men of many countries went into bringing the money for TV's and V8's—and even vitamin B's—to the French Broad. Strict solid Dutchmen, precise Frenchmen, indefatigible Germans and Jews, American Northerners and Midwesterners mingled in this region with the inheritors of traditional Anglo-Saxonism. The industries they created are the new cash crop of these ancient hills.

# 18

## Who Killed the French Broad?

"My Grandpa, back after the Civil War awhile, heard about the land out yonder. Folks all a-saying how rich the ground was, how flat and wide all the fields, and it might' nigh free for the taking. More he thought about it away from here, more dissatisfied Grandpa grew at being here, so one day he told Grandma to get her things together and fix the younguns for travel cause they were going to put the hills of old North Carliny behind them. They were a-going out yonder. Well, to whittle it short, they loaded up their big old wagon with all the plunder they could take and set out, with my paw and the other younguns, to find a new home.

"Weeks they was on the road. Something would break down, they'd stop for a little visit, first one thing and another. Crossed the Mississippi, kept a-going, finally reached Texas, I reckon it was. Land was flat and cheap, like they'd told him, all right—but my Grandpa just said one thing. 'Ma,' he said to my Grandma, 'the water here ain't fit for a body to drink.' And the next day he turned his team around and headed for home again. When he got back here to the mountains he settled down on this little farm again, and after that nothing could budge him. Hot summer day you'd come up the path, find him drinking a deep gourdful of water out in the shade around the springhouse. 'Finest water in the world.' He'd offer you a draw. 'And how about Texas?' I'd tease him later on when I was old enough. 'There's some say that the folks that went out there and stayed got rich as cream. Rest of us back here in the hills got blue-john.' Grandpa'd look at me sharp. 'Rich?' he'd snort. 'What's "rich" if a man can't get decent water to wet his thirst?' "

That's the way it used to be. This mountain man has told you more than a family story: he's told you a legend. A legend of people who knew that if the fundamental ingredients of living were sound and good, the furbelows could be done without. Old-timers knew the flavor of wheat in bread; knew the taste of water fresh from the earth. Tastes as rare today as the sight of wool carding or the sound of a waterwheel. For somewhere along the way from their time to ours a bargain was struck. We exchanged the purity of simple necessities for complex luxuries which were never meant to satisfy, but to stimulate our hungers.

The French Broad country is particularly a region of springs. The water of most of the brooks and streams and rivers they form is as nearly pure, in its pristine state, as water can be. But when we turned away from the spring at the edge of the kitchen yard and turned on the faucet in our porcelain sink, we turned off our interest in what came out of the spigot. One by one we allowed ourselves and others to begin the rape which finally (in places) ended in the murder of the French Broad. And it had come about precisely because the headwaters were so pure, so nearly perfect.

The sole blame for the river's fouling could be laid to no one person or group. Because the river belongs to everyone, it is the possession of no one. Those rights today legally known as riparian rights go as far back in man's history as the Institutes of Justinian, when running water, like the air, was *res communes:* that is, "common to all and property of none." Even the Napoleonic Code and the

Spanish law embodied this concept; it became a part of English common law. And today we reap the effects of man's very natural impulse to seize his rights and use this common property without equally assuming his responsibilities in regard to that property. It will be the highest awareness of democracy when men realize that freedom must be nourished by justice and rights can only be preserved by fulfilling the obligations they incur.

In the early days of settlement one of the most heinous crimes a man could be guilty of was the littering or despoiling of another man's water supply—the spring or stream that fed him. Feuds or killings had a sort of unwritten approval when a man was defending a resource so vital to him and his family. But, odd as it seems, when the people began to cluster together in towns and cities and the despoiling became really large and ugly, it began to be overlooked. Villages and factories dumped their trash and turned their backs. Farther down the river people held their noses (and their tongues) and added their waste. And finally, part of the river was "killed."

Water is a living thing; it is life itself. In it life began. And everything that lives in water requires oxygen. It is also a moving thing. A burden bearer, water can carry off great loads of humanity's leavings—but here the struggle between life and death begins. For it can carry only so much, and as the oxygen in water is used up by waste, organic or inorganic, the living creatures in water begin to die. First, of course, go the higher types—until finally only the rat-tailed maggots and other such low pollutional forms are left—and then, nothing.

Not only the life *in* the river suffers; there is all the life along it, all the network of creatures that live by water, including man himself. These, then, are the two aspects of dead waters: the life in, and the life along the river. Let's look at each.

On September 6, 1939, the Asheville *Citizen* reported that fish were dying in the Swannanoa River just above its junction with the French Broad. "Hundreds of dead and dying fish were taken from

the river yesterday by both children and grownups. Some carried
away large baskets full and others had strings of a dozen or more."

A dozen years later, on September 5, 1951, the Asheville *Times*
reported a similar situation below the junction of the Davidson
River and the French Broad:

> State Wildlife Resources Commission game protectors
> and fish biologists opened investigation today to determine
> cause of the death of thousands of fish in the past 24 hours.
> . . . The greatest kill of both game fish and rough, forage fish
> took place late yesterday but this morning the banks of the
> once-famed bass stream were dotted with dead and dying fish.
>
> Witnesses told investigators that the small streams feeding
> into the French Broad were churned into a muddy froth last
> evening by fish fighting their way to clean water. Eighteen and
> twenty inch trout often failed to get over the miniature sand-
> bars at the mouths of the streams and flopped back into the
> main river to die, they said. Small trout, panfish and minnows
> got through to the comparative safety of the little feeder
> streams. . . . The big stream looked no differently this morn-
> ing than any other morning. It was its usual darkish color
> with flakes of foam floating aimlessly along on it. The only
> thing different were the number of fish flopping feebly on the
> surface.

The final verdict on this particular mass extinction of fish was
reported a month afterward, October 9:

> Excessive pollution caused the death of several thousand fish
> in the French Broad River several weeks ago, Clyde P. Patton,
> executive director of the State Wildlife Resources Commission,
> said yesterday.
>
> He said this was the finding of the commission and the U.S.
> Fish and Wildlife Service following a study of water samples

taken from the river. . . . He said that some fish placed in sample water taken from the river died in as short a time as one minute.

The story might have been news but it was not new in the French Broad watershed. In 1945 an extended study of the basin had found:

> The Pigeon River below Canton, North Carolina also at one time must have been a popular fishing stream. At the present time its condition is entirely unsuitable for fish life above Waterville Lake, and only the coarser fish are found below the lake above Newport. . . . Due to the nature of the principal waste . . . the stream is black from Canton to its mouth and carries a considerable amount of foam in the turbulent sections.

It had also been pointed out by various authorities that "approximately 92 percent of the pollution discharged into the rivers in the French Broad River Basin originates within North Carolina" and that its basin there "contains sources responsible for more than one-fourth of the total pollution of North Carolina." Of this enormous load of waste, 21 per cent is raw sewage from towns and villages and cities along the river, many of whose citizens apparently never stop to wonder where the water flushed down their drain empties, and 79 per cent is manufacturing offal from industries who daily bring millions of gallons of clear clean water into their plants, use it, and turn it back into its channel discolored, bestenched and loaded with oxygen-consuming litter.

Talking with a man who probably knows as much about the forests and waters and people of the upper French Broad as any person in the region, a former forester and a present business administrator, you particularly notice the way he says, "I first came to North Carolina in nineteen three. I was born in Missouri but

I'd been living in Oklahoma working in lumber yards there when I contracted typhoid. My brother sent me a bulletin Dr. Schenck, on the Vanderbilt Estate, had published about forestry. It was the only bulletin he ever published and I read it while I was still in bed. It set me afire. I vowed if I got well I'd come to North Carolina and see what forestry was about. And I did. I remember my ride on the train up the French Broad River the morning of January second, nineteen three. It was the first mountain river I'd ever seen. Clear and sparkling! I've never seen it so clear since. But I'll never forget the way it looked that winter morning."

There are those who can describe how the Pigeon once was, too. Like a crystal you could look through to the glinting sand, the shiny round pebbles on its bed. Down the boulder-strewn canyon from North Carolina into Tennessee, green mountain water tumbling and then swirling into deep quieter pools where fish fed and darted under overhanging rocks. And a man could sprawl on his belly and bury his face in the good cold water—and drink.

No one dares hope for the return to such a time and condition. There are elements of beauty and purity that apparently must be sacrificed if modern life is to be satisfied. Since streams have the dual purpose in man's organized society of supplying water and carrying off refuse, it is unintelligent not to recognize each function. Likewise, as a North Carolina state official recently observed, "Both of these purposes can be fulfilled and civilization can still go forward if the waste is properly treated so that the stream is not overloaded." But it can do no harm, it might possibly be healthy, for us to give a moment's thought and memory to what we have lost.

For most people the important question is: What are we losing now? Let us not be poetic but practical. Let us not be softhearted but hardheaded. If there is a gulf between the ideal and the real, let us be "realistic." As real as the riverbank and the ghost-trunked sycamores that grow there, as the liquid beauty of the river's sweeping curves, and as real as the white scum that caps the water's blackness for mile after mile. Besides beauty of sight and sweetness of smell and goodness of taste, what important are we losing? What possibilities, what dollars and cents, have been killed along with stretches of the river?

Before we discover what is being lost, perhaps we should determine what has been gained by the free use of the French Broad, the Pigeon, the Davidson, the dozens of other tributaries. There have been remunerations. Cities along the waterways have been able to dump their sewage in running water that could, after a while, if the load was not absolutely insupportable, repurify itself. One of the miracles of water is its constant renewal. So, up to a point, this was a quick, sanitary and cheap method of disposal for communities "just growing" like Topsy. The gain here came to the town's citizens who had a free service: no taxes, no money to pay.

From industry, the remuneration was their payroll. When paper plants, cellophane manufacturers, tanners, canners, rayon and textile plants, and others took their stands along the headwaters of the river, they and the people around them realized the benefits that were to be gained by a diversified economy. Small farms supplemented by industrial payrolls made for a well-balanced community. None of the companies was shy about mentioning this part of its expenses, either. At any time any one of them would willingly explain how much their payroll meant to the "mountain people" in their realm of influence. It was more of a fact than a joke when someone replied to a visitor who had complained of the bad odor permeating the air for many miles in the vicinity of one plant, "We don't mind that. It just smells like money to us."

There was another ingredient behind that remark too. An ingredient which lurked behind much of the talk of payroll as well. Threat. The covert but unmistakable threat that if industry were required to deal with its more obnoxious manifestations it might be forced to close down operations and move to a more hospitable clime. The margin between profit and loss seemed by

implication always to be just about the amount that any effective pollution-control measure would cost. Most of the projects that had been introduced—and there were industries making a move toward waste reduction—were ineffective because just about the time the waste load per unit of production was cut in half, production itself doubled, leaving conditions, if no worse, also no better. For the moment, however, we must clearly recognize the payroll, the money with which industry benefited the French Broad country; we will recognize the actualities of city growth made possible by free municipal disposal. These are the gains realized from allowing any amount of pollution in the French Broad.

Now: What is it costing us?

First, and to begin with the least important (but no less pleasurable) of the losses, there is the part of the river and its tributaries that have been killed of any game fish. In a region like Western North Carolina and Eastern Tennessee, widely advertised as a resort area, such a loss is more real than might probably be the case in other places. In fact, the split personality of a locale trying to be all things to all people is showing increasing strain in the French Broad country. In luring tourists to the mountains, clean air, clear water, swimming in something besides pools drenched in chlorine, natural scenery unmarred by dirty streams have been primary attractions listed in the folders. In luring industry to the mountains the pure water, natural surroundings attractive to executives and labor, and the general climate have also been primary considerations. The time has arrived, it would appear, when a choice must be made. Either tourists or industries must be courted unless —and this is surely the wise decision that will finally be made— industries and municipalities accept their responsibilities to other industries and municipalities and to the region as a whole and embark on a program of each cleaning up its own waste. Until that time, pollution will be depriving the French Broad country of some of the revenues that would accrue from the $4,500,000,000–$5,000,000,000 spent annually by the hunters and fishermen of the United States. Broken down to its share of this expenditure, either North Carolina or Tennessee should have something like $150,000,-000, and further reduced to a regional share with either Western North Carolina or Eastern Tennessee considered one of the three major divisions of its state, this would mean about $50,000,000 spent on two outdoor sports that have become one of the nation's (and could be one of the region's) biggest businesses. It is obviously not good business, then, to put out of circulation even a single mile of good fishing stream in a countryside capitalizing on its assets as a tourist and sportsman's paradise. To so kill the waters for dozens and dozens of miles and to impair Douglas Lake which was supposed to be one of the recreational Great Lakes of the South, is eventual suicide for a tourist area.

Second, pollution of the river by a few industries and towns is costing the introduction of new industries. Water has been described as "one of the greatest natural resources in the French

Broad River basin. No other resource is more abundant or can serve the public in more beneficial ways, yet no resource is subject to as much misuse." Because of bad cutting habits, because of woods fires and overgrazing and a half-dozen other related malpractices, the constant flow of water is decreasing every decade. That it seems to be dwindling even faster than is actually the case is an illusion created by our increased demands. Needs for water have spiraled. Consequently, if we cannot create more water, we can do the next logical thing and make the water we do have serve several uses. If factories upstream take in clear water, use it, treat it for the wastes disposed of and then send it on downstream in condition for the next fellow to use, the effect—to all practical purposes—has been to add more water to the present supply. Water once used has been made available to someone else and creates possibilities for new industries all down the river. The problem has been brought up in North Carolina before the Resource-Use Education Conference in the state capital: "Although North Carolina is described as an agrarian state, it has achieved its prominence as a result also of a sound diversified industrial development. North Carolina rightfully extends a cordial right hand to industrial prospects, but in the past few years has too frequently waved farewell with the left hand as the prospect moved on in search of clean water and of a clearcut water resources policy." The people of the French Broad basin, as well as those of the other river basins of North Carolina and Tennessee, therefore owe it to themselves to make sure an adequate supply of suitable water is available for new industries, and they owe it to the industries, old as well as new, to present them with a firm policy of pollution-control by which they can chart remedies and their course of production and costs.

The third large loss is that to any municipality at present facing a water shortage while, in many instances, a river flows by its very door. In the whole French Broad watershed, only three small towns rely on a ground-water supply. All three of those supplies are from springs and are in North Carolina: Hot Springs,

Bakersville and Little Switzerland. The other cities and villages depend on surface water, and many of them are being forced farther and farther back into the hills to build their reservoirs and maintain supplies. Might not the taxes spent on laying many miles of pipe line and on the construction and maintenance of new and costly dams be saved—or used elsewhere (perhaps on disposal plants for their own wastes)—if the closer, more abundant source could be tapped? As an example, the town of Newport, Tennessee, about twenty miles across the state line, is now faced with just this situation. The Big Pigeon River cuts right through its middle, but still the town is thirsty. The Water Resources Commission appointed by the President of the United States noted, in 1950: "Newport, on the Pigeon River near its confluence with the French Broad, is badly in need of additional water. . . . Pollution in both these two large streams is so serious as to make their use unfeasible."

A smaller, concrete experience came to light in the summer of 1953 when, during a prolonged drought, a farmer near the mouth of one of the North Carolina streams emptying into the French Broad turned to irrigation to save ten acres of cabbage he was raising as a truck crop. Local health authorities found the water from the stream to be unfit for use on vegetables and the farmer lost his crop, the nearby city lost a source of food supply. And all within sight and reach of thousands of gallons of water running away.

More and more, as droughts descend and populations increase and water becomes what it has never been in this region before—a valuable commodity because of its scarcity—people will begin to realize the simple logic and necessity of "washing our waters."

These are three practical ways in which all the people of the French Broad are losing by even a partial killing of their rivers' living waters. Pollution is an ugly word. A sick word. A dead one. And the French Broad is a beautiful river. But there is no health in ignoring sickness and merely hoping it won't spread. There is no honesty or courage in denying death and hoping it won't be noticed, won't reach any farther. There is only one respectable course for a free citizen and that is to shoulder his share of the responsibility for the "killing," for the pollution. Because, just as the river belongs to no one, it belongs to everyone—and everyone is held accountable for its health and condition. Some certainly more so, for as one national writer has observed, "Where does the responsibility lie for cleaning up our water? The answer is plain and simple. Every city and town, and every industry, is responsible for cleaning up the pollution it creates." And the least that those who are fortunate enough to be dwellers of the French Broad country can do, out of humble thankfulness for nature's bounty to them, is make certain that their town, their city, and the industries around them at last shoulder this responsibility.

These dwellers can become familiar with facts rather than bogey tales, particularly the bogey tale that begins: "We'd like to clear the water so you could see the rocks on the bottom of your river bed again, but we're afraid it would mean you won't be feeling another kind of rocks in the bottom of your pockets." This is the falsehood of inevitability. And it is time every individual shook himself from lethargy and probed for the truth obscured by that falsehood: the truth that filth is not inevitable. Pollution is not the price we have to pay for securing industries in our midst or for building great cities. We can have factories and we can have towns and we can have clean water. Filth is the price we pay for apathy.

Disposal plants and processes are expensive. They lack glamor. Their P.A. (Public Appeal) quotient is low. They cost cash, and taxpayers and stockholders must eat. But they must drink too. They must wash. And so, we are back at the beginning of the circle. Back to the purity of living water.

A native wit remarked, "The Bible says that 'cleanliness is next to godliness,' but in parts of North Carolina it seems next to impossible." This was more humorous than accurate, we must believe. Cleanliness will not prove an impossible financial problem to cities that have withstood shattering depressions and regional upheavals and come through strong and growing. Cleanliness will not pose an impossible financial problem to industries that have overcome so formidable a hurdle as that of being forced to find a whole new raw material from which to manufacture their very product. The citizens of Knoxville who drink the water of the French Broad will not think it an impossibility to secure cleaner drinking water when many of them have worked on the project at Oak Ridge where man unraveled one of the secrets of the universe and split the atom.

Depressions would not have been overcome, raw material shortages would not have been resolved, the atom would never have given up its secret energy if the people involved had accepted their problems as insoluble, or at best capable of only long and modified study. It is not typical of the legendary American that he will accept any bad situation as inevitable. Why then have we allowed ourselves to suppose the scum on our river inevitable?

There is one answer: the apathy of each of us. Our cities and our industries are lagging because we lag. The engineering technicalities of pollution control can be overcome; the financial stresses can be lightened by Federal and state agencies that stand ready to help by loans and other assistance. Only the people are not yet aware of what can be done—of what has been done in such cases as that of the poisonous textile dyes used in Piedmont North Carolina where the people and their law said, "These shall not be dumped direct into our rivers," and it was not done. The industries complied with the voice of their neighbors.

In a democracy, there is no stronger regulator than the will of people—simple people, fine people, clean or dirty people—the people. And when we realize what our apathy is costing us, we will realize it is too expensive a luxury and exchange it for enlightened self-concern and public concern. We will realize we had rather raise our own voices to cleanse our own evils than to wait until emergency has brought other pressures to bear.

Let the people's will, then, speak with a law saying this killing of the French Broad must cease. A law for both of the states of the river affirming that each shall clean its portion of the river. A law requiring each agency—town or village, factory or plant— to come of social age now in the middle of this twentieth century and assume its responsibilities along with its rights. Such a law, fitted to the varying pollution problems of city or industrial wastes, would give the cities a sense of unity, all fulfilling the same requirements for the same rules of decent citizenship, and it would give the industries a framework in which to present to their stockholders the reasons for a necessary expense which might, for the moment, reduce annual dividends from 7 per cent to 6 per cent, net profits for the year from seven millions to six millions. The request is just; if the terms are plain and firm and established to preserve the life of the river and its people, there can be no avoiding such a law.

For law has a certain poetry too. Law in its own purity, like the French Broad in its purity, has a logic and an inevitableness that dwarfs all dispute. A law is the logic of man, a river is the logic of nature: when the two are fused for the benefit of both, the result is one kind of beauty.

# 19

# The High Sheriff

"Ever know Jesse James Bailey?" you ask the old farmer mending fence with baling wire along the road in Madison County.

He spits. "Well now I reckon. Back nineteen twenty–twenty-two, when he was sheriff of this-here county, things was humming. He worked at his job twenty-four hours a day and ate and slept in his spare time."

"Ever heard of Jesse James Bailey?"

A wide grin creases the face of the ancient Negro woman rocking in her chair on the littered porch of the shack on Velvet Street. "You mean ole Sheriff Jess Bailey? Lord! Lord! Ever' moonshiner and liquor peddler in Buncombe County breathed easier when he done laid down his sheriff's badge. Them was high days, back then."

The town politician sets his glass half full of bourbon and "plain ole branch-water" on the weatherbeaten desk in front of him and props his feet up on either side of the glass. His cunning eyes peer at you over flyspecked glasses. "Jesse James Bailey." He rolls the name slowly along his tongue as if savoring some lost relish, some tart and authentic flavor that the words recall but that is missing now and has been for years. "I knew the old rascal." The way he says it makes Bailey's incorruptibility a legend, seals —by its negative compliment—the positive alienation of the man from his usual cohorts in office. "He'd start on somebody's trail, he'd catch 'em or break hell loose a-trying. At the start of his term in the sheriff's office, he went out and brought the criminals in, but along toward the end of his term they just come in and surrendered. Least, that's what folks used to say. And money couldn't touch him."

The man they remember is half legend, but the man named Jesse James Bailey is wholly alive. So you go down to the office of Chief Special Agent for the Asheville, North Carolina, division of the Southern Railway—detective, in nonofficial jargon. Behind the chief desk is a gray-haired oval-faced man with ruddy complexion, lively eyes that pick up details and assimilate their meaning, rugged tough-skinned hands with pink immaculate fingernails. When he shoves back his chair and stands up, the whole six feet two and two-hundred-ten pounds of him are behind the grip of his handshake. There is old-fashioned pride and style in the wide dove-gray felt hat, the carefully buttoned vest adorned by a watch chain and the handsome scarab stickpin in his silk tie.

"Mighty happy to see somebody from up on Beaverdam. Guess the first thing you'll want to know is how I got my name. Well sir, it's a long story, and I just missed being named Samson Bailey by a few days. You see, I was born in a kindly remote section of Madison County, down there at the big bend of the French Broad River—since then they've named it Bailey's Bend on account of my family—and we had a good farm there and all, but it was pretty well cut off from roads.

"Back in that day they had preachers would ride through the country preaching and selling Bibles. They'd carry their Bible around for a sample and sign up everybody that wanted one and send it or bring it to them later. Well, along about a week after I was born, my father was out working his field one day and this minister came riding up along the river. When he saw my father, he rode over to the field and they set to talking. Erasmus Bailey, that was my father's name. After a little bit, the preacher told him who he was and said, 'My friend, wouldn't you like to have a new illustrated Bible?'

" 'What's that?' my father asked. He was a great hand to tease.

" 'My friend, you don't mean to say you've never heard of the Bible?'

" 'No.' My father shook his head. 'I've just got one book and it's not that.'

" 'Well, what book is it you have if it's not the Bible?' the preacher asked.

" 'It's a life of the James boys,' father told him.

" 'Well, I'll make you a simple proposition, friend. I want to leave this Bible with you and you read it, and if you don't like it better than the James Brothers you can give it back to me. If you do like it better, you can buy it from me then. Ain't that fair a-plenty?'

"Nothing my father could do with a proposition like that but take it. So the preacher left the Bible and rode on his way. About a month later when he come back through, he asked, 'Well, how'd you like the Bible, Mr. Bailey? Get a chance to read any?'

" 'Yes. Yes, I read a good bit.'

" 'Like it as well as your James boys?'

" 'Well, I'll tell you. I used to think the Jameses were some fighters, about the best anywhere. But after reading that Bible I seen they couldn't hold a candle to Samson and those Phillips boys!'

"So I reckon if I'd been born the week after, instead of the week before, that preacher come, I'd a-been called Samson Phillips Bailey!"

His laugh is as big as himself, it shakes his shoulders, lifts his eyebrows, rumbles free and hearty from his belly.

"I'm just a rough mountain fellow, didn't get past the fourth reader—they called them readers back then instead of grades—in school, but I went to work for the Southern Railway back in nineteen six when I was eighteen years old and I've been with them ever since. They give me two leaves of absence, and one term I was sheriff of Madison County and another term I was sheriff of Buncombe County. The only man in North Carolina ever to be elected sheriff of two different counties in the same state.

"I was sheriff of Madison County from nineteen twenty to nineteen twenty-two. Bloody Madison, you know. Marshall's the county seat. Right on the French Broad with river on one side and mountain on the other. Folks say it's the town that's a block wide, a mile long, sky high and hell deep.

"When I come in as sheriff, Madison County was in the grip of the prohibition movement that was sweeping the country. I wasn't going to make it an issue in the campaign but my main opponent thought the liquor element was so strong and would spend so much money, he'd win with me in the prohibition camp. Everybody knew I never drank myself. So first thing I knew, I was campaigning on a prohibition ticket. The moonshiners and fellers behind them began pouring out money like rainwater down a drain spout. Just to show you what a man's up against running for public office, there were these two townships back up on the Laurels; one, down lower, run by this man who controlled all the whiskey traffic around there. Oh, he never touched the business himself—he ran the general store, was postmaster, had a gristmill, the biggest farm in that section, was a deacon in the Baptist church—but he put up the money and protection for all the moonshining and made a big share of the profits. Oh, he had lots of influence and I felt like I had to have him in my camp for that election.

"The other township up there, way up in the hills, didn't have any keyman like that. The Presbyterians had put a mission up there a few years before, and they were all pretty civilized folks. I did a little campaigning up there. But what I really thought I needed was that big man in the lower township. So one day I made it a point to run into him while I was riding up through there. After we'd talked around a little bit, I said, 'Now, my friend, I reckon you've heard I'm running for sheriff this election coming up.' He said he'd heard some talk about it. 'Well,' I said, 'I just wanted to tell you I know you've got lots of different interests up in this section of the county, and as long as everything's quiet and not causing anybody any trouble up here, I don't see there'd be any need for me to interfere in your affairs.' Oh, my opponent said he wanted to be sheriff so he could be of service to his fellow man, but to me that office looked just like a great big piece of strawberry shortcake topped with whipped cream! Never wanted anything so bad in my life. Then I put it to him, 'So, if you think we could get along all right, I'd be glad if you could see your way clear to supporting me. Say a word for me around here in your territory.'

"He heard me all through and then after while he said, 'Bailey, I like you. But the other feller's *been* sheriff. I *know* what he'll do for me and I'd just have to gamble on you.'

"Oh, I never felt so sunk. I needed those votes. And when the election come, I lost almost every vote in that township. But you know what happened? Up where that Presbyterian school had been, they marked for me so strong it canceled out every one of the other votes I'd lost and a few to boot. Where that big feller's influence had been against me in one place, it had worked for me in another, just knowing he was for my opponent. That's the way things are in politics. I won by a majority larger than my three opponents combined. Prohibition came in strong that year. Madison still drank wet, but it felt dry." A grin, and a twinkle in the keen eyes.

"You know there's three things you've got to do to be a sheriff. First, you've got to promise to make everybody a deputy. Of course, they don't want to do any work, you can never find them when you need them. They just want to carry a pistol.

"And then, the second thing you have to do is give away plenty of guns. People write asking for a nice little pistol, or a nice big revolver, the next time you take one off some criminal.

"Third thing you've got to do is be a prescription agent for the whole county. Why, I bet I doctored everybody in Madison and Buncombe counties for everything from ingrown toenails to falling hair—and a few cows too."

He reaches inside his files and hands us a yellowed prescription sheet. It reads:

Sir—Hollis Mason is very sick and I have advised him to use whiskey. If this is legitimate consider me as prescribing for him as often as he sends for it.

—— M.D.

"When I finished my two-years' term, I had twenty-three thousand of those liquor prescriptions in my desk drawer. Seemed like every time you made a raid the whole county got sick."

He pushes the big-brimmed hat on the back of his head and it gives him a jaunty careless look. You know he isn't a careless man, however, or he wouldn't be here now—he'd be dead from one of the dozens of bullets that missed by a hair's breadth during those hundreds of raids on hidden distilleries. Or from the crash of his car as it hurtled off the road more times than once giving chase to a blockade-runner or transporting prisoners down to the North Carolina state penitentiary at Raleigh and facing emergencies of slipped handcuffs, mutiny and violence. Or the times he confronted knives and the quick, well-honed razors. It took caution and courage in equal parts to be a successful sheriff in Madison County at the beginning of prohibition: courage to face ambush, courage to do the work for less pay than the moonshiners would give you for not doing it, and caution to read the trails with care, know your opponent's methods, go in after him and come back alive. Dead law was no law.

Sheriff Bailey captured stills up and down the hills and hollows; from Paint Rock where the French Broad River crosses the

North Carolina line into Tennessee to Paint Fork, at the remote head of one of the tributaries, his men cut down barrels and furnaces, brought boilers and jugs in as evidence of their success. Headlines in the Marshall newspaper would boast: "Sheriff locates another O-Be-Joyful Fountain," or "Citizens of Paint Rock all take French leave just before call by Sheriff. Fly the coop for parts unknown. Take to tall timber." Or, later, items such as these appeared in the Asheville *Citizen* and *Times:*

> Sheriff Bailey is not a sea-faring man but yesterday he used a pair of powerful prism binoculars to spy out a liquor cache on Riverside Drive in the cliffs on west side of the French Broad. The sheriff, suspicious for some time, mounted with his glasses to the fifteenth floor of the new courthouse and spied activity from there. Later went and made arrests.

Or the story telling about Bailey's first twenty-eight days as sheriff of Buncombe County. From December third to the thirty-first, his department seized twelve stills and confiscated 137 gallons of whiskey, captured three automobiles transporting, and 800 gallons of beer. Considering the preparation that must go into a raid, that is quite a schedule.

The raid was born when someone reported to the sheriff's office that there were suspicious, or definitely proven, activities taking place in their part of the county. Sometimes these reports came from neighbors, sometimes from disgruntled co-workers or friends of the moonshiner. Occasionally they were grudge rumors not worth investigation, often they were funny. Like the time a man came into the office demanding that the still near his house be seized. Sheriff Bailey asked him where the still was in relation to his house. He didn't know. Sheriff asked which general direction it might be in. He couldn't say. Well, then, how did he even know there was a still anywhere near? It was this way: He did a lot of fox hunting, kept a good pack of foxhounds so he could make a real chase when he started out on the mountains. But two days before, just when the weather was right and he was all set to go out for a day and night too, maybe, he couldn't find his hounds anywhere around the place and couldn't bring them in with his horn. After while the hounds came home—drunk! They'd been drinking mash from a still. Those lazy hounds just lay around all day. Getting a man's hounds drunk and knocking him out of a good fox chase was too much!

When the reporters were fellow moonshiners, the work of a raid was about half as hard, for they could tell the schedule of the still's operators and the easiest and least suspected approach to its location. Such informers risked their lives. The sheriff protected them and would lose a case before he would divulge the name of an informer. During a raid,

the spies had to be covered for, too. Officers were careful to shoot at them—and miss; they were rounded up with the rest of the band —and allowed to escape.

After the still was located, the sheriff picked his deputies and they set a day for the raid. Long before daylight they parked their car in some inconspicuous place and made their way over mountains, up densely wooded coves, along trails that had been carefully camouflaged with bits of brush and leaves.

"They were a cautious bunch, I tell you," Sheriff Bailey says. "Sometimes they'd have weeds bent across their path till it'd fool the sharpest eye. And you'd have to get in there and get your men scattered around at strategic points a good while before daybreak. Then there was nothing to do but hunker down there in the chilly damp dark and wait. Soon as the first streaks of light began to break through, the picket would probably come. Many's the time I've watched a picket come up the trail and choose him a post under a big oak or poplar and set there with his rifle across his knees, ready to shoot a warning at first sign of strangers, and say he was shooting at squirrels. Sometimes when the still was near a house, I've even heard them beat on the side of the house to warn their folks to get away from the still.

"Well, after the picket's there and the rest of the crew had come and started laying their fire or stirring the mash, you could move in on them any time. Once in awhile they'd shoot it out, but most the time when you had them barehanded like that they'd give up."

One of the lawyers defending his moonshiner client against the sheriff, made a statement in court which became known through the region. "My client's chief crime was bad calculation," the lawyer said, "trying to run a still in Madison. When he tried to make whiskey in Bailey's county, he made more of a mistake than he did whiskey."

As the sheriff struggled against odds to make the mountain people obey a law they did not recognize as law because it infringed on their liberties, and as he captured and demolished still after still, someone told him that if he didn't ease off on his activities against the bootleggers he'd never be elected to the office of sheriff again. Bailey replied, "I'm not running for sheriff now. I'm filling the office of sheriff." And the day he retired from that office in Madison County, at two minutes till noon he brought in his last still and two moonshiners.

The position of high sheriff was one of honor to Jesse James Bailey and he brought all his personal pride to it. When he appointed the deputies who were to serve under him as law enforcers, he inserted a new clause into the acceptance blanks each deputy was compelled to sign before receiving his badge. In that clause the deputy agreed to shave and brush his teeth once a day, to have his clothes pressed once a week and to shine his shoes as often as necessary. Since deputies were chosen more often for their hardiness and knowledge of the rough back country of the county, than for their appearance and manner, this added a new dimension to the deputies' duties. And when the sheriff moved into the offices of the new expensive courthouse at Asheville, the Asheville *Times* ran this headline and item:

> Spitoons and Bibles will be in order in the Sheriff's office.
> Saturday, after the office had been moved to the spacious quarters on the ground floor of the new courthouse, Sheriff Bailey announced: "Any deputy sheriff who spits on this fine floor will be dismissed. Any visitor who does the same will be arrested." . . . The sheriff said that he had issued orders to his men, requesting them to attend Sunday School weekly.

Bailey not only created new respect for his office but played its human interest for all it was worth—and that was plenty. People were his meat, and he had a gusty appetite.

"There was old Maggie Jones," he grins, leaning back in his heavy oak chair, "black and smart too. She'd been selling liquor down there in Darktown for years and nobody could catch her. She had sharp eyes and a big iron bar half as big as my arm across the front door. There was a little peephole in the door, and somebody would open it and see who was knocking while Maggie looked out of the window upstairs and made sure who it was. Then if it was the law—and she knew every one of us at a glance—she had a very clever system. She kept her jugs sitting in one of those big old-timey bathtubs up on second floor and she had a half gallon of Lysol there too. At first sign of trouble, Maggie's girls would begin pouring, and when the liquor was all down the drain they'd empty that bottle of Lysol right on top of it. Kill the smell. Well, my friend, it looked like I'd never catch her. So one day I decided to try a little camouflage. I got the biggest size dress I could find that was a-tall stylish looking and I put it on, and a big wide-brimmed hat that I could pull way down over my face, and some silk stockings, gloves, a nice big handbag to hang on my arm, and I powdered my face all up and I started down to Maggie's. When the car drove up, I could see her sitting up there at that window. So I pulled the hat down and I minced along as well as I could to the door and I knocked. Maggie leaned over to look out. About that time I stepped back a little from the door. The window above me was open, it was along in August, as I heard somebody ask Maggie, 'Who dat big-foot gal?'

"Then Maggie called out. 'Dat ain't no gal. Some you downstairs open the door and let Mr. Dressed-up Sheriff Bailey in.'

"Course, we got in just in time to smell that Lysol again. Oh, I reckon it was all a joke much as anything. I never did catch Maggie."

He takes off the wide hat and smoothes down his shocky hair; humor crinkles the corners around his eyes. "Ever hear about riding the broom? Now that was something. Learned about it in Buncombe County, while I was in office there. Women up in the jail made up a charm, supposed to work against their enemies or anybody they didn't like. One would take the broom and straddle it and prance up and down across the room while all the others stood around and helped her chant. They'd make up verse after verse and sing it—or plain holler it—about the person they were against. This was supposed to work like a snare and bring their enemy into jail right away. My matron's name was Jennie Grey and one day I heard about half dozen of the women up in our fifteenth floor hotel just riding the broom and singing this little song:

> " 'Ole Sheriff Jess Bailey!
> Come git in the jailhouse.
> Ole Sheriff Jess Bailey!
> You're a mean ole louse.
> Ole Sister Jennie Grey!
> You called me a pig.
> When we git you behind the bars,
> You won't talk so big.' "

"Well, we had us a time back then. There was my trusties too, you know. They were the petty offenders, been up in jail a good many times, we'd let them have the run of the courthouse, mostly the fifteenth floor, that was the jail, and the basement, that was my office. Had two or three handymen over the length of a year or two—Negro boys I thought I could trust, they'd carry messages, help keep the place clean, kind of act as jack-of-all-trades. There was Jim Greasy and Big Gambler and Tooflies—all of them sooner or later left out and had to be arrested all over again. Then Chunn's Cove come. He was nicknamed after that place just outside the city, and I thought he'd stick to me awhile, he liked being around the office so much. But I guess he must have heard those bones a-rolling one Saturday evening, cause he just up and took off. The next week come a letter to my desk addressed: 'Mister Jesse James Bailey, high sheriff of the new courthouse.' Inside was a note from Chunn's Cove. 'I done wrong to run away and I want to be took back.' But somehow by that time my faith in handymen was kind of shattered."

One of the main difficulties in being sheriff anywhere along the French Broad, on either the Tennessee or North Carolina side, was the proximity of the neighboring state. Bootleggers gained sanctuary by fleeing across the state line in remote and thinly settled areas. Bailey dealt with this problem in typically forthright fashion that might not withstand close scrutiny by law codes, but which was pragmatically a large success. In Unicoi and Cocke counties in Tennessee, Bailey had those two sheriffs make him a deputy, and he in turn deputized the sheriffs of those counties so they could operate in Madison County, North Carolina. That way the bootleggers didn't have a nearby "safety goal" or "demilitarized zone" where the law pursuing them from one state was powerless in the bordering one.

"Liquor was the big problem, both my terms of office," Bailey says. "Liquor and what it done to folks. Just to show you the misery and waste that one family can bring on a community, let me tell you about the Lances. They lived up in the Laurels in Madison County and the old man 'Red' Nick Lance had made whiskey all his life, saved up a little fortune, maybe twenty thousand dollars, which was a lot of money in that time and that place. Red Nick had three boys, Dock and Luke and Bill. He taught all the boys how to make liquor, but the trouble was they weren't quiet, wanting to keep to themselves and tend to their own business like Red Nick did. They were a mean bullying crew. Well, to begin with, Luke went down to the voting place one election day, full of liquor and meanness, started making fun of this boy James Nelson that was there, feller about his own age, kept on bullying him around till finally things got pretty serious and ended up by Luke shooting Nelson. Course they arrested Luke, but before he could be brought to trial he escaped.

"All this was before I took oath of sheriff for Madison County, but I hadn't been in long till it developed that Luke was around home, and he and Dock started terrorizing the whole community around them. Reports began coming in to me about their distilling and drinking and threatening. Now there was an upright citizen named Barlow lived up there in the thick of the Lances. He had a good farm, a good name, and one day he come to me and told me how things were. He said he thought he'd located where their still was, knew where most of the trails run, and could help me work out a plan to capture it and them too. Well, I made Barlow a deputy, we went on our raid, but we didn't find nobody. Somehow they'd got wind that it was Barlow who helped us. One night a little while after that, it was in February, Barlow waked up to see his big barn in blazes. He stood in the door of his house and saw four fine horses and six cattle burned to death. Afraid to try to go and help them because there were two men out there at the barn dancing around it like wild Indians and firing shots.

"Barlow come down and got me the next day. I picked up those empty shells around the barn, where they'd kicked up such a time, and trailed them right to their house. The shells were just like those in Dock and Luke Lance's guns. Well, we took them in, released them till trial under bond Red Nick made.

"Now Barlow had a tenant lived on his place name of Arthur Snapp. A few days after the Lances left jail on bond, Snapp came down to Barlow's place and told him he'd had word the boys were going to try to burn Barlow's house, maybe kill him too, that night. Barlow was a gritty man. He didn't scare. He and Snapp armed themselves, and when dark came they went out in the yard beside the house where Barlow had some big stacks of lumber he'd been sawing off his place during the winter. They hid behind those lumber piles where they could see whoever came in the yard. Bright moonlight night in February, but cold too. After they'd been crouched there hiding for a while they got pretty chilled. So they made it up to take turns going into the house to warm. As each one come out, he'd give a signal so the watcher would know to hold his fire. Well, they took turns for a while, then somehow there was a mix-up on the signals and Barlow shot Snapp. Killed him right there. It was an awful tragedy. Barlow felt terrible about it, took care of Snapp's family, and of course the Lances tried to build up the killing against Barlow every way they could.

"Along in April, I got this letter." He hands a cheap narrow sheet of child's tablet paper across the desk. The lame penciled lines march up and down the page like the curved outlines of the Smoky Mountains.

Mr. Jessie Baley I will rite you a few line to let you know that at Luke Lance is over here. And if you Dont come and get him we ame to kill him he is up at Ben King a making old Liquor and Laying out in that Larl there Ben King and Laying over at they old man Nick Lance with that Watson girl she is at Nick Lance now and Luke Lance is over here at Ben King. Now and you can hide and watch them go to him and you can catch him for he is ridding around and the road so time of a night and you can come and get him are came to kill for he is so mean we can't stand him he is in all the meanesse at he cane bee in up here and so now if you will put a Sheriff at Nick Lance and I at Ben King you will get bee for he leaves here. So now you Do as you please to D.

Mrs. Darlene Lance R 5 Marshall NC

"Barlow still wasn't afraid to help me, so early one Monday morning he and another deputy and me set out to find that Lance still and cut it down. Barlow knew where the main trail was and we picked it up as we went. When we finally come to that still, it was all ready for a run. The mash was in the still and the fire was laid ready to have a match struck to it. But there wasn't a soul around. It was still before daylight so we had hopes maybe they'd come in a little bit. We stayed hid around that still till about two o'clock in the afternoon, no breakfast, no dinner, we's getting weak, so we started on back. When he come to the forks at the foot of the mountain, Barlow could go right up this footpath to his house, but he had to go by Dock Lance's. He had his gun with him, though, so the other deputy and me started on down to the main road and Barlow went toward home. It was about five minutes I guess, before we heard a shot. We thought maybe Barlow had taken a try at a squirrel. Well, I hadn't been back in my office any time a-tall till somebody brought word Barlow had been killed. I went back up there and you could see the place, right along under a bank by the creek that ran alongside this path, where somebody had laid in wait for Barlow. He'd been shot in the back of the head. We arrested Dock Lance. His sister-in-law, little girl fourteen years old, was our main witness against him. She'd seen him come running down that path right after the shot. He didn't have his gun, though, she said. We never did find the gun. Luke and Dock were tried in same term of court, Luke for killing young James Nelson a couple of years before, Dock for murdering Barlow. Luke was sentenced to eighteen years, Dock to twenty.

"Well, that was the last I had to do with any of them, but the youngest boy, Bill, he went ahead and got into trouble too. After he'd been in prison about five years, Luke escaped, was loose two years, the police in Harlan, Kentucky, captured him but before they could bring him back to North Carolina he escaped again. This time him and Bill went to New Mexico and it was April, nineteen twenty-nine, before they captured them. Fight just like a Western movie, up and down canyons and desert around Alamogordo, Luke and Bill still trying to shoot their way out. They were brought back to prison, though. A few years later they let Dock out on parole to go home to die. Had t.b. Their pappy, old Red Nick, had died the first year they went to the penitentiary. He died penniless. But he'd never tried to teach the boys anything but stilling, even though he was peaceable enough himself." Bailey's face is still and thoughtful, recalling all the wasted lives.

Then, just as it has carried him over so many rough places in the past, humor picks up his spirits again. A wide smile creases his face and he parts with one final reminiscence. "Back in twenty-two, my last year in Madison. We'd been tipped off about a new stilling outfit up on one of the Laurels, and that Friday night I took a couple of my deputies and we went up the creek. Found the cove and the still all right, nobody around; we scattered ourselves behind some ivy bushes and waited for day. Right after sunrise they come in, four young bucks all set for a big run of week-end liquor. It was a pretty outfit they had, I'll have to admit, and they were mighty proud of it, too. After they got their fire built, one of the boys just stood back looking at all that fine copper and he said to his cronies there, 'Damned if I ain't sorry ole Sheriff Bailey can't know we got a fine setup like this right under his nose. Believe I'll just phone him up and tell the ole rascal.'

"Telephones were just coming into use in Madison then, and this feller strolled over to the bush right in front of where I was hiding and cranked his arm around and around. He held a little branch up to his ear and grinned at his buddies over by the still. 'Hello, Central,' he hollered, 'let me speak to Sheriff Jesse James Bailey.'

"I stood up from behind the bush. 'Right here, son,' I said.

"We didn't have a bit of trouble taking them four fellers. They were plum speechless. I've been a lot of wrong places at the right time, during my life, and a lot of right places at the wrong time, but I never was at a better place at a righter time than that morning." He chuckles.

# 20

## No Cokes in Hell

On a simmering mid-July Saturday along the river, the county seats ebb and flow with a tide of people in from the surrounding countryside. The counters of the chain dime and clothing stores, the booths of odorous lunch stands, shady street corners or the cool porch before the crowded doctor's office: these overflow with the women in their town ginghams and rayons, the men in their best overalls and serges exchanging news, trading sharply, finding human contact. Slowly the tide comes in during the morning by truck and bus and battered family car, even yet occasionally by wagon; through the stifling hours of late afternoon it recedes back into the hills, the level farms, the upland coves. From noon till two o'clock the Saturday tide has reached its fullness. And the fervent preacher on the courthouse lawn has reached his highest peak.

Shirt-sleeved, armed only with a large loudspeaker and a small Bible, red of face, with a voice he will not admit is susceptible to the human frailty of exhaustion, this minister is a one-man army hurling himself against all the age-old Powers and Principalities of Darkness. In a mighty and mounting monotone, his voice overlays the town, reaching beyond the trampled courthouse square and its human swarm around him into stores and offices, into the houses beyond where children lie taking fitful naps and the languor of a hot long afternoon permeates the very air.

"Hit's a bold time we're a-living through, folks, a bold dark time, and I'm here to tell you today that the day and the hour is a-coming when the sheep are going to be separated out from the goats, and brother it won't make no matter then who you are—you may be one of the deacons in these-here fine city churches that go walking around like they had cucklebeers in their hair with faces pickled in prune juice, or you may even be one of these city-slicker preachers that's got a shoestring with a few knots tied in it where his backbone ought to be, you may be fine society folks wearing low-cut dresses, dancing all squeezed up in some other man's arms and both of you as full of lust as an old dead dog that's blowed up and full of maggots: and if you're any of these, brother you're lost and damned to hell and it don't matter what your name or address has been here in this poor old sinful world.

"Oh-h I'm so proud I've got the old time salvation, the real soul-splitting, happy-shouting kind of religion. Why I wouldn't pay tax on that other kind of mincing, namby-pamby, low-voiced stuff that passes itself off for salvation. Because, brother, I'm a-telling you straight, you've got to take the tonic of God and eat the whole word; that'll put some zip in your soul, brother, when you know that there ain't nothing but the hand of God can knock the devil out of you. Some say my kind of preaching is 'sensationalism' but let me tell you I'd rather have sensation than stagnation. Hit's the putrid old stagnant ponds have the wiggle-tails, and wiggle-tails breed mosquitoes and mosquitoes make malaria and that malaria, brother, brings death—and death's what I'm working against: the black everlasting death set up against eternal life. Oh-h I'm a-telling you plain, on that final judgment day when the Lord comes on earth a-riding that pure white stallion bred in the stables of God, and when He begins to choose up His own, there's a-many of you going to be a-weeping and hollering and begging for mercy—but brother, the time to beg is now. Get right now, pull your feet out of the muck and mire of hell, cause hit's a place of pain and sorrow everlasting, burning forever, and, brother, when you're burn-

ing and sweating down there let me tell you there ain't no relief. There ain't no fans nor no rest and, brother, there ain't no Cokes in hell."

His voice, which has made no pause but has risen steadily to a hoarse cry of mingled threat and plea, rests momentarily so that his picture of eternal fires sinks into the already heat-oppressed crowd. Just as Coca-Cola was a Southern product which became part of the national way of life, so this religious appeal is also part of a place and born of a long past. Both the drink and the philosophy offer satisfaction to a thirst bone-deep. Each is a combination of sharp sweetness, chilled warmth, and languid zest that slips down easily and somehow seems to renew the energy to carry on for awhile longer. Hell is as real as the green glass bottle of a Coke; perhaps even a little easier to believe in than the limitless joy of heaven.

It is a brisk autumn evening in the semimetropolitan city of

Asheville. The modern facade of the low-slung auditorium in the hotel area of this tourist town is splashed with banners. Inside and out thousands of eager followers jostle for seats, settle for standing room or the loudspeaker in the lower floor annexes, wait patiently for the message from the dynamic young wavy-haired evangelist who became known a few years ago throughout America as the Gabardine Gabriel, the Barrymore of the Bible. He has conferred with presidents, converted movie stars and racket men and attracted record crowds in the major cities of the nation, and he more recently swept through the world's largest city, that capital of calm reserve and judicious reflection, London, with a Crusade so efficiently organized and effectively presented that Wembley Stadium itself was finally required to accommodate his listeners. Billy Graham's home is here in the mountains, and his theology is also at home here. With burning eyes and tense leashed body, Billy Graham stands on the stage under the floodlights and tells the people:

"No man since Adam who has not believed on Jesus Christ will be in heaven. . . . Women, keep your house clean . . . don't gossip . . . all some children have for Sunday dinner is roast preacher . . . and take time with your children. If you want to lick the devil, hit him over the head with a cradle." When it is time to ask for "love gifts" to carry on his Crusade, Bill Coeur de Lion points out, "The gospel is free but the pail you carry the water of life in costs money." To the sad sweet familiar music of "Almost Persuaded," he collects cash for his Crusade and saves souls, revives fundamentalist religion far beyond any dreams of the ignorant courtyard evangelists who are designated by the city dwellers as strictly for "the mountain folks." The personal sincerity and conviction of this young preacher are as much the essence of his appeal as the methods of his campaigns are the essence of the century and social climate in which we live.

But the French Broad country has always been a region of religious activity. Perhaps that is why its people have always resented so bitterly the accounts of writers who have "come in from

off apiece" and related any of the tales of its religious practices.
Among themselves they will laugh lustily at the story of the mountain traveler who went to piedmont North Carolina and, when
one of the lowland natives there asked him what the altitude was in
Buncombe County, replied, "Baptist by a damn sight."

But they will not smile at the story in print of a traveling
preacher in the early days who asked one of the mountain women
if there were any ministers in that country, to which the woman
replied, "You can just go 'round to the gable end of the house and
see for yourself. John's got the hides of ever' kind of varmint in this
county tacked up there."

The French Broad highlanders have always wanted to be
friendly—but never patronized. Socially, economically, religiously,
they have come from a tradition of independence and individual
worth that would tolerate no inferior status. They did not want to
be "uplifted." They wanted to go along on a mutual journey and
pull their own weight. So they have clung to their religion and
regarded suspiciously any who came to examine it.

Actually the history of the churches on the river was a natural
result of the settlers' backgrounds and their physical environment.
Because much of the region was difficult to penetrate, because roads
were few and even those few had stingy upkeep for many years,
preachers and congregations found it impossible to get together.
When churches finally were organized, each meeting was a tribute
to the religious zeal and social hunger of both minister and audience.

Being predominately Scotch-Irish in origin, most of the French
Broad people were also Presbyterian ecclesiastically. At least at the
time of their arrival here. The older settlements through which they
passed on their migration to East Tennessee and Western North
Carolina—Abingdon, Virginia, on the northwest, Morganton,
North Carolina, on the east, and Jonesboro, the oldest town in Tennessee—had been heavily Presbyterian from their beginning.

As early as 1778 the Reverend Samuel Doak located in Washington County, Northeast Tennessee, and established a Presbyterian church. It was five years later before the first Baptist church assembled in that county and the Methodists began their work. In adjoining Greene County, the first preaching in Greeneville was done in 1780 by Samuel Doak and the first church was certainly Presbyterian. Farther southwest, on the main stem of the river, at a site where the town of Dandridge would come into being eight years later, the Hopewell Presbyterian Church was organized in 1785.

One of the prime movers of Presbyterianism in East Tennessee and an arch rival of Samuel Doak's, Reverend Hezekiah Balch was probably the founder of this Hopewell Church. He was certainly its pastor shortly afterward, as well as pastor of another congregation organized some two years later about ten miles northeast of Dandridge. In 1786, the Baptists had established themselves. Two and a half miles east of Dandridge at Coon's Meetinghouse, their French Broad Baptist Church was formed.

Pushing farther south across the river, in September of 1789, a Baptist church was organized in the vicinity of the future town of Sevierville. And the coming of the last decade of the eighteenth century was to coincide with a growing number of denominations organizing all along the lower French Broad, although the Presbyterians remained in the lead.

In the autumn of 1790, a preacher named Samuel Carrick came to Gilliam's Fort located in the wide fork where the French Broad and Holston rivers meet to form the Tennessee. Carrick, like Doak and Balch, was a Presbyterian from Virginia and eager to establish churches through this region. In 1791 he returned to Gilliam's Fort with Hezekiah Balch, and the two ministers stood upon an Indian mound and delivered their message. That same year Lebanon-in-the-Fork was organized with Mr. Carrick as its pastor.

Also about 1790 one of the first Methodist societies in Tennessee made its appearance at a neighborhood named Earnest on the Nolichucky River. It was named after a settler, Henry Earnest, who had come there eleven or twelve years before. This same man also provided, with his wife and five sons and six daughters, four fifths of the membership of the new Ebenezer Church.

Although some Friends, or Quakers, had emigrated from Pennsylvania and Eastern North Carolina prior to 1790, that year saw the beginning of an even larger influx into Greene County, along the Nolichucky and its big tributary, Lick Creek, and eventually southwest into Blount County to give their name to a community still called Friendsville. From this group was to come the first society for the abolition of Negro slavery in America, with branches in the largest counties up and down the Tennessee portion of the French Broad, and its first general convention was eventually held at the Lick Creek Meetinghouse.

Many of these church groups on the lower French Broad, particularly the Presbyterian and Baptist, had come before any church organization on the upper, or North Carolina part of the river. Settlement was slower there, travel decidedly more difficult, and it was probably about 1790 before the first congregations were established. In 1792 a Baptist church on the French Broad River, in the present Henderson County, was admitted to the Bethel Association of Upper South Carolina. Its eighteen members—traditionally organized in 1789—doubtless represent the first denomination established in the North Carolina west of the Blue Ridge.

George Newton, the earliest Presbyterian preacher in the area, was also a schoolteacher, and the first log schoolhouse in Buncombe County served as his church. By 1793 there were seventy Methodists on the "Swanino Circuit," and it is judged that the Baptists had a church on North Hominy Creek about 1791. So here, as in Tennessee, the Presbyterians and Baptists came first—it is difficult to be sure about the Baptists because of the more informal nature of their gatherings and the scarcity of written records—with the Methodists in close running and then, in certain sections, Quakers also. But the

Episcopal church arrived later. It was this Church of England many of the first Scotch-Irish and Huguenot settlers had especially disliked. Besides, to become a leader in this church a trip abroad was practically required, and although there were many natural leaders in the new country there were few who could afford such a journey. In addition, the formality of the Episcopal service was scarcely adapted to this pioneer surrounding. Even a half-century later, when Bishop Otey did arrive on the French Broad circuit, the general lack of understanding with which his services were attended was illustrated by the man who invited a friend to "Come on, let's go down and hear that feller read and his wife jaw back at him," referring to the fact that Mrs. Otey was sometimes the only member of the congregation who could serve as respondent during the litany.

Slowly, in time however, Episcopal and Catholic, Jewish and Christian Science and the other Protestant churches were added in the two or three largest urban centers along the river. But the religious picture today remains surprisingly like the very earliest development: fundamentalist and Protestant, with eager interest in personalities and no shrinking from quarrels of doctrine or individual interpretations of the Bible.

No personality the churches produced was more intrepid or influential than that of the Methodist bishop who had his first encounter with the French Broad watershed in 1793 in Tennessee when he "rode to Nolachucky . . . where I had about 200 hearers," and his last encounter in 1814 when he hastened "to camp-meeting away on the bleak hills of Haywood," in North Carolina. Bishop Francis Asbury gave Methodism in the old Southwest a boost from which it has not yet ceased to benefit. Year after year he came through the mountains winning new converts, broadening and deepening his influence. His journals are marvels of candor and complaint, ardor and anger—and always interesting. By 1797 he had begun to have some idea of this new area he was embracing, for after coping with the wild Toe River in North Carolina he wrote on a Saturday in March:

After riding three miles we began to scale the rocks, hills, and mountains, worming through pathless woods, to shun a deep ford. . . . I am of the opinion it is as hard, or harder, for the people of the west to gain religion as any other. When I consider where they came from, where they are, and how they are, and how they are called to go farther, their being unsettled, with so many objects to take their attention, with the health and good air they enjoy; and when I reflect that not one in a hundred came here to get religion, but rather to get plenty of good land, I think it will be well if some or many do not eventually lose their souls.

The following year, upon arrival at the resort of Warm Springs, he was able to comment further on the people: "My company was not agreeable here—there were too many subjects of the two great potentates of this Western World; whisky, brandy. My mind was greatly distressed."

As the years passed and Asbury came again and again into these backwoods settlements, his awareness of the stern demands of nature and the inherent eagerness of the people grew. He gave up trying to travel by chaise ("this mode of conveyance by no means suits the roads of this wilderness"), but horseback was not easy. In October 1801 as he pushed from East Tennessee toward Buncombe courthouse, "man and beast felt the mighty hills." And five years later when he was once more leaving Buncombe, crossing through Mills Gap down to Rutherford, he wrote, "one of the descents is like the roof of a house, for nearly a mile . . . I rode, I walked, I sweat, I tumbled, and my old knees failed: here are gullies, and rocks, and precipices; . . . bad is the best."

Four years later his struggle with nature had abated not a whit. On a November Sabbath in western North Carolina, he recorded:

Friday our troubles began at the foaming, roaring stream, which hid the rocks. At Catalouche I walked over a log. But

O, the mountain—height after height, and five miles over!
After crossing other streams, and losing ourselves in the woods,
we came in, about nine o'clock at night, to Vater Shuck's.

Perhaps the depth of the good bishop's feeling against the
hardships of travel here was reached when he said, "I will not be
rash, I dare not be rash in my protestations against any country;
but I think I will never more brave the wilderness without a tent."
Apparently the bishop suspected that to provide himself with a
tent would be in some way to question the ministrations of Divine
Providence.

As to the people among whom he labored in this tangled vine-
yard, Asbury was always torn between concern for their untutored
fervor and despair over their faults. On Mud Creek in November,
1802, he wrote:

I was happy to find that in the space of two years, God had
manifested his goodness and his power in the hearts of
many upon the solitary banks and isolated glades of French
Broad: some subjects of grace there were before, amongst
Methodists, Presbyterians, and Baptists. [Seven years later, he
observed:] At Buncombe I spoke on Luke 14:10. It was a
season of attention and feeling. We dined with Mr. Erwine,
and lodged with James Patton: how rich, how plain, how
humble, and how kind! [In the next breath, however, he was
lamenting:] What heights, what hills, what rocks! Lord, thou
preservest man and beast! The disagreeable part of this western wandering is the necessity of stopping at night. Ah! how
different are the taverns here from the houses of entertainment in the Atlantic States! And the keepers of these poisonous
liquor shops—Is there one who fears God and encourages prayer? One or two; the rest are drunkards. [In 1812 it was encouraging to learn that] God hath wrought upon the vilest of the

vile in the fork of Pigeon and French Broad Rivers, and He will
yet do wonders.

In laboring across "these Alps" and preaching his "awful
truths," Bishop Asbury left behind him a firm foundation of Methodism. And despite such remarks as, "once more I have escaped
from filth, fleas, rattlesnakes, hills, mountains, rocks, and rivers:
farewell, western world for awhile!" the affection he felt for this
"western world" was implicit in each pilgrimage he made as regularly as the year came around.

Like the early Baptists and Presbyterians, Bishop Asbury had
to preach in such accommodations and surroundings as he could
discover. In those earliest beginnings, it was truly the people and
not the building made a church. At first, homes were the com-
monest meeting places and the man with the largest, most cen-
trally located house was obliged to provide room for the annual
preaching of his denomination's representative. Such a house was
Jacob Shook's on Pigeon River in North Carolina.

Jacob's father had left the Netherlands in 1740 and nine years
later Jacob had been born in Pennsylvania. After the Revolutionary War, Jacob moved to Western North Carolina and on the flat
acres of the Pigeon River bottoms built the first frame house in what
is now Haywood County. Since there were no sawmills the Dutchman cut his lumber with a ripsaw and fashioned his own nails by
hand. His workmanship was stout; its product still stands. And the
third floor of this house was dedicated to the worship of God. Probably the first Methodist church in this present county of Haywood
congregated there, hung their hats on wooden pegs around the
room, and gave strict attention to Bishop Asbury, McKendree and
others. When he died in 1839, at the age of ninety, devout old Jacob
Shook left behind him three religious mementoes: the large Dutch
Bible from which he had always read aloud to his family; a will
which began, "In the first place I give my sole to Christ who re-

deemed it . . ."; and the land which he had donated for a camp-ground for his denomination's use.

On one of his journeys, Bishop Asbury had noted passing "two large encamping places of the Methodists and the Presbyterians: it made the country look like the Holy Land." These permanent sites of large annual revivals of religion were one of the most typical and interesting developments of the nineteenth century. Camp meetings answered many needs in the lives of these people and it is surprising that an institution of such human interest, with so much color and enough vigor to outlast the better part of a century, should have been so completely ignored in the annals of our region.

The Presbyterians may have inaugurated these camp meetings, but it was the Methodists who appropriated them into their history and made them their own.

The third or fourth week in August, when crops were "laid by" and "garden truck" was at its most plentiful, families within a radius of many miles put finishing touches on their arrangements to attend camp meetings. For weeks the best clothes had been readied, any delicacies of food saved back, and a neighbor had been approached about looking after the livestock and farm while the men were away. Through hot August days the mother and girls had been baking and preserving and stewing and drying and fattening, for as much of the food as possible was prepared ahead of time to leave the females as well as the males some leisure at the meeting in which to contemplate the state of their souls.

At last, dressed in clothes that might be worn only three or four times a year, with a wagon heaped full of produce—a hog or sheep perhaps, and a crate full of chickens, plus sacks of vegetables, melons, pans and plates and silver—with bedding piled high and extra clothing carefully packed, children fidgety with excitement and curiosity, and the mother guarding the Bible that was a necessary attendant at the sermons: at last the family set out for camp meeting. The journey might last hours or days, roads might be almost impassable from washing rains or mud, or they might be choked with dust. But arrival at the grounds, with hundreds, often thousands, of other people already there, was ample reward. The wagon was unloaded before one of the "tents." These were actually rough cabins or shacks built of logs at first and later of lumber. Around their walls were built-in sleeping bunks of scaffolding, and the floors were usually of dirt covered with straw. If the "tent" was overcrowded, the father or some of the boys might sleep in the loft above or out in the wagon. Then the time for renewing old friendships, embracing long-remembered relatives, and meeting new folks, arrived.

The heart of the meeting ground was the "arbor," an open-air structure with a roof supported by stout locust posts, and no sides at all. The tiered seats were made of slabs: their occupants were supposed to have come here for edification, not comfort. Not far from the arbor was the tent reserved for the ministers. Here they slept, such time as they had for sleep, which was little enough. These were strenuous occasions, with three or four services each day.

At daylight the trumpet sounded. In the earliest days a horn fashioned from the horn of some prize steer was used, but as years and wealth accumulated, a trumpet was added at some of the camps. This first blast was the signal for rising, and the second trumpet half an hour later was the signal for family worship. After breakfast another trumpet blast summoned everyone to public prayers in the arbor. At eight o'clock there was a sermon and another at eleven. At three o'clock in the afternoon and again in the evening "at early candle-light" there were more sermons. This was an average schedule, but there were more enthusiastic ones, and at least on one recorded occasion as many as eleven sermons were delivered in a single day.

Such a schedule required energy of both audience and speakers, and the lean-to for cooking therefore remained a busy place. Any family that could afford it brought a servant to help with these chores, but for the most part the women themselves picked and dressed chickens, boiled hams and sliced sides of beef, swung the black bubbling pots of coffee over the embers and mended their open fires. With their food as with their religion, these people liked it served plain and plentiful. Almost as scandalous as being a back-slider was being stingy at your table, and probably a good deal more likely to cause comment among the women.

So the preachers preached, the men and women listened, everybody sang, some shouted and many were moved to reform their lives. New experiences and friendships were shared and the young boys and girls courted. Many a marriage was made—if not directly in heaven, at least at camp meeting. And if, after these revivals, as one chronicler observed, "the reaction set in" and "there had been a harvesting; now there was sifting," still "Methodism had come to stay, and the pioneers were sowing in hope, whether it rained or shined."

That everything was not completely calm in the religious world, as might at first glance seem to be the case, was merely, however, another phase of the democracy that had birthed the camp meeting. The early days of the churches in the French Broad country were characterized by tremendous disputes over doctrine and shattering quarrels between creeds. Within the same denomination differences arose, such as that between the illustrious Samuel Doak and his equally illustrious fellow Presbyterian, Hezekiah Balch. Upon the latter's return from a trip to New England in 1796, he began to affirm a complicated code known as the "Hop-kinsian doctrine," a doctrine which the Reverend Doak immediately and heartily denounced. A schism in the church resulted. Eventually, over a period of years, Balch was tried twenty-one times for heresy—the accusations stemming mostly from Doak. So steadily did their enmity increase that it is related when these two men of God met face to face on a street of Greeneville one day, Doak said to Balch, "I will not move. I never get out of the way for the devil." Whereupon Balch replied, "Well, I always do," and stepped smartly to one side and up the street.

The Presbyterians in East Tennessee were not alone in disagreeing over creed among themselves. The early history of the French Broad Association of Baptist Churches in Western North Carolina is riddled with such rifts. Matters of discipline would dissolve into divisions over doctrine, and like amoeba multiplying by simple fission, the Baptist churches were always dividing to make room for a variation of creed or belief. Such was the situation when Stephen Morgan and Garret Deweese had their difference over the "doctrine of Election." Morgan was an Election man, believing some individuals were called by God to eternal life and they were the Sanctified; the rest were doomed to damnation, and nothing could alter that condition. Opposed to this was the Free Will in which Deweese believed. There were "criminations and recriminations" and the usual final splintering of congregations.

If Stephen Morgan was representative of interchurch quarrels, he was even more typical of interdenominational feuds. His main target was Methodism, and he "met his opponents with the Sword of the Spirit" for many a year. His best remembered piece of wisdom was stated in many a sermon: "Brethren, there are three things God-Almighty never made and never intended should be: a mule, a mulatto and a Methodist."

For sheer rapture of invective, however, no three men in the area could equal the bright and steady burning of the Methodists' Parson Brownlow. From the first early days of his preaching in North Carolina through the famous years of a lifetime in Knoxville and vicinity, the Parson (whom we've already met during the Civil War as a Republican editor and during the Reconstruction as Governor of Tennessee) covered the area, and the country, with tracts, speeches, books and sermons attacking "an enemy compounded of Baptists, Presbyterians, the devil, Democrats, and finally the Confederates."

When he denounced Presbyterianism he did not spare the rod. "For these futile jackalls [Presbyterian, Congregational or Hopkinsian missionaries], who, during the long hard winters of the North, sit perched up in the chimney corner of some theological seminary, snuffing the delicious fumes of the mush-pot; or, dozing over a Latin primer, to sally out into the west in the spring and summer seasons, to enlighten the inhabitants thereof, is too intolerable to be borne any longer." At the same time he took a swipe at the Baptists: "The Baptists are a people whose theory is so narrow, and whose creed is so small, that, like their shoes, they seem to have been made for their exclusive use."

Since the Baptists seemed to rise more readily to refutation of his exaggerations—one North Carolina minister, Humphrey Posey, actually indicted and convicted him on charges of slander, and execution was levied on the Parson's "dun mare, bridle, saddle bags and umbrella"—it was the Baptists who soon became his prime target.

Brownlow reached the height of his denunciation in this delicate bit of hairsplitting: "When Presbyterians, Methodists, Episcopalians, and others, baptize either infants or adults, they introduce their subjects *faces foremost!* Our Baptist brethren are almost alone in their vulgarity in *backing into the Church of God!*"

So creed debated against creed, Free Willers opposed Electioners or Hard Shellers, there were revivalists and antirevivalists, Missionary and antimission Baptists, Hopkinsians and anti-Hopkinsians, and only by remembering Lord Bacon's dictum that "controversy is the wind by which the truth is winnowed" could many a man understand the hot air "winnowing" all around him.

Nevertheless these were the more sensational aspects of religion. Less spectacular, but doubtless much more effective, were the humble steadfast ministers of all denominations who covered large territories and visited sparsely settled regions, rode horseback when they owned a horse and walked when they did not, and during part of their time had to farm or otherwise scrabble a living as best they could, because part of the Protestant heritage of these mountain people was certainty that the word of God was free and, unlike Billy Graham, these old-time ministers had not yet learned to point out that nonetheless the vessel which carried that word cost.

There was affection between these people and their preachers, and there were often love gifts of food or goods. In return, these Methodist, Presbyterian and Baptist ministers brought companionship and news into many a lonely mountain cabin, often combined teaching with their preaching and on many an occasion used the same small building for both. They often worked for not only heaven-after-death but a better-life-on-earth as well. The editor of the first newspaper in Western North Carolina, a weekly called *The Highland Messenger*, was David McAnally, a Methodist circuit rider with headquarters in Asheville, and a Knoxville minister named Charles Charlton was the first person to bring Jersey cattle into East Tennessee, and by his interest in progressive farming established the first creamery and owned the first reaper in that area, also.

Their hours of laborious travel went unrecorded, although the winters were as cold and the hills as steep for them as for the more eloquent Bishop Asbury. Their poverty of goods was often real but they felt rich in spirit and zeal. There are no monuments left to them except in the memories of a few old-timers. Like the watery-eyed, quavering octogenarian you pick up just outside of Asheville and give a ride down the river to a crossroads called Alexander. He speaks of his Baptist church and on some impulse you ask him if he ever knew your great-grandfather, John Henry Ballard, who lived many miles away from this spot, but who covered many a mountain county in his ministry for the Baptist Church (Free Will division). The old eyes turn to look at you anew and there is a sudden light in their blue depths. "Preacher Ballard? Did I know Preacher Ballard?" The unsure chin quivers for a moment. "He was the finest old man I ever knew. Many's the sermon of his I've listened at. Quiet and reasonable, that's the way he talked—but what he said, it was food for your everlasting soul. He was in that War Between the States, you know. Maybe that give him a difference over some of the other preachers. I don't know." The old man is quiet, looking out the car window at the river as you drive along. "I've got Preacher Ballard's picture at home now, laid safe between the leaves of my Bible."

So there are memorials of various kinds to the "old-time religion." Perhaps the most apparent outgrowth is in the ten large religious assembly grounds that swarm each year with people from all parts of the world and bring modern dress to the old impulse that summertime was meeting time in the mountains. At Ridgecrest and Montreat, Lakes Junaluska and Kanuga, Blue Ridge and Ben Lippen, Cragmont and Bon Clarken, Lutherridge and Osceola, all within a twenty-five mile radius of Asheville, over one hundred thousand people assemble on a June-through-August schedule. The old trumpet blasts are no longer part of the ritual, but there are still sermons and good fellowship in plenty.

In fact, much of the religious life along the French Broad is essentially the same as it was a century ago. This has been a source of bafflement and amusement and speculation to many a tourist in the area, be he a permanent newcomer or a transient passerby. What he usually fails to understand is the long racial past of these people, bred on the moors of Scotland, in the wild seabound counties of Ireland, their superstitions and premonitions transmitted from generation to generation like a color of eyes or a quality of skin.

What these strangers have not known is the loneliness of mountain winter, with wind rushing like a dark unfathomable evil through the hills, and endless unfilled nights of time for a man or a woman or a child to sit by the fire and wonder on the simple strangeness of life. In the cities, where all seems man-made and man-controlled, man's logic and reason may provide answers sufficient to the needs of man. But here, where even yet, in some of the remoter coves and ridges, a man may seem the least significant part of life, where there is still manifestation of a large design counterpointed against a great chaos, here there are and will be the primary gropings of religion seeking truth. Often comical, occasionally inspiring, the insights into Christianity of the people on this mountain river are sometimes simple to the point of absurdity, sometimes profound to the point of wisdom. If they believe that there are no Cokes in hell, they also grant human beings the dignity of a soul that can experience hell. As in so much else, here they are a paradox, a sort of symbol of all human wonder and perverseness.

# 21

# The Chattering Children

Long Man, the Cherokees called the river. Long Man whose head rested on the mountains, whose feet lay along the valleys, who was fed by the Chattering Children of all his tributary streams.

You cannot know this river by simply sitting on the level banks of its lower body or by striking out on any straight road up its course; you must judge the "lay of the land" and follow a wandering path that will take "rounders" on its sources high in the mountains. Likewise, to know its people you cannot adopt quick attitudes or secondhand generalities, a frontal approach forespells failure in any friendship; you must take "rounders" here, too, and find your way by easy conversation into their sources of character and life. As each odd characteristic little branch finally drains the fullness of its stream into the French Broad, so each individual person finally pours the ripeness of his personality into the region where he dwells. There is no one creek, there is no one person, representative of the river or the region. But there are a few of the little creeks and little people whose lives and words bespeak with special force some particular feature of the French Broad: Mister Jason and Granny McNabb and Cousin Fanny and Uncle Wash, each as different from the other as the part of the river on which each lives differs from the whole. Yet as alike too, in their large regional kinship and humanity.

Mister Jason's folks have been in the mountains of Mitchell

330

County, North Carolina, a long time. He is a mountain man by birth and breeding and belief, but cartoonists and itinerant sociologists would be disappointed to know it. Mister Jason has the handsome assurance of a successful industrialist and the quiet thoughtfulness of a poet, and perhaps it takes something of both to be an effective superintendent of schools in this rugged county. The county seat of Bakersville, where his office functions, has been dwindling in size for years, since flood wiped out a length of its homes and the mica industry moved its center ten miles away to Spruce Pine, but it remains the hub of justice and education. Slow as a summer afternoon, with a little cluster of men on the street corner in front of the courthouse, somehow faintly New England in the homogeneous aspect of its houses and the lack of commercial specialization in its dozen or so stores, Bakersville offers a surprise in the reserved dignity of its leading school official.

The title "Mister Jason" combines the familiarity and respect in which he's held. For Jason Deyton's family are older to the county by half a century than the name it bears. "My great-grandfather Nathan by seventeen ninety had gathered up a good deal of land in the bend of Toe River where Cane Creek joins it—after a while it came to be called Deyton's Bend. It was virgin country then. Nathan had married Mary Knight. Her father, my great-great-grandfather that would be, was killed in a horse race. Racing was one of the main sports in those days, you know. Mary's father had won the race, but just as his horse crossed the line it hit soft ground, threw him against a tree and broke his neck. Makes them come alive for you, doesn't it, to know how they died, your ancestors."

Mister Jason's soft voice pauses. His dark, almost humorous eyes light the olive complexion beneath soft graying patches in his brown hair. "Those are some of the little things made me come back here after college, I guess. Other places had more money, more people. This was the place I knew best, the place where I might help out, like my grandfather or great-grandfather did." He smiles slightly so that you will not confuse reminiscence with conceit, then says, more briskly, "A project we have here in the schools is designed to show the pupils history is alive and let them learn something about their own past. One year they helped write a pageant about our county. Maybe the drama technique wasn't faultless but we all learned a lot about where we live and about ourselves. It's well to learn about yourself, you know."

He goes on to tell about these mountains and their little valleys he knows so well, filling in dates and figures with loving knowledge born of concern, moving through generations and recounting experiences easily, as if they had assimilated into his own experience. Mister Jason has another quality rare today and perhaps it is the natural result of this fusion of past and present: a calm that seems utterly remote from that gnawing deadly modern disease—harassment. His voice seems utterly patient and imperturbable. It is appropriate that this high northern corner of the French Broad watershed, guarded by the towering heights of Roan and Mitchell and the Blacks, should produce a man who had absorbed some of their quiet self-possession and sense of timelessness, and set him to work with a younger generation.

On the opposite side of the French Broad watershed, where bold Allen's Creek rushes down out of the Balsams, anyone you talk with up or down that creek and many adjoining ones can tell you who Granny Sarah McNabb is and where she lives. In a weathered little house yon side of the creek. There are still pockets of snow high up in the mountains around the narrow valley, but the buds on the cherry trees in Granny's yard are swelling toward spring. There are shocks of fodder and stacks of green wood in the yard too, for a son and his family live in part of Granny's house. Nevertheless, she does all her own cooking and keeping in the two front rooms she set aside for herself after she'd finished her life work as a midwife and divided up the farm among her children. Her face is round and webbed with fine lines and full of light. Its strength of character matches her lean body's strength of muscle.

"Law, child, I've had to be strong. I'm eighty-four years old now and I've catched babies ever since I was twenty. The last one was when I was eighty. I slipped out in the night, none of the family knew about it, and I got back before morning. None of them know about it to this day.

"I waited on two or three doctors at different times while I was growing up—everybody always said I had the turn to be a nurse—and after a while women started sending for me if they couldn't get the doctor, and pretty soon some of them wanted just me, wouldn't hear to a doctor looking after them. I couldn't count all the babies—five, six, seven hundred?—there was over a hundred I guess, that I never turned in at Raleigh. It was before I ever had those forms to fill. But out of all that number, over all those years, I never lost a baby or a mother. Oh, it wasn't none of my doing. It was the work of the Lord. I was just an instrument for Him to use.

"During those years I got married and had children myself. There was ten of them, five boys and five girls, all still living today but one, and I've got forty grandchildren and fifty-two great-grandchildren and four great-great-grandchildren. And my husband was only fifty-two years old when he died. My baby was under five and there was four of the younguns just tots. It was hard going for me, sometimes we went short, but I never begged for anything. We always made a crop. I never stopped under a thousand cans of food, not counting pickles and jellies, and we had apples in the cellar.

"And for thirty years I made wreaths for the Farmer's Federation over at Asheville. They'd ship them up North and all around. I'd go up on the Balsams and get my green stuff. I'd hitch up my wagon and team and put the children in and go up into the mountains and gather greens all day long. The Federation furnished me all the wire and materials I needed. I'd get a dollar a wreath.

"But many's the time I've put it aside to go on a call. One of my boys asked me once, 'Mama, what if you had a contract for a hundred wreaths and they was due the next morning and you were running short, but someone came asking you to go to a woman whose time had come, what would you do?' 'Why, I'd lay them wreaths down,' I told him. 'Wreaths can wait. A woman can't.'

"There's no time in the world like the hour a woman's bringing a baby. There's nothing like somebody coming into the world, a new life. And nobody ever come and knocked on my door and asked me to look after their wife that I didn't go. Snow or rain or cold, it never hurt me to go out in weather when I went on a case. I remember one electric storm, the man led the way up over a high ridge, the thunder was crashing and the lightning was so close the horse would just squat and tremble every time it come. But we made it through all right.

"One of the hardest and pitifulest places I ever went was to a lumber camp way back there in the Balsams. The man come after me and we rode just about all night before we got to the house, one of those poor little throwed-together lumber shacks and it already full of babies. The woman was having a hard time. I straightened up the house and took care of the children and gave the mother a little quinine in two ounces of castor oil—that's all the medicine I ever gave, and the best doctor I ever waited on showed me about using that if the baby was lingering. But I stayed a week there. I always saw my woman through, no matter how long it took, and there wasn't a scrap to cover the baby's nakedness whenever it did come. So while I waited I had to make it a belly band and some little shirts and gowns. I'd always take flannel in my bag and if they didn't have any fixings, I'd make what they needed. Sometimes I'd take food too, if I knew it to be a place where the folks were in need. There was seven babies I caught in that lumber camp before I was through there.

"Pay? Once in a while they'd pay me. That wasn't what I went for. At first I charged ten dollars. Later on I asked twenty. But mostly it was just whatever they could give, and I never dunned anybody in my life. They never paid in produce, though, 'cause usually I had more than they did. I'd be carrying them food.

"One of the doctors let me read up in his books and after a while I signed up in Raleigh to be a midwife. They sent out somebody to teach us and give us a test. From that time on, I always got my Permit, and with a Grade A on it too. I carried all my necessaries in a denim bag with a drawstring top: washbasin and handbrush, nail file, soap, Lysol, cotton cord tape and dressing, boric acid and eyedrops, two pad covers, four towels, a white coverall apron and cap and the birth certificate and report cards on the mother and baby. It had to all be boiled in disinfectant water and wrapped in clean rags. And I always kept my special dress and slip and shoes and stockings cleaned and ready at hand for me to step right into night or day whenever a call came."

Granny McNabb leaves for a moment and goes into the next room. She walks slowly because in the past year she's broken both hips. When she comes back her bright blue eyes are shining above the faded blue denim of the bag she's clutching. On her lap she sorts through the remnant of necessaries left in the little bag that has gone with her over so many lonely trails during so many strange hours, helping deliver life in the French Broad country. The white cap that folded to cover her head, crowned by a bit of yellowed lace sewed with tiny stitches. As she handles the flannels and cottons and bottles, a smile creeps across her face.

"Some folks think the moon changing has something to do

with the time a baby's born. It don't have anything to do with it. When the apple's ripe, it'll fall. The baby wasn't got in the moon, it'll not be had there, neither." Remembering something else, her face sobers. "A few times I had to tend a girl as young as fourteen. That's not right. A man ought to stay off that marriage till the girl's of age to have a baby. No matter what age, a man can't ever be too good to a woman has had his children. I've seen them come to their time and I know. I remember once a father came after me to help his daughter. She wasn't married, but her folks were looking after her all right. They don't always, when it's like that. I went and stayed with her and when her baby come, it was black. What'd I do? Just what I did for every one of my babies. Spanked the breath of life in it and put drops in its eyes, give it a bath and dressed it and put it to the breast. It was another soul, and its mother was another mother. I'd never lower her name none either. But I watched that baby grow up, and sometimes it pretty near broke my heart seeing him neither black nor white and neither side claiming him. He went away from North Carolina finally. I don't know where he is now but I hope he's found his Lord, wherever he is.

"My babies are scattered all over. Whenever I go to our church up here I can sit and count folks I helped bring in the world. That was my talent. I never had an education but the Lord give me my talent. And I never heard a knock come on that door at night that I didn't start talking to the Lord. He can do anything. He made the leaves of the herbs for the healing of the nations, and He can carry a body through any trial. I'd ask Him to help me. I'd tell Him it was a mother I was going to help and He'd have to show me what to do. All the way going, on horseback or walking, riding behind mules or maybe even oxen, I'd call on the Lord. This was my mission in life and I did it with His help the best I could. Because there's nothing on this earth like seeing a new life come into the world."

Standing on the porch of her little house, looking up toward the hardy mountains as crowned with white as she, and down the valley toward all the houses clustered close as fox grapes, Granny McNabb folds her careful hands over the black dressy apron she wears and says, "Nowadays I'm the poorest woman on this creek, far as money counts. But I'll never want."

Going up or down Allen's Creek, and many adjoining valleys, anyone you talk with can tell you who Granny Sarah McNabb is —who she is and what her eighty-four years have been.

And for miles up and down the lower Tennessee part of the river, from Knoxville to the North Carolina line, almost anyone can tell you about the big white house with the colonnade connecting to a smaller house, on the hill above the river and the main highway West. About the big house called Swannburne and the tiny woman who was mistress there until a little while ago.

Cousin Fanny wasn't quite five feet tall. Her bones were small as a bird's, and her face was bright and inquiring and gentle. Sometimes she seemed so fleshless that it would have been no surprise if the wind had caught in one of her pink or lavender shawls and billowed her completely away to some never-never land of milk and honey. Delicate as the Dresden treasures that adorned her piano and library table and whatnot shelves, pale and perfect, Cousin Fanny was more than her appearance would admit. She was a tough-sinewed, lively woman who gave birth to eight children, withstood fire (her first home on this same site burned completely) and flood (the Douglas Dam lake of TVA covered the hundreds of acres of farmland surrounding her home) and death (of husband and children). And from it all she tried to wring a token of meaning and a memento of beauty. For despite the fact that she lived in comparative ease on a large plantation, she was one of the few of the world who respected the attainments of the mind above the accumulations of the flesh. Herself from the Burnett family (one member by marriage was author of *Little Lord Fauntleroy* and *The Secret Garden*, and a brother wrote the definitive history of *The Continental Congress*), a family who valued learning

and believed that reminiscence can be as valuable as an antique cupboard, she read old and modern classics and unashamedly wrote poetry.

When Tennessee Valley Authority chose Douglas, on the French Broad, as site for a dam, and when President Roosevelt asked Congress to approve its construction, Cousin Fanny, in pale silk and chiffon, turned her pen and ink against the yards of concrete mixing in the hoppers. She wrote letters to Senators, and sent poems to the President's wife. The multiple purposes of the TVA, with its dedication to flood control, navigation, reseeding of the eroded hills, and extension of electric power to remote areas may have eluded her poetical imagination. But her faith in the dark teeming acres of land her husband had planted and reaped, land that had meant a way of life to her for so long, never wavered. The land never had a stranger, more earnest, spokesman than this little bundle of emotion and determination, who throughout a sheltered life had grappled with most of the realities of experience. Her letters and poems did not save the acres her Colonel Swann had accumulated and worked, once with the help of the Stokely boys before they started their cannery, but she did get, by Presidential decree, a levee around the little French Broad Baptist Church that had been part of her life and the community life for generations. It stands today in a hidden corner at the water's edge.

It was typical that this little incident should happen to Cousin Fanny: Working her flower beds one day with a man from one of the farms—a helper who undoubtedly felt, as most mountain men

do, that he had lowered his masculine status in some way by "fool-
ing around with flowers"—she tried to be friendly and at the same
time share an insight that might make them both enjoy their work
more. "These bulbs, Walter, will be beautiful when they bloom. I
want you to be sure and come back to see them then. You know
the Bible says that man does not live by bread alone."

"He sure don't, Miss Fanny," Walter agreed, "he's got to
have a little meat along with it."

Her humor would have carried her across the gulf between
them. For Cousin Fanny was a mountain woman with a mountain understanding, and although she lived in a typical plantation
house, she was no typical plantation mistress. She could do whatever seemed to her must be done, including bury her dead and
fight with words and accept her defeats, and seem all the while
as fragile as a Dresden figurine.

Farther up the river, above Cousin Fanny who was and her
Swannburne that is, bordering on North Carolina, is Cocke County,
bisected by the French Broad River. South of the river the county
edges toward the Smoky Mountains and takes in part of their blue
and lofty preserves—but north of the river lies the knob country.
The knobs are as different from the Smokies as brown sparrows are
different from eagles. One is a homely, man-familiar thing, while
the other is wild and aloof.

It has been a long time since the knobs boasted any timber of
respectable size. Rounded from decades of erosion, they are laced
with dozens of cowpaths winding up and down the steep trampled
slopes. Where they have been altogether abandoned the growth is
scrubby, bushes and briars clinging to the poor soil which many of
the local farmers say "ain't fit for nothing but to hold the world together."

In the midst of this knob country is a little oasis. Down a red
clay road from a lonely one-room white frame church set among
pines, lie two adjoining farms. They are small in acreage—thirty or
forty acres each—but the fields are heavy with alfalfa, the pastures

are prosperous with cows and hogs and goats, the garden lot is a
medley of greens: lettuce, cabbage, mustard, peas. One small house
sits neatly on a hill between the fields and another, older one, is
settled in the valley just below it. Two of Uncle Wash's children
own these homes and these fields they tend. Not many Negroes
own farms in the French Broad back country. Uncle Wash lives
here at his old house in the valley but he doesn't tend any more
crops. He was born the thirteenth of March, 1859. He's ninety-
six years old and ready for a rest.

"I was born up at Del Rio, on the French Broad. My mammy
belonged to Mr. Matthew Weathers there and so whenever I come
along I belonged to him too. It's a quare thing to look back on: one
man owning another one. But that's the way it was. Matthew
Weathers bought my mammy at auction up at Warm Springs,
North Caroliny. They used to hold slave auctions there ever once
in a while. Mammy had walked all the way from Mexico—she
told me about it when I was a little youngun—but she never said
whether she was born there or if she'd come on a boat and just
been landed off there. But her and all the others they sold at the
Springs that day had been fetched from Mexico barefooted. Mammy said her feet was cut to pieces by the rocks. She and Lou was
put up for sale together. Mammy's name was Angeline. They always sold slaves in pairs if they could. Mammy went on the block
first. Mr. Matthew looked at her and said, 'That's the one I want.'
He paid twelve hundred dollars for Mammy. Lou just brought
eleven hundred. Mr. Matthew wouldn't pay no more for her.

"Mammy lived at Mr. Matthew's the rest of her life, even after
the War. Not two years after she come there she had me. I was her
first youngun. Not long after, she got married to a young slave Mr.
Matthews brought new on the place. All the rest of the younguns
she had was just half-kin to me.

"I growed up doing work on the farm. One thing I could always do better than anybody else on the whole place, and that was
break a drove of hogs to the road whenever they set out for South

Caroliny or Georgia. They're mean to drive but that was my job. I'd start out with about thirty and take them as far as Warm Springs—it's Hot Springs since then, ain't it?—and then whenever they were going good on the road I'd let the regular drivers take over and I'd start back to break another batch. I never did get all the way to South Caroliny myself. Just the beginning of the way. After you once get hogs broke to the road, you can't get them off, no matter how contrary they were at the start.

"Then one summer Mr. Matthew's daughter, Miss Jettie, went up to North Caroliny to a big Methodist Camp Meeting and met a man she wanted to marry. He was from near Asheville, and after the wedding I moved up there with her. She come and said to me, 'Wash, I know who you are and I want you to come and stay with me.' I went and I stayed ten years. I'd a-been there till yet but I had to come back to save a man's life. I was working in the field with two other Negro men one day, and they got in a fuss, then into a fight, one of them picked up a stick and busted it over the other's head. Nearly killed him. Well you know how it is when we get in any kind of trouble. First thing we know we get put on the roads. Miss Jettie and her husband talked to me about it, said they hated to see me go, but I was the only witness and if I wasn't there nobody could prove a thing about the fight, nobody would be sent to the gang. So I left. Miss Jettie shook my hand and there was tears standing in her eyes. We both knew who we was but we couldn't say nothing about it.

"I wasn't in North Caroliny but once after that. And that was when I went to work in lumber back in Lost Cove way up in Yancey County. I helped with the logging. Big virgin poplars and chestnuts and spruce trees. We used mules and horses to log the flats, and steers on the mountains. It was rough work but the country was fine. There was lots of different men working there. One I remember telling about how he helped drive the Cherokees from the mountains in Georgia and North Caroliny and Tennessee out to Oklahoma in eighteen thirty-eight. Like a cattle drive. Or my hogs. Or the time my mammy come from Mexico. Mighty quare to think back on it all."

Mighty quare for a fact, Uncle Wash. How many currents in French Broad life have touched you; how your own small buried story recapitulates in flesh the large history of the river's people. Even to the winning of this farm in the poor knobland back to green fertility, so that you and your sons living on it seem in a sense pioneers. A cycle is complete. And perhaps the meek, after all, do inherit at least large corners of the earth. One of the newest comers to the French Broad could know your story, Uncle Wash, more deeply and truly than many an old-timer. For really, Carl Sandburg is not a "newcomer" in any part of America. When he left the sunburnt Midwest for the mountains of North Carolina, he was just coming back to some of the land he'd sung about in ballads, to some of the people he'd written about in poems. The man who put a handle on Chicago as "Hog Butcher to the World" has come to live on the headwaters of a region which, before Chicago really got going, was the corn-and-hog capital of the continent.

In the winter of 1944–45, Sandburg with his wife Lillian (sister to camera artist Edward Steichen) and daughter Helga and their herd of prize Toggenburg and Nubian goats came from the blizzard-swept dunes of Michigan to the comparatively gentle Southern mountains. In a large white house cresting a pine-fringed hill above 240 acres of rolling woods and pasture and a private lake, once the dwelling of the Treasurer of the Confederacy, Sandburg laughs and says, "Ain't this a hell of a baronial estate for a proletarian poet?" But Connemara is not a "showplace estate"—it is a working farm, just as its owner is no "showcase poet" but a living spirit. His definition of poetry is understood by the French Broad folks—"a synthesis of hyacinths and biscuits"—although they might have phrased it differently to suit their geography: "a synthesis of trillium and corn bread."

The rugged character of his face and the white shock of hair is understood by his new neighbors too, for they can appreciate a man

who refuses to be pigeonholed: an artist who celebrates both tough
and gentle, large and small; a poet who is perhaps even greater as
historian-biographer. For if Abraham Lincoln was buried in noble
song by Whitman, he was resurrected in magnanimous prose by
Sandburg.

If Carl Sandburg is the most distinguished dweller in the
French Broad country (letters addressed simply "Sandburg, Level
Pebble, U.S.A." have reached him at Flat Rock, North Carolina),
he is also one of its friendliest farmers and most understanding
neighbors. There are no "important" or "unimportant" people in
his horizon. There are only people, all of some interest and each
of some worth. He has been around for three quarters of a century now, and when he holds out his hand in greeting to you at
Connemara, you feel you are sharing time with one of the real
men of the century—or as the Cherokees called their leaders, one
of the old chief men of the nation.

So the tiny streams and little folks gather to make a river and
a people. Even the little stream I knew best, Beaverdam Creek
just northwest of Asheville. This Chattering Child has in its own
small pattern duplicated, too, the life of the Long Man. It is astonishing to look back and remember and realize how everything in
this story of the river was foreshadowed, really, in the simpler personal story of Beaverdam.

Even the course of this little creek is like that of the French
Broad: starting high in the mountains at the head of the valley,
past gray boulders and laurel clumps, it reaches the farmland and
travels more slowly, past level fields, and then into a man-made
lake. Beyond the dam it flows quietly to its merging with the larger
river. Along its twisting banks, not so long ago, a man or a child
could kick up an occasional arrowhead and feel the thrill of antique discovery, remembering that Shawnees and Cherokees once
traveled here.

Resting on its stream bed and bolted to nearby rocks, are the
pine sills, over a century old now, that supported an early gristmill

for the settlers and later held a sash sawmill. Over the gap that crosses the mountain rim near the Blue Ridge Parkway, the herb and galax gatherers used to come each winter, trudging, tenacious people determined to overcome the Depression; and up the valley, from far places, strangers sometimes came and stayed. Like Mr. Hydie, the Dane, who had been gardener to His Majesty the King of Denmark and in America drove his horse and buggy on the left side of the road; who planted, probably for the first time, asparagus on Beaverdam, and created of his little farm and modest house a sight so green and rich and pleasant that children believed a mansion stood behind those shrubs and garden paths, and were dismayed years later, when some new owner slashed away the living greenery, to see only an ordinary stark little home.

There was, and is, the weathered log Swain house, oldest in the valley, where two cousins were born in 1801, who became governors of states a continent apart—David Swain of North Carolina and Joseph Lane of Oregon; where Swain remembered seeing, as a boy, a regular four-wheeled farm wagon for the first time, and fleeing before the frightening rumble of its wheels as it jolted up the rocky creek-bed road. There is the Killian house, mentioned more than once in the journals of hard-pressed Bishop Asbury; and the crumbling rock piled under magnificent old oaks, where an uncle of Thomas Wolfe's, Bacchus Westall, lived when a diphtheria epidemic struck his children. There is the house of Republican politician Hezekiah Gudger who flourished under Theodore Roosevelt's administration, and not far away the house of Captain Baird, who served the Confederate States of America and was the gentleman-soldier of its legends.

There are a few of the old-time bear hunters who can relive the tales of Davy Crockett, born over on the Nolichucky, and Big Tom Wilson, who was kin to some of them. There are many of the workers who catch the industry buses out to the nearby plants. Up and down the creek there are retired residents who have come to this little valley from all parts of the country. Writers drift in and out.

An eminent musician is permanent now after thirty years. There are dairy barns and beef cattle and broiler houses and little patches in the burley tobacco allotments each year. There is a skilled wood-worker who studied at Vanderbilt's Biltmore under Miss Vance and Miss Yale. There is the man whose father drove a "sea of hogs" to South Carolina many a year and whose aunt (daughter-in-law of President Andrew Johnson) gave a scarab pin to Sheriff Jesse James Bailey because he'd fought the moonshiners. And occasion-ally, up the hidden inlets of this valley, there have been moon-shine stills, too. There has been much living on Beaverdam—it is one of the oldest settled outskirts of Asheville, meaning one of the oldest cleared too, and evidence still runs red and thick with every rain.

For the stream that was there twenty-five years ago is no longer there today. Once upon a time the summer sound of it through open windows caused strangers unaccustomed to a front-yard stream to think that rain was falling; last summer the trickle that seeped beneath its leaves and rocks was noiseless as dust. On the lower part of the stream there is a lawsuit pending over pollution of its water. The lake it forms has been drained to a mudhole twice during recent seasons to cart away the silt washed down by every rain. And last summer, as drought hovered for the third consecu-tive year over this region usually so rich in rainfall, even some of the oldest boldest springs deep in its mountains faded to their orig-inal unseen sources. I stood beside the damp sand of one of the best and most ancient of these springs, beneath a clump of high straight poplars and a ledge of rock, and I remembered the wonder of the clear flowing water that had always filled the basin there. How right that we should say a spring is fed by veins—tiny threads of water leading from many sources—and that we can destroy a spring by probing too deeply for its delicate feeders. From its veins and thousands like it, the life of Beaverdam Creek and French Broad River and the waters to which they run are made. Gradually the springs and streams and rivers have changed before our very eyes. A few of the springs have gone completely; many of the streams have dwindled irreparably; most of the rivers have diminished. They need, like the people of the region, our concern and respect.

For it is a rare region, this country of the French Broad that boasts so much variety of beauty and species and experience. How can a sentence sing it or a chapter describe it or a book give it full life? To paraphrase in prose a poem Robert Frost once wrote in a part of the country he too loved:

I'm going out to clean the spring and wait for it to flow clear again; I may taste its sweetness. I'm going out to feel the soft yield of winter moss and mulch beneath my woods' feet. Won't you come too?

I'm going out to hear the slow talk of some stranger becoming friend as I listen to his life; to see the wide sweep of the river's silent power around a certain bend beneath the sycamores. I'm going out to smell fresh rain on summer dust and the prehistoric water odors of the old French Broad in flood.

Won't you come too?

# Acknowledgments

Many of my acknowledgments for help in writing this book are either explicit or implicit in its text. The task of naming others to whom I am indebted seems at once limitless and necessary. Although I cannot name them individually, I must remember all those men and women who were my first source material for true and inner knowledge of the river region, who gave me at first their friendly attention and often afterward added their friendship. I thank each of those who gave me five minutes or five hours or, in fine generosity, the fruits of labor that have cost five years, or much more, of their devoted concentration. Whether we talked in the carpeted comfort of an office, leaning on a fence by the dusty roadside, among the turning wheels of industry or in camp along the upper reaches of the river, no matter where or when, it is the conversation and knowledge of these varied people who have given my story of the French Broad any of its quickening to life. Of course neither they nor any of these others to whom I am indebted are responsible for the book's shortcomings.

Particularly I should like to mention Mr. Jesse Stokely of Newport who, during his last illness, spent much time and energy relating to me facts and remembrances of some of the last great hog drives up the French Broad River. Also Mrs. A. A. Arthur of Knoxville, who, at 94 years of age, shared her memories with me through many long hot summer hours; and Mr. Verne Rhoades of Asheville, whose knowledge of western North Carolina is only equaled by his admiration for the region. Dr. Charles Hursh, formerly with the U.S. Forest Service in Asheville, and Mr. Van Court Hare, for-

347

merly with the Engineering Department of the Tennessee Valley
Authority in Knoxville, were most helpful in sharing their broad
knowledge of the whole river basin. Mr. James McClure Clarke
of Fairview, N.C., was generous with introductions to a wide and
varied circle of friends. And Mr. Gilbert Govan, of Chattanooga,
who was my first well-wisher, must know he has my appreciation.

Next I thank those librarians who worked with ability and
zeal in helping me gather information that was accurate, consequential and fresh—and often quite buried in obscurity. They were
Miss Ida Padelford in the Sondley Reference Room of Pack Memorial Library in Asheville, and Miss Margaret Ligon, Head Librar-
ian of Pack Memorial Library in Asheville; Miss Pollyanna
Creekmore in the McClung Room Collection at Lawson-McGhee
Library in Knoxville; the reference librarians at the University of
Tennessee Library, also in Knoxville; and Mrs. Lela Pearce in the
library of the *Citizen-Times* newspaper offices in Asheville.

There was always the encouragement and interest of friends
and relatives whose family histories are part of this river's long
past, or who are newcomers to the French Broad land but who
appreciate it no less, indeed perhaps more, than any of us. I wish
I could name each of these old-timers or late-arrivals but I am
sure many of them will find something of their own image, or contribution, in the pages of my book. And because my mother, Bonnie Cole, came of a family whose roots have been in the French
Broad hills for over a century and a half, and because my father,
Willard Dykeman, was drawn in middle life from New York state
to make a new home in the French Broad country, perhaps something of both the ancient awareness and the new-found delight
have fused in my perception of this native region. And whatever
there is of merit in this book, much of the credit must justly go to
James Stokely, my husband.

# Bibliography

## LETTERS, ACCOUNT BOOKS, AND DIARIES

Account Books, Ledgers and Register as well as Letters of the Sherrill Inn. Loaned by Mrs. James McClure Clarke, Fairview, North Carolina.

Letters of the McDowell Family. Loaned by Miss Margaret Ligon, Asheville, North Carolina.

Letters, Account Books and Various Papers relative to the early days of the canning business. James Stokely.

Day Book of Peter Fine. 1797–1804. Loaned by Mr. William Crawford, Newport, Tennessee.

Letters of the Civil War. Loaned by Miss Pauline Jones, Knoxville, Tennessee.

Minister's Account Book and various old newspapers. Loaned by Mrs. L. S. Allen, Newport, Tennessee.

Civil War Diary. Loaned by Mr. Iliff McMahan, Newport, Tennessee.

Various Papers and Information. Given by Miss Odessa Chambers, Asheville, North Carolina.

Civil War Diary of E.H. Rennolds. January to December 1863. In the University of Tennessee Archives at Knoxville, Tennessee.

## BOOKS AND PAMPHLETS

A *History Of Navigation On The Tennessee River System.* U.S. Government Printing Office, 1937.

Allen, William Cicero, *The Annals of Haywood County.* Asheville, N.C., The Inland Press, 1935.

———, *Centennial of Haywood County.* Waynesville, N.C., 1908.

Ammons, John, *Outline Of History of the French Broad Association And Mars Hill College.*

*Appleton's Illustrated Hand-Book of American Winter Resorts.* D. Appleton and Company, 1877.

349

Arthur, John Preston, *Western North Carolina*. Raleigh, N.C., Edwards and Broughton Printing Company, 1914.

Asbury, Francis, *Journals*. New York, Lane and Scott, 1852.

Ashe, Samuel A'Court, *History of North Carolina*. Greensboro, N.C., C.L. Van Noppen, 1908.

Ashe, W.W. and Ayres, H.B., *The Southern Appalachian Forests*. Department of the Interior, 1905.

*A Water Policy for the American People:* A Report of the President's Water Resources Policy Commission. 3 vols. 1950.

Battle, Kemp P., *History of the University Of North Carolina*. Raleigh, N.C., Edwards and Broughton Printing Company. 1912.

Biggs, Riley Oakey, *The Development Of Railroad Transportation In East Tennessee During The Reconstruction Period*. Unpublished Master's Thesis at University of Tennessee, 1934.

Bowman, Elizabeth Skaggs, *Land Of High Horizons*. Kingsport, Tenn., Southern Publishers Inc., 1938.

Boyer, Marie Louise, *Early Days All Soul's Church and Biltmore Village*. Biltmore, N.C., 1933.

Brown, John B., *Old Frontiers*. Kingsport, Tenn., Southern Publishers, 1938.

Brownlow, William G., *Helps To The Study of Presbyterianism*. Knoxville, Tenn., 1834.

————, *Portrait and Biography of Parson Brownlow, the Tennessee Patriot*. Indianapolis, Ind., Asher and Company, 1862.

————, *The Great Iron Wheel Examined*. Nashville, Tenn., 1856.

Bryant, William Cullen, Editor, *Picturesque America*. New York, D. Appleton and Company, 1872.

Bryson, Herman J. *The Story of the Geologic Making Of North Carolina*. Raleigh, N.C., 1928.

Buckingham, J.S., *The Slave States of America*. London, 1842.

Buckley, S.B., *Mountains of North Carolina and Tennessee*. 1859.

Burnett, Edmund Cody, *Big Creek's Response To The Coming Of The Railroad*. Agricultural History. July, 1947.

————, *Hog Raising and Hog Driving In The Region Of The French Broad River*. Agricultural History. April, 1946.

————, *The Railroad Comes to Big Creek*. The Railway and Locomotive Historical Society Bulletin No. 68.

Cameron, J.D. and Cushman, W.S., *Glimpses of A Land Of Beauty*. 1899.

Campbell, Robert F., Rev. D.D., *Mission Work Among The Mountain Whites In Asheville Presbytery, North Carolina*. 1899.

Carhart, Arthur H., *Water or Your Life*. Lippincott, 1951.

Chapin, George H., *Health Resorts of the South*. Boston, 1891.

Cleveland, John B., *Controversy Between John C. Calhoun and Robert Y. Hayne*. Spartanburg, S.C., 1913.

Colton, Henry E., *Guide Book to the Scenery of Western North Carolina*. 1860.

Coulter, E. Merton, *William G. Brownlow, Fighting Parson of the Southern Highlands*. Chapel Hill, University of North Carolina Press, 1937.

Davidson, Theodore F., *Reminiscences and Traditions of Western North Carolina*. 1928.

Deyton, Jason B., *History of Toe River Valley to 1865*.

Dick, Everett, *The Dixie Frontier*. New York, Knopf, 1948.

*Discovering Mitchell County*. County Board of Education, 1940.

Dunaway, Wayland F., *The Scotch-Irish of Colonial Pennsylvania*. Chapel Hill, University of North Carolina Press, 1944.

Eaton, Allen H., *Handicrafts of the Southern Highlands*. New York, Russell Sage Foundation, 1937.

*Flood Control Plan for the French Broad Valley*. Tennessee Valley Authority, June, 1949.

*Flood Control Plan for the Upper French Broad River and Tributaries*. Tennessee Valley Authority, 1942.

Folmsbee, Stanley J., Ph.D., *Sectionalism and Internal Improvements in Tennessee 1796–1845*. 1939.

——, and Deaderick, Lucile, *The Founding of Knoxville*. 1941.

Ford, Bonnie Willis, *The Story of the Penland Weavers*. 1941.

Foreman, Grant, *Indian Removal*. Norman, University of Oklahoma Press, 1932.

Gatchell, E. A., *The Standard Guide of Asheville and Western North Carolina*. 1887.

Gilman, Caroline, *The Poetry of Travelling in the United States*. New York, S. Colman, 1838.

Goodrich, Frances Louisa, *Mountain Homespun*. New Haven, Yale University Press, 1931.

Guerrant, Edward O., *The Galax Gatherers*. Richmond, Onward Press, 1910.

*Guide to the Summer Resorts and Watering Places of East Tennessee*. East Tennessee, Virginia, Georgia Railroad Company, 1879.

*Handbook of North Carolina*. State Board of Agriculture, 1893.

Hayne, Robert Y., *Address in Behalf of the Knoxville Convention*. 1836.

Haywood, John, *The Civil and Political History of the State of Tennessee*. Nashville, Dallas and Richmond, 1915.

Helper, Hinton A., ("Guy Cyril") *Asheville, Western North Carolina. Nature's Trundle-Bed of Recuperation.* 1886.

Henderson, Archibald, *The Campus of the First State University.* Chapel Hill, University of North Carolina Press, 1949.

*Histories of the Several Regiments and Battalions from North Carolina in the Great War 1861–65.* Written by members of the respective commands. Edited by Walter Clark, Lieutenant Colonel of the 70th Regiment, NCT. Goldsboro, N.C., 1901.

*History of Tennessee.* Goodspeed, Chicago, 1887.

Humes, Thomas, *Loyal Mountaineers of Tennessee.* Knoxville, Ogden Bros., 1888.

*Hydrologic Data on the French Broad River Basin 1857–1945.* North Carolina Department of Conservation and Development, 1950.

Jervey, Theodore D., *Robert Y. Hayne and His Times.* New York, Macmillan Company, 1909.

Johnson, Clifton, *Highways and Byways of the South.* New York, The Macmillan Company, 1903.

Kephart, Horace, *Our Southern Highlanders.* New York, The Macmillan Company, 1914.

King, Edward, *The Great South.* Hartford, Conn., American Publishing Company, 1875.

Lanman, Charles, *Letters From the Allegheny Mountains.* New York, G. B. Putnam, 1849.

Lefler, Hugh T., Editor, *North Carolina History Told by Contemporaries.* Chapel Hill, University of North Carolina Press, 1934.

Lindsay, Thomas H., *Guide Book to Western North Carolina.* 1890.

Longstreet, James, *From Manassas to Appomattox.* Philadelphia, J. B. Lippincott Company, 1896.

Mason, Robert Lindsay, *The Lure of the Great Smokies.* Boston, Houghton-Mifflin Company, 1927.

Mead, Martha Norburn, *Asheville in Land of the Sky.* Richmond, Va., The Dietz Press, 1942.

*Message from the President of the United States Transmitting a Report of the Secretary of Agriculture in Relation to the Forests, Rivers and Mountains of the Southern Appalachian Region.* Government Printing Office, 1902.

Michaux, F. A., *Travels to the Westward of the Allegheny Mountains, in the States of Ohio, Kentucky, and Tennessee, in the Year 1802.* London, 1805.

Mims, Cora Massey, *The Scottish-Carolina Timber and Land Company.*

———, *The Mims Family.*

———, *The Massey Family.* Privately printed Pamphlets.

Mooney, James, *Myths of the Cherokee.* Nineteenth Annal Report of the Bureau of American Ethnology 1897–1898. Government Printing Office.

Moorman, J. J., M.D., *The Virginia Springs and Springs of the South and West.* Philadelphia, Lippincott and Company, 1859.

Morley, Margaret W., *The Carolina Mountains.* Boston, Houghton Mifflin Company, 1913.

*North Carolina: Its Resources and Progress.* North Carolina Board of Immigration, Statistics and Agriculture, 1875.

*North Carolina's Natural Resources.* North Carolina Department of Conservation and Development, 1952.

O'Dell, Ruth Webb, *Over the Misty Blue Hills: The Story of Cocke County, Tennessee.* 1950.

Olmsted, Frederick Law, *A Journey in the Back Country.* London, 1860.

Patton, J. W., *Unionism and Reconstruction in Tennessee, 1860–69.* UNC Press, 1934.

Patton, Sadie Smathers, *The Story of Henderson County.* Asheville, 1947.

Peattie, Roderick, Editor, *The Great Smokies and the Blue Ridge.* New York, Vanguard Press, 1943.

Phillips, Charles, and others, *A Memoir of the Reverend Elisha Mitchell, D.D. Together with Tributes to His Memory.* Chapel Hill, J. M. Henderson, 1858.

Pollard, Edward Albert, *Southern History of the War.* New York, C. B. Richardson, 1866.

Price, R. N., *Holston Methodism.* Nashville, Tennessee, 1906.

*Proceedings North Carolina Third Annual Resource-Use Education Conference.* Chapel Hill, August 10–12, 1950.

Ramsey, J. G. M., *The Annals of Tennessee.* Charleston, Walker and James, 1853.

———, *Autobiography.* Typescript in University of Tennessee Library. Knoxville.

Reniers, Perceval, *The Springs of Virginia.* Chapel Hill, University of North Carolina Press, 1941.

*Report of the Stream Pollution Study Commission State of Tennessee.* July 1, 1950.

Rothrock, Mary U., Editor, *The French Broad-Holston Country: A History of Knox County, Tennessee.* 1946.

Royce, Charles C., *Cessions of Land by Indian Tribes to the United States.* First Annual Report of the United States Bureau of American Ethnology 1879–80. Government Printing Office.

Rule, William, *Standard History of Knoxville, Tennessee.* Chicago, The Lewis Publishing Company, 1900.

Scott, S. W., and Angel, S. P., *History of the Thirteenth Regiment Tennessee Volunteer Cavalry*. Philadelphia, P. W. Ziegler, 1903.

*Sevier County, Tennessee. Census of 1850.* Transcribed by Pollyanna Creekmore and Blanche C. McMahon.

Sheppard, Muriel Early, *Cabins in the Laurel*. Chapel Hill, University of North Carolina Press, 1935.

Sondley, Foster A., *A History of Buncombe County, North Carolina*. 2 vols. Asheville, N.C., The Advocate Printing Co., 1930.

*Stream Pollution in Tennessee.* State of Tennessee Stream Pollution Study Board. Nashville, Tenn., 1943–1944.

Stringfield, William Williams, *Memoirs of the Civil War.*

Stuckey, J. L., and Steel, W. G., *Geology and Mineral Resources of North Carolina*. Raleigh, N.C., 1953.

*Summary Report on Water Pollution. Tennessee River Basin.* Federal Security Agency, 1951.

Swiggett, Howard, *The Rebel Raider: A Life of John Hunt Morgan*. Indianapolis, Ind., Bobbs-Merrill, 1934.

Tatum, Georgia Lee, *Disloyalty in the Confederacy*. Chapel Hill, University of North Carolina Press, 1934.

Temple, O. P., *East Tennessee and the Civil War*. Cincinnati, Robert Clarke Co., 1899.

Tennent, Gaillard S., M.D., *Medicine in Buncombe County Down to 1885*. Charlotte, N.C.

*The Douglas Project on the French Broad River.* Final Completion Report. Tennessee Valley Authority, 1946.

*The Floods of July, 1916.* Southern Railway Company, 1917.

*The Land of the Sky and Beyond.* Southern Railway, 1893.

*The Territorial Papers of the United States.* Compiled and Edited by Carter, Clarence Edwin, vol. IV. *The Territory South of the River Ohio, 1790–1796.* Government Printing Office, 1936.

*The War of the Rebellion: A Compilation of the Official Records of the Union and Confederate Armies.* 130 vols. Government Printing Office, 1880–1901.

Thornborough, Laura, *The Great Smoky Mountains*. New York, Thomas Y. Crowell Company, 1937.

Trenholm, Alicia Middleton, *Flat Rock, North Carolina*. 1908.

Truett, Randle Bond, *Trade and Travel around the Southern Appalachians before 1830*. Chapel Hill, University of North Carolina Press, 1935.

Vance, Zebulon. *Sketches of North Carolina.* 1875.

Warner, Charles Dudley, *On Horseback, A Tour in Virginia, North Carolina and Tennessee*. Boston, Houghton Mifflin and Co., 1889.

*Western North Carolina.* Charlotte, N.C., A. D. Smith and Company, 1890.

*Western North Carolina Railroad to the Mountain Resorts of Western North Carolina.* 1882.

Williams, Samuel Cole, *Dawn of Tennessee Valley and Tennessee History.* Johnson City, Tenn., The Watauga Press, 1937.

———, *Early Travels in the Tennessee Country. 1540–1800.* Johnson City, Tenn., The Watauga Press, 1928.

———, *History of the Lost State of Franklin.* New York, Press of the Pioneers, 1933.

Woodward, Helen Beal, *Washing our Water: Your Job and Mine.* Public Affairs Pamphlet #193.

Woolson, Constance Fenimore, *Horace Chase.* New York, Harper and Brothers, 1894.

Works Projects Administration. *North Carolina, A Guide to the Old North State.* Federal Writer's Project. Chapel Hill, University of North Carolina Press, 1939.

———, *Tennessee, A Guide to the State.* Federal Writer's Project. New York, The Viking Press, 1939.

Ziegler, W. G., and Grosscup, B. S., *The Heart of the Alleghanies.* Raleigh, N.C. and Cleveland, Ohio. Williams, 1883.

MAGAZINES

*American Forests.* October, 1952.

*American Illustrated Methodist Magazine.* December, 1900.

*The Asheville News and Hotel Reporter.* 1896.

*The Chautauquan.* June, 1895.

*The Chemist and Druggist.* June 28, 1930.

*Daily Tar Heel.* October 23, 1938.

*Drug Markets.* July 27, 1926.

*Forbes.* November 15, 1940.

*Fortune.* January, 1949.

*Harper's New Monthly Magazine.* April, 1875.

*Harper's Weekly.* August 23, 1879.

*The Living Wilderness.* Winter 1951–52.

*The Lyceum.* Asheville, N.C. Issues of 1890.

*North Carolina Historical Review* .

*The Pharmaceutical Era.* June 30, 1923.

*Publications of the East Tennessee Historical Society.* Vols. V, VII, VIII, XIX.

*Scribner's Monthly.* March, 1874.

## NEWSPAPERS

Asheville *Citizen*.
Asheville *Citizen-Times*.
Asheville *News*. September 19, 1861.
Asheville *Times*.
*Eastern Sentinel*. Newport. 1881.
Knoxville *Daily Journal*.
Knoxville *Journal*.
Knoxville *News-Sentinel*.
Knoxville *Register*. July 13, 1836.
Newport *Herald*.
Newport *Plain Talk And Tribune*.
Newport *Times*.
*The Knoxville Whig*. September 5, 1866. May 1, 1867. November 20, 1867.
*Tri-County News*. Spruce Pine, North Carolina.

Old copies of the *Eastern Sentinel* were loaned to me by Mr. and Mrs. James A. T. Wood of Newport. Files of the old Newport *Plain Talk* and *Times* were loaned by Mrs. Tom Campbell of Morristown, and the old Newport *Herald* by Mr. Dooley Roadman of Knoxville.

# Index

357